MW00440459

VIRGINIA STATE PENITENTIARY

VIRGINIA STATE PENITENTIARY

A NOTORIOUS HISTORY

DALE M. BRUMFIELD

INTRODUCTION BY EVANS D. HOPKINS

THE
History
PRESS

Published by The History Press
Charleston, SC
www.historypress.net

Copyright © 2017 by Dale M. Brumfield
All rights reserved

Front cover, clockwise from top left: VCU James Branch Cabell Library Digital Collections;
Library of Virginia; Library of Virginia; Alexander Macaulay.
Back cover: Dementi Studios.

First published 2017

Manufactured in the United States

ISBN 9781467137638

Library of Congress Control Number: 2017945014

CONTENTS

Foreword, by Evans D. Hopkins   7
Author's Note   11

1. On the Possibility of Opening a Penitentiary-House   15
2. Growing Pains: 1805–1859   30
3. Corporal Punishments   56
4. "Bite and Be Damned": The Penitentiary
   and the American Civil War   62
5. The Black Codes and Legalized Slavery   66
6. "Let the Children Suffer"   86
7. Public Awareness and State Farms   97
8. Eugenics Cover-Up   102
9. The Electric Chair and Notable Penitentiary Electrocutions   117
10. Reform Years: 1920–1940   144
11. The Charge Against Flogging   150
12. The Powhatan Thirteen to the Martinsville Seven:
    Assembly-Line Execution   159
13. Great Escapes and Not-So-Great Attempts   169
14. Culture Inside the Pen: Sports, Art, Music,
    Theater and Literature   182
15. Reform, Legal Setbacks and a Major Inmate Victory:
    1950s–1970s   196
16. Odd, Strange and Curious   215

CONTENTS

17. Never Stomp the Kitten: 1978–1992   230
18. Fact Check: Separating Fact from Rumor
    at the Virginia Penitentiary   239

Bibliography   245
Index   259
About the Author   269

FOREWORD

Herein are untouched traces
Of men who are not yet without love or mercy
Though loathed and tormented daily
For it is 1984, and has been for years…
—"Herein," Evans D. Hopkins (1984)

"The degree of civilization in a society can be judged by entering its prisons," Fyodor Dostoyevsky, the renowned Russian author of *Crime and Punishment*, wrote in 1861. In that respect, with Dale Brumfield's most thorough history of the Virginia State Penitentiary, we are provided with a valuable overview of the evolution of our civilization and the incarceration culture that still plagues our nation. That culture, in large measure, began in the newly formed America, at 500 Spring Street in Richmond, Virginia.

I did not know Dale Brumfield when he asked me to take part in a dedication ceremony for the historical marker of the site of the Virginia State Penitentiary. I was incarcerated there for the first seven years of a life sentence for armed robbery, meted out to a then twenty-six-year-old by an all-white jury in my hometown of Danville, Virginia. But I had relegated memories of the hell that had been "The Wall," as we called it, to the pages of a book and had no desire to dredge up repressed memories. In addition to fearing the return of the nightmares of the place, I was apprehensive that a historical marker might somehow be seen as a monument, of sorts, to a symbol of man's inhumanity to man.

Arthur J. Probst Jr.

I told Dale of my misgivings and that I was concerned that a book of history might not do justice to the humanity of those forced to live within. He responded by saying that this book was his effort to remind people of that humanity and to remind them of the inhumanity, as well. He asked me to read his manuscript and decide for myself.

What I found, and what the reader will find, is a fascinating story—or, rather, a compendium of fascinating stories that make up a microcosmic saga of a place in time, across time. From Thomas Jefferson's vision of a place of penitence; to the use of the institution as slavery by another name; to brutal floggings, forced sterilizations and medical castrations; to the steady and racist use of the electric chair, Dale Brumfield paints a portrait of punishment that, indeed, was often criminal in and of itself.

But he also shows men who, as my poem of 1984 expresses, "are not yet without love or mercy." From the remarkable prisoner who playfully kisses the cheek of a bound and blindfolded guard before leaving him unharmed and escaping to a man who is condemned to die but protects guards during the infamous Mecklenburg escape, we are often surprised by the humanity of the men about whom he writes. He tells of writers, reporters, musicians, artisans and artists. As one of those men, who found his voice as a writer and regained his humanity as an artist, I am grateful for his nuanced depictions.

And he writes of volunteers and teachers from the Richmond community who came into the prison regularly and provided counseling, friendship and meaning. I—and countless others—benefited to a degree that cannot fully be fathomed.

There were bonds of brotherhood formed by most of us who lived—and died—at the Virginia State Penitentiary. And it would be remiss of me not to make mention of those who came to visit the incarcerated at 500 Spring Street—family members, friends and loved ones. Three of those loved ones lost their lives in late 1988 in a prison visitation van accident in which twenty-one people were also injured. Most of those in the van were Richmonders, traveling to Nottoway Correctional Center, to visit prisoners who had recently been transferred to the rural prison, as the penitentiary was closing down and emptying its population. Two of the dead, Nancy LeLasheur and her toddler son, Ben, were on their way to see me.

While some of my memories of that place called "The Wall" can forever stay repressed, thinking of Nancy and Ben reminds me that there are thousands of men and women in this state who will find interest and meaning in this work by Dale Brumfield. And for that, we can be thankful.

Evans Hopkins is the author of the acclaimed memoir Life after Life: A Story of Rage and Redemption, *published by Simon and Schuster/Free Press. From 1982 until 1997, Hopkins became one of the most widely read incarcerated writers in America. His social justice and incarceration op-eds have been published by the* Washington Post, *the* New Yorker Magazine *and Slate.com, among others. In 2015, on behalf of the Swanson Legacy Committee, Hopkins presented a special Swanson Courage Award for Civil Rights to Virginia governor Terry McAuliffe for his restoration of rights to former offenders.*

AUTHOR'S NOTE

Someone must have slandered Josef K., for one morning, without having done anything truly wrong, he was arrested.
——*Franz Kafka,* The Trial

There is far more left out of this story than there is in it. Everyone in Richmond prior to 1992 has a Virginia Penitentiary story, whether they were an inmate, corrections officer, psychologist, vendor, contractor or visitor. Those who spent their Saturday evenings in the 1950s watching shadows of inmates boxing, or who held vigil during a strike in the 1960s, or who spent a Thursday in the 1970s inside teaching a class, or who walked (faster than normal) or bicycled past that great wall in the 1980s on their way to work have a story to tell. I wish I could have told them all. I really do.

Many thanks to the following for their assistance and enthusiasm for this project: Charles McGuigan, Doug Dobey, the amazing Bruce Smith, Caryl Burtner, David Stover, Richard Moss, Dr. Edward H. Peeples Jr., Danny Link, Clyde King, John Whiting, Bruce Hazelgrove, Eric Gregory, Arthur J. Probst, Brian Sterowski, Jerry Givens, Thomas Haynesworth, Alan Katz, Beth Myers Yamamuro and all the Brumfields.

Also, huge thanks to:

Ben Cleary, F.T. Rea and Jerry Williams for their great help and insight with literature, sports and film.

Latrobe's original penitentiary building, with an added fourth floor, circa 1920. *Dementi Studios*.

Virginia State Penitentiary, 1971. *Library of Virginia*.

Roger Christman, Gregg Kimball and the entire staff of the Library of Virginia.

Frank Green, Michael Paul Williams, Bill Lohmann and Bob Rayner at the *Richmond Times-Dispatch*.

Ron Hall at the Carroll County Historical Society.

Michael Stone and Virginians for Alternatives to the Death Penalty.

John Ulmschneider and the staff of the VCU James Branch Cabell Library, especially Ray Bonis and the helpful staff upstairs in Special Collections, Ken Hopson and the staff downstairs in IT and everyone in between.

Kari Bruwelheide at the Smithsonian Institution.

Evans Hopkins for his guidance, insight and friendship.

CHAPTER 1

ON THE POSSIBILITY OF OPENING A PENITENTIARY-HOUSE

Sec. 17. The Executive of this commonwealth are hereby requested as soon as may be, to cause as much land in or near the city of Richmond, to be purchased for the use of the commonwealth, as will be sufficient for the building of a jail and penitentiary house, which shall be constructed of brick or stone, upon such plan as will best prevent danger from fire, and sufficient to contain with convenience, two hundred convicts at least, at an expense of 30,000 dollars...
with a yard sufficiently capacious adjoining thereto for the said convicts occasionally to walk about and labor in, which said yard shall be surrounded by walls of such height as without unnecessary exclusion of air, will be sufficient to prevent the escape of the prisoners.
—session act of 1796 to amend the penal laws of the commonwealth, chapter 2, paragraph 4. Revised code 355. Passed December 15, 1796

A Bold New Idea in Penal Reform

In the fall of 1785, while serving in Paris as ambassador, Thomas Jefferson wrote a letter to Virginia governor Patrick Henry of a new prison and a radical new theory of incarceration he had witnessed, in which he stated, "With respect to the plan of a prison...I had heard of a benevolent society in England which had been indulged by the Government in an experiment of the effect of labor in solitary confinement, on some of their criminals, which experiment had succeeded beyond expectation."

Jefferson went on to explain that the same idea had been suggested in France, and an architect in Lyons had proposed a plan of a "well contrived edifice" for incarcerating prisoners. He obtained a copy and, finding the French facility too large for Richmond, personally drew a scaled-down version, leaving room for additions as warranted. "This I sent to the Directors instead of a plan of a common prison," he wrote, "in the hope that it would suggest the idea of labor in solitary confinement…which we had adopted in our Revised Code."

At a time when capital and corporal punishment, such as executions, whippings and confinement in stocks, were common in America, the idea of incarcerating criminals for long periods of time in an institution was an unusual one. In Pennsylvania, just after the Revolutionary War, the Philadelphia Society for Assisting Distressed Prisoners formed and first took an interest in alternative incarceration methods. In 1787, Dr. Benjamin Rush published and then read at Benjamin Franklin's house an innovative report suggesting that the principle of imprisonment should be to make the prisoner penitent—the source of the word "penitentiary." Thus, the Quakers of Philadelphia, between 1787 and 1793, began substituting imprisonment for all offenses except first-degree murder.

Jefferson was influenced by the Philadelphians and agreed with the Quakers that the legitimate object of all punishment should be discipline, repentance and reform rather than vengeance, but he had many profound ideas of his own regarding crime and punishment. As early as August 1776, he had written to Edmund Pendleton that he believed the punishments of the time were much too severe. "Punishments I know are necessary, and I would provide them, strict and inflexible, but proportioned to the crime," he wrote. "Death might be inflicted for murther [sic] and perhaps for treason."

While serving in the Virginia General Assembly from 1776 to 1779, Jefferson drafted an early revision of the penal laws, called "A Bill for Proportioning Crimes and Punishments in Cases Heretofore Capital." While he still embraced some seemingly odd punishments (women found guilty of polygamy, for example, were punished "by cutting thro' the cartilage of her nose a hole of one half inch diameter at the least"), he added that all other non-capital crimes could be punished by "working on high roads, rivers, and other projects in time proportionate to the offense." His belief in labor in confinement made the reformation of the offender the groundwork of his theory.

The General Assembly, however, had doubts about the efficacy of extended incarceration, labor and solitary confinement, and Jefferson's bill went nowhere. Another bill introduced by James Madison in the 1785 General Assembly session to amend Virginia's outmoded laws and incorporate "labor by public works" lost by one vote. "Our old bloody code is by this event fully restored," a disappointed Madison wrote to Jefferson in 1787.

Pennsylvania attempted a system of labor by public works (highway labor, without prison confinement) from 1786 to 1789, but it failed in a flurry of escape attempts and enforcement difficulties. Another system of total solitary confinement, used from 1790 into the nineteenth century at Philadelphia's Walnut Street Jail, also failed due to mismanagement, overcrowding and administrative corruption.

It was then believed that a concept of total solitary confinement, based heavily on monastic life, was an answer to the incarceration problem. According to Negley Teeter in his 1969 study "The State of Prisons in the United States, 1870–1970," this system included "subsistence upon coarse food or shortened rations; the wearing of distinctive, and in certain cases humiliating, clothing; abstinence from sexual and other excitements; the contemplation of past transgressions, accompanied by resolutions to make future amendment; the use of a cellular form of living accommodation; and the encouragement or absolute requirement of silence."

George Keith Taylor, who helped author the penitentiary law, was a fan of "cellular living," writing that "a silence surrounds [the prisoner], profound and uninterrupted as that of the grave. During all this time he sustains the torture of having nothing to do....Will he not in bitter remorse implore the pardon of heaven and resolve on reformation of conduct?"

Author Charles Dickens, however, personally visited the Walnut Street Jail on a trip to America and was horrified at the "gaunt, hollow-eyed stares" of prisoners confined in dark, damp lockups with only a Bible and no contact with another living soul. Solitary confinement failed when those "hollow-eyed" felons either went insane or died.

Out with the Old Ways

On December 5, 1796, Virginia legislators finally amended the outdated penal laws and embraced Jefferson's now twenty-year-old suggestion. This revised code eliminated many archaic "Divine, Moral and Martial Laws," some of which lingered since Thomas Dale's Jamestown days. The revision eliminated the death penalty for all crimes committed by free persons except for first-degree murder (the idea of grading murder by degrees was also a Quaker concept). No longer was it punishable by death to speak out against the articles of Christian faith, trade with the Indians, steal an ear of corn, render a false account of colony supplies or kill a domestic animal without consent of the general counsel. The code did away with whipping for refusing to seek religious instruction with a minister or failing to keep regular work hours. Fishermen and bakers no longer had to worry about having their ears cut off for committing business fraud.

Under the new law, convicts would labor eight hours per day (Sundays excluded) in November, December and January; nine hours per day in February and October; and ten hours per day every other month. Clothing would be identical, and heads and beards would be "close-shaven" once per week.

"Experience has convinced me," Jefferson wrote in a letter from Monticello in 1809, "that the change in the style of the laws was for the better, and it has sensibly reformed the style of our laws from that time downwards."

A PENITENTIARY SITE IS SELECTED

With the law passed, by the end of 1796, the General Assembly executive, Governor James Wood, and a council consisting of gentlemen named Goode, Dawson, Bunley, Brenton and Pendleton began receiving inquiries from architects and even applications for superintendent for a new "Gaol and Penitentiary-House" that could hold two hundred inmates.

Since at that time Richmond was a small city confined to Shockoe and Church Hill, the council wanted the penitentiary in a remote place, yet accessible. After considering several locations, a twelve-acre "steep gravelly knoll" was purchased far west of the city on March 30, 1797, from a gentleman farmer named Thomas Rutherford. The parcel overlooked the James River, situated between two ravines that merged and emptied into the canal. It was hoped in this location easterly breezes would cool the facility during the summer. Across and southwest from the penitentiary site on a huge tract was William Byrd III's mansion, Belvidere, which had been built in 1750 and named for its beautiful views of the river to the south.

A petition against the proposed location of the penitentiary, signed by eight Richmond residents and presented to the council, warned of some of the hazards that would be encountered by that location. "Even water to supply the prisoners to quench their thirst, cook their provisions, and clean their garments cannot easily be procured," the petition stated. "The place itself is most unfit for the purpose [of a penitentiary], and may occasion as certain tho' less sudden death to the prisoners themselves, as the gibbet could do."

Samuel Dobie submitted an architectural application on December 30, 1796, and a proposal shortly afterward. Ebenezer Maud submitted a proposal around February 1797 and was remitted $20 for his work. Then, on March 14, Herbert Cain submitted a proposed plan to the council drawn by an English-born architect and engineer named Benjamin Henry Latrobe. Latrobe was paid $100 for his plans in May 1797 before they were even accepted.

Jefferson's sketches were disregarded.

Benjamin Henry Latrobe

Benjamin Henry Latrobe. *AOC.gov.*

Latrobe was an accomplished architect, fine artist and socialite who had studied in England under such well-known British architects and engineers as Samuel Pepys Cockerell and John Smeaton. After suffering a series of personal setbacks, including an emotional breakdown and losing his wife in childbirth, he immigrated to Virginia in November 1795.

The grueling four-month winter journey across the Atlantic aboard the ship, the *Eliza*, was plagued by cold, violent weather and a food shortage that led to many passengers almost starving to death. After settling in Norfolk, Latrobe's first job was a house design for Captain William Pennock.

After moving to Richmond in April 1796, Latrobe designed a new theater, which was rejected as too ambitious for Richmond, then designed and built a house for Colonel John Harvie. The penitentiary, however, was his first major American project, leading to more work in Philadelphia, including the waterworks and the Bank of Pennsylvania. In 1803, he was appointed by Thomas Jefferson to work on the still-unfinished U.S. Capitol building in

Washington, D.C., and is considered the second architect of that structure behind William Thornton—a man Latrobe considered "an idiot savant" of architecture.

The seven penitentiary drawings created by Latrobe were submitted on board stock and consisted of:

1. A plot, or "ground" plan, labeled I.
2. First-floor plan, labeled II.
3. Second- and third-story plan, labeled III.
4. Color illustrations of the south and west elevations, labeled IV.
5. Ground- and second-story plans of the fore courts, not numbered.
6. Elevations of the external and internal façades of the semicircular court, labeled VI.
7. Internal elevation of the west wing infirmary, internal elevation of the east wing women's court and color perspective drawing of the front gate, not numbered.

The designs—loosely based on the 1791 publication of Jeremy Bentham's *Panopticon, or the Inspection House*—were revolutionary for the time, albeit more formal than functional, and the structure may be considered the first modern prison in America, predating New York's Auburn Prison by over sixteen years. The main building was a semicircle, with three stories of cells and workshops facing an interior commons area behind a rectangular section composed of three courtyards, a workroom and the women's section—features unheard of for a prison. Cells were various sizes, with some accommodating several inmates.

Another innovation was the addition of individual solitary confinement cells in the basement level. These cells were a necessity, since every inmate was required to spend no less than one-twelfth and no more than one-half their sentence in solitary. Locked in a small windowless cell, the unfortunate inmate saw no one but the guard and did absolutely nothing but try to read a Bible in the clammy darkness, meditate on his or her crime and try to maintain sanity.

The front of the building was a huge stone gateway arch. Originally, Latrobe indicated that the arch crown was to be decorated with masonry chains linked together, reminiscent of London's Newgate Prison, but that decoration was never added.

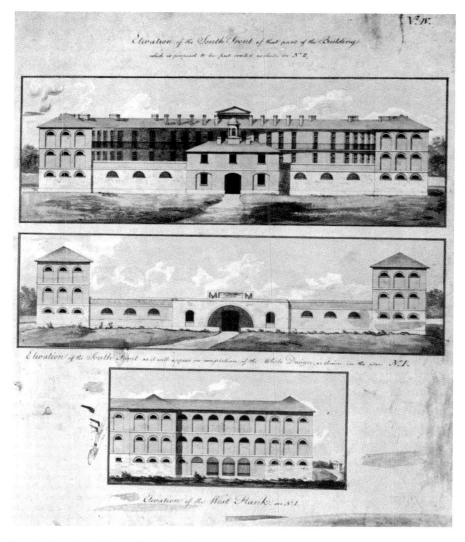

Latrobe's south and west elevation plans, 1796. *Library of Virginia.*

1797: CONSTRUCTION BEGINS

On March 23, Thomas Callis was appointed superintendent of the penitentiary for an annual salary of £200. On April 3, Robert Cowley was contracted to lay out and mark the property with landmark stones, and John Harvie and George Winston were contracted to furnish bricks and lime for the proposed structure. Then, on June 23, the council—after considering many plans—adopted those of Latrobe and formally hired him as the architect, paying him another £150.

In mid-July, carpenter John Shortis was paid £55 for digging the foundation, and William Giles was compensated for leveling a platform for receiving the large amounts of lime that would be arriving. Martin Mims was awarded the contract to lay the approximately 600,000 bricks. Numerous brick- and stonemasons, smiths and carpenters were hired. While setting foundation markers, Latrobe wrote of his frustrations of dealing with wandering cattle, snakes and "poisonous lizards with a red head and a green body."

On August 3, Superintendent Callis sent a letter to Governor Wood expressing concern about the shape of Latrobe's prison foundation. "I am willing to allow Mr. Latrobe all the credit due to his superior abilities, but I do not conceive that they are any further requisite in the execution of the business in question. This, however, is humbly submitted to the wisdom of the honorable Executive."

Not appreciating his designs questioned, Latrobe sent a stern letter to Callis informing him of his intention to inform the council that he was an incompetent. It was one of several unpleasant encounters the two had during construction.

By late summer, the initial preparations were complete, and the cornerstone was laid on August 7, 1797. An inscription, composed by Latrobe, read:

Of the Commonwealth of Virginia
Having abolished the ancient sanguinary criminal code,
The first stone of an Edifice
The monument of that Wisdom
Which should reform while it punishes the Criminal
Was laid on the 7th day of August
In the year 1797, and of American Independence the 22nd.

Because of heavy winter rains, an "unfavorable spring" and a late severe frost, work on the penitentiary was halted and not resumed until May 6, 1798. During the delay, Latrobe wrote a play in January, called *The Apology*, which was performed only once at a benefit by a Richmond theatrical company. The poorly received comedy apparently spoofed not only Alexander Hamilton but also Philadelphia-based British journalist William Cobbett, whom Latrobe called a "Skunk newspaper editor."

In a status report to the governor, Latrobe and Callis reported that by the end of 1797, the basement story of the east wing, containing six solitary cells, a washhouse and store cellar, had been built up to the ground line. All the arches had been turned and their centers pinpointed and marked. Considerable progress had also been made erecting the front gate and attached offices.

By June 1798, Latrobe was dismayed to find the only well that was supplying construction and drinking water had gone completely bad. In a July 9 letter to the governor, he wrote, "I beg most seriously to represent to you the necessity of thinking soon of supplying the house with water. Mr. Mims receives only two Hogsheads per day of bad water from [the well]." On a positive note, he did write that if they could figure out how to get water there by August, the facility could start receiving prisoners as early as November.

Also in that letter, Latrobe indicated that he knew that Superintendent Callis—by then a major thorn in his side—had pointed out to his honor that a stonemasonry mistake at the base of an arch under the kitchen had caused about four inches of settlement. But after personally examining that part of the arch, Latrobe concluded that while a stonemason named Beard had indeed "hammered a base stone" out of position, it was not directly under the arch and thus not a hazard. He even invited Governor Wood to examine the stone himself. "You will be convinced that the pressure of that stone has done no mischief," adding somewhat acerbically that "I have requested Mr. Callis, to point out to you the mode by which every possible danger may be avoided."

Latrobe included in this correspondence details of the extensive carpentry work of the original facility. He indicated that the cell walls would be one-and-a-half-inch oak planks, "ploughed and tongued" and "driven full of clinched nails." He specified kew-nailed straight plank pine flooring (northern pine, not Virginia pine, which he considered inferior) and six-paneled, two-inch bead and flush doors with a plate of iron, among many other instructions.

In September 1798, Latrobe again reiterated the need for funds to supply the penitentiary with water. He also argued that a plan suggested by Callis to change the roof from a hipped to a gable form would be a "sacrifice of taste and professional feelings."

He had hoped to start receiving inmates by that December but had to amend the completion date to early spring of 1799.

QUALIFICATIONS QUESTIONED

At this time, Callis's drumbeat of criticisms directed at Latrobe to Governor Wood came to a head, and Latrobe admitted that he had heard the council was considering removing him as penitentiary architect, possibly because of the stonemason error, his distracting work on the Philadelphia waterworks and other discrepancies reported to the council by Callis. Latrobe explained that he had gone above and beyond the call of duty in the design of the facility and was actually also functioning as construction supervisor. "Knowing that I have now educated a set of workmen capable of finishing the work, who when I first met them, were unable to execute anything beyond the commonest arch," he wrote on September 9, "…that I have done the duties of two situations ever since I was appointed—that it is impossible with justice, to charge me with the slightest infidelity or neglect, and that in fact no such charge has ever been made."

Journalist William Cobbett admonished Latrobe's unusual work ethic (possibly not appreciating being called a "skunk" by him) and commented that if the architect did not get the penitentiary finished in a timely manner, "he would very likely be the first tenant."

Whatever the charge against him, Latrobe kept his job, and construction under his leadership continued. Around October 24, a blacksmith named Henry Featherstone apparently went temporarily insane and attacked several other workmen. Featherstone was fired and drafted into the army's Seventh Regiment, which he promptly deserted. An ad in the September 8, 1799 *Virginia Gazette* offered ten dollars' reward for his capture.

By late November 1798, the east, or female, wing had been built up to the roof eaves. The arches of the ground story—which contained the solitary confinement cells, the guard room of the women's ward and one workroom—were "fully turned." The roof of the east wing was finished and ready to be raised and placed as soon as the upper arches were turned.

The ground floor of the west wing contained the kitchen, a bakery and an open area designed to admit some circulation into that part of the building. The second floor contained a men's infirmary and more cells, all measuring roughly twelve feet by six feet, six inches by nine feet tall, lighted and ventilated by an open, barred window but not heated. The "warm climate" of Richmond, Latrobe believed, made heating an unnecessary extravagance—to prisoners' later regret.

The main gate containing two apartments for a porter and guards, a bath and a storeroom was nearly complete. The penitentiary had no toilet facilities, other than buckets kept in the cells, so a waste runoff trough was dug so the buckets could be emptied through it into a holding pond beside the river. A road from Richmond to the main gate was completed. Latrobe also wrote that as of November 9, the ironsmiths were making the iron grates to the external windows, and during the winter, they would complete all the work necessary to "render the east wing and south front secure."

Latrobe estimated the cost of completing the penitentiary at $39,832.80. A few days later, he wrote that he had urgent business in Philadelphia and left town, promising to return after Christmas.

Almost no records exist of construction progress in 1799, only that Latrobe's duties in Philadelphia and continued confusion and disagreements finally led to his and Callis quietly leaving the project. John Clarke, an amateur architect, was appointed to fill both positions and simultaneously complete the Richmond armory. Clarke strayed from some of Latrobe's original concepts—for example, he put the "keeper's house" on top of the gateway instead of inside the central court, which altered Bentham's Panopticon theory of central surveillance.

Opening Day

On March 25, 1800, Governor Wood proclaimed the commonwealth's penitentiary system in operation and appointed Martin Mims the keeper of the still unfinished penitentiary-house. The *Journal of the House of Delegates* and an official roster compiled by Superintendent Abraham Douglas in 1810 states that twenty-one prisoners were admitted between April and December, including eighteen whites and three blacks. The first female prisoner was a lone black woman admitted in 1802.

Convict #1

The very first convict admitted to the brand-new penitentiary was Thomas Merryman, who had received a sentence of five years for murder in Cumberland County, near the town of Effingham.

In February 1800, Merryman heard there was going to be a wedding at the farm of a man named Minter, whose daughter was marrying Albert Jones. Merryman was well aware of Minter's daughter—he had proposed several times to her, and she had rejected him every time.

Merryman traveled to Minter's farm and snuck inside. After the ceremony, Merryman congratulated them both and then enjoyed a dance with a Miss Talley, a cousin of the bride.

Then, as Jones and his new bride stepped to the center of the room for the next dance, Merryman drew a recently sharpened knife and stabbed Jones deeply under the ribcage. Blood reportedly spurted from the groom's side, and as the women and men screamed in panic, Merryman sliced his way through the crowd, jumped on his horse and escaped. Jones died at the feet of his bride. One hundred years later, the bloodstain was supposedly still visible on the estate's wood floor.

Governor Wood offered a reward of £100 for the capture of Merryman, and he was eventually caught in what is today West Virginia. He was brought back to Cumberland County and tried by Justice Marshall Booker before being sent to District Court in Prince Edward County, where he was found guilty and sentenced to five years in the penitentiary.

But since the penitentiary was not completed, he had to wait about a week in the Prince Edward Public Jail. Then, when the governor announced the penitentiary open, he was registered on April 1, 1800, as convict #1.

Food and Clothing

According to a report dated May 12, 1800, Merryman and the other twenty inmates, upon their admittance to the penitentiary, each received "a bunk to lay on, a bed made of German oznabrig [a coarse, cheap fabric] stuffed with straw, hay, juniper or cedar shavings, a dutch blanket, also a chest, tin pan, and water bucket."

The original food allowances were set at around eleven cents per prisoner per day. On Sunday and Wednesday, each inmate received one pound of Indian or rye bread and one pound of coarse meat made into soup. On Monday and Friday, each received one and one-quarter pounds of Indian or rye bread and one and one-quarter pounds of Irish potatoes. On Tuesday, Thursday and Saturday, each received one quart of Indian meal made into mush and one "gill" (about a half cup) of molasses, mixed with water.

For clothing, male convicts were issued "two short jackets, two pair of overalls and two shirts made of oznabrig for the summer." A waistcoat was later added. Female convicts would be issued "two short gowns, two petticoats and two shifts made of oznabrig for the summer." Both males and females were also issued two pairs of shoes and two pairs of stockings each year, with an additional suit of coarse wool for the winter. Clothing was originally yellow cloth, but because of difficulties attaining that color, it was changed to blue and drab. It wasn't until the 1820s that the notorious Elam Lynds, superintendent at New York's Auburn Prison, standardized convict uniforms nationwide into the familiar black and white horizontal stripes.

Gabriel's Rebellion: Impact on Penal Reform

In August 1800, as final construction neared completion, a crowd of almost one thousand slaves led by Gabriel Prosser ("Prosser" was the last name of his owner) planned a well-coordinated uprising against Federalists, slave owners and Richmond merchants. Planning to march under a banner that read "Death or Liberty," the attack—known as Gabriel's Rebellion—was scheduled for Saturday, August 30 (mere weeks before a hotly contested presidential election), but was ruined that day by hours-long torrential rain that made roads impassable and created mass confusion.

Two slaves reportedly saw the storm as an omen and told Mosby Sheppard, the brother of their owner, Philip Sheppard, of the planned attack led by "Prosser's Gabriel." An alarm was sounded, and the Richmond Light Infantry Blues were called up by Governor Monroe. Gabriel tried to flee but was caught aboard a ship in Norfolk a week later, and he and twenty-six other co-conspirators were briefly incarcerated in September at the penitentiary and in the Henrico Jail.

The hangings of the conspirators began on September 12 and continued intermittently over about six weeks. Gabriel—who was taken to the penitentiary and placed in solitary—was hanged on October 7. The final seven were executed in locations other than the penitentiary.

After the first ten hangings, Governor James Monroe wrote to Thomas Jefferson, asking if in his opinion more executions were needed to prevent similar rebellions. Jefferson responded that "there is a strong sentiment that there has been hanging enough. The other states and the world at large will for ever condemn us if we indulge a principle of revenge, or go one step beyond absolute necessity." His concern was that Virginia presented the appearance of executing out of revenge rather than justice and could undo the reforms he was working so tirelessly to promote.

Gabriel's Rebellion prompted the General Assembly to pass several laws to deal with future slave conspiracies. One directed the governor to create a militia unit to protect Richmond and to move an arms supply into the city as needed. Another law, passed on January 15, 1801, empowered the governor to transport condemned slaves, when deemed expedient, out of the country.

According to the law, if a slave were condemned to death for such crimes as conspiracy, insurrection "or other crimes," the state would have had to compensate the owner for his "property" so the owner would not shield the slave from the justice system. Under the new law, the owner paid a cash penalty to the governor, who then had the slave transported out of the United States, amounting to a reprieve for the criminal and a cash savings for the state. An estimated nine hundred slaves were transported out of the country in this manner until the law was changed in 1858. If the slave ever returned to Virginia, he or she would be captured and executed.

UNANTICIPATED COSTS AND EVENTS

Almost immediately, the penitentiary started incurring unanticipated costs, to the aggravation of the governor and the council. The law for conveying prisoners from around the state to the penitentiary stated that local judges or justices of the peace had to retain "so many men, horses and boats as shall be necessary for the safe conveyance of the said prisoner or prisoners to the said jail and Penitentiary-House." One day was allowed for every twenty miles traveled, and the sheriff and guard attending the prisoner(s) each received $1.04 per day plus $0.04 per mile travel stipend both to and from the penitentiary, upon presentation of receipts. The sheriff or deputy also had to swear an oath that he had used as few men and horses as possible.

In 1804, ninety-nine men escorted a total of thirty-four prisoners to the penitentiary, most "from distant parts of the state," incurring an outrageous expenditure of $3,132.09. Cost notwithstanding, considering the significant size of the state in the pre–West Virginia era, coupled with almost nonexistent mountain roads, it may have taken a law enforcement officer up to two weary weeks or longer to escort a prisoner to Richmond from such remote western Alleghany areas as Clarksburg, Kanawha or Green Briar.

Labor Added to Confinement

In 1801, as Democrats celebrated the inauguration of President Thomas Jefferson and Aaron Burr as vice president, Superintendent John Clarke reported to Governor Monroe that most of the brickwork, flooring and roofing of the penitentiary was completed, and he "could conceive of no doubt" that the entire structure would be fully completed by the end of the year. Also this year, the General Assembly authorized the executive to appoint an on-call surgeon to the prisoners, for a salary of $400 annually.

In 1801, twenty-eight white and five black prisoners were admitted to the penitentiary.

While outside construction still continued, a nail manufacturing facility under the supervision of Assistant Keeper Henderson Stile was set up as part of the "labor in confinement" strategy. This was followed soon with a shoe-making operation. The creation of these somewhat limited penitentiary manufacturing processes in 1802 predates New York's celebrated "Auburn Plan"—considered the archetypal labor in confinement system—by almost eighteen years.

On January 28, 1803, the General Assembly further amended the penal laws of the commonwealth, with the most crucial being the distinction between first- and second-degree murder, as it meant the difference between hanging and eighteen years' confinement.

On May 8, 1804, a group of six prisoners attempted to set the penitentiary on fire and escape in the chaos. At 11:00 p.m., three inmates took several keepers hostage in cell 110. Afterward, they went to hall no. 7 and broke into the women's yard, where they were joined by the others. Fire was then discovered in the north wing. A prisoner named Barnes swore he would "perish in the flames or get his liberty," but another unnamed prisoner chose to go back and liberate the keepers, "lest they should perish in the fire."

Assistance finally arrived from Richmond, and the fire was under control after the top of the northwest wing burned down to the lower story. Damage was estimated by the May 16, 1804 *Richmond Inquirer* newspaper at a wildly exaggerated $25,000.

In late 1803–04, when forty-four new prisoners were admitted, $500 was appropriated to enlarge the wooden perimeter fence to accommodate an even greater influx of prisoners that sooner than they realized would strain the facility to the breaking point for decades to come.

CHAPTER 2
GROWING PAINS
1805-1859

PROBLEMS AND DEFICIENCIES

It became apparent there were problems, both with the theory of labor in confinement and with the penitentiary building itself. In late 1804, a committee was appointed by Governor John Page to examine the expenses and the applications of reform practiced by the facility. The report filed on January 18, 1805, was heavily critical:

> *The success of the institution essentially depends upon principles which, in practice, have not been duly regarded....In several of the workshops eight or nine of them labor together, there are four of them lodge* [sic] *in the same apartment, and enjoy an opportunity of unreserved communication....The result of this arrangement has been conspiracy against the keeper and the guards, and the formation of repeated schemes of escapes.*

In addition, the committee found that the convicts were not confined to their labor with sufficient strictness and that they walked the grounds and galleries "with little restraint." Worse, they felt the facility did not strike fear in the hearts of criminals. "These defects, however, it is believed are not attributed to the officers of the institution, but by the provisions of the law by which it has been established," the report stated, going on to say:

When the new penal code was adopted in 1796, it was affirmed and believed, that the certainty of punishment, which was to be expected under that system, would operate powerfully to deter men from crimes.... The penitentiary at present has few terrors nor is it the opinion of your committee, that the association of profligates with each other, can in any degree conduce to their reformation.

Despite the misgivings, the committee ultimately elected to give a fair trial to the experiment, which was still considered lofty in its ideals and far better than the brutal and unforgiving colonial-era alternatives.

As for the penitentiary structure, there were several difficulties, all attributable to the fact that no one really knew what they were doing. There was no perimeter security, and contraband was frequently passed through the first-floor cell windows by outsiders. The solid oak cell doors had no windows, so guards had to open them to check on the prisoners inside, leaving them vulnerable to ambush. There was also no convenient place for a night security guard to walk past the cells "for the purpose of preventing evil communication" between the prisoners.

It was necessary to carry a torch for light to enter the basement solitary cells, as most of them had only a small opening near the ceiling that allowed a tiny bit of dim natural light. The Prison Discipline Society Report of 1827 stated that in those solitary cells "the water stands in drops on the walls, and no provision is made for warming the cells at any season of the year." It mentioned an undated instance where a prisoner's feet had frozen to the cell floor during his term of solitary confinement. Even Superintendent Samuel Parsons admitted the cells were "imminently dangerous to the health" of the convicts. In the first few years, empty solitary cells served as a temporary armory, but the weapons frequently rusted in the dampness.

Cells on the first and second floors quickly filled past capacity; as early as 1803, a cell intended for two inmates contained six. Since there was no dining or mess hall, prisoners ate meals in their cells. There was no well or spring-fed running water, so it had to be carried from the James River. Inmates marched single file to empty their toilet buckets through the trough to the holding pond near the river, and the drifting stench was unbearable in the summer.

Latrobe had seriously miscalculated the severity of Richmond winters, and from December through February or longer, prisoners spent nights and Sundays shivering in their unheated cells, wrapped only in cheap oznabrig overalls and thin blankets as cold winds, freezing rain and sometimes snow howled across the James River through open, barred windows. The prisoner mortality rate in 1806 was the highest in the six-year history of the facility, with 5 total deaths out of 118 prisoners, all attributed to exposure.

"The situation of this place is truly disagreeable and dangerous," Superintendent Mims wrote to the governor. Mims was correct in this assessment but was hardly qualified to manage the penitentiary. He had no experience in incarceration, his guards were lax and he thought his job was further hampered by undue statutory requirements, including one that the mayor of Richmond and two inspectors had to be present when corporal punishment was administered.

Worse, the council found that slipshod regulations, a shortage of raw materials and the ease with which a prisoner could go on sick leave caused the facility to run a financial deficit. In April 1806, the "exemption of convicts from labor on their own suggestion of indisposition" resulted in 29 out of 118 total prisoners being bedridden with self-diagnosed sickness, usually "biliousness" (upset stomach) or gastritis. Since a physician was only called as needed, the council saw the need for a daily physician so that no prisoner could be exempt from labor unless personally placed by him on a list of invalids.

In February 1807, Mims resigned in frustration. He was replaced by someone with actual penitentiary experience this time: Abraham Douglas, from Philadelphia's Walnut Street Jail.

IMPROVEMENTS IN LABOR

By 1806, there were two industries at the penitentiary, nail manufacture and shoe-making, but the facility was still a financial liability. Since most of the convicts were farm laborers with no specialty skills, they had to be taught these trades from scratch, resulting in low productivity and inferior products. There were at least two convicts skilled as wheelwrights and wagon makers, but there was no work in that trade. It thus became apparent to the council that the variety of manufacture would have to be expanded so the labor by confinement theory could involve as many convicts as possible. Within two years, the penitentiary was also making horse collars, wagon wheels, farm implements and other items.

In the spring of 1807, Governor William Cabell and the council had an idea to motivate the keeper (assistant superintendent) and the turnkey (chief jail guard) to increase production: grant them a 15 percent commission of the net proceeds of any goods sold. This arrangement worked exceptionally well; by 1810, labor and manufacture at the penitentiary had diversified and improved to the point that Superintendent Mann S. Valentine opened a Penitentiary Store on Richmond's Shockoe Hill. Items for sale included cut nails, springs, hammers, chains, fire buckets, even cloth, yarns and especially boots and shoes.

Later, it was discovered that the commission arrangement worked *too* well. In 1813, the total proceeds of goods sold was $18,974, with the keeper's cumulative commission $2,979—more than his annual salary. Mortified, the council immediately abolished that rate structure, and by 1815, the keeper's salary was raised to $1,800 annually and his commission cut to 2½ percent. All other employees received a 50 percent raise.

Still, productivity remained high. A report to the House of Delegates from the council-appointed Inspection Committee showed that from April 1, 1807, until December 1811, manufactured stock on hand from all manufacturing totaled $49,851 in value, although the profit margin was still minimal. "The convicts are clothed in articles of their own manufacture," the report concluded. "They appear healthy, and are furnished with wholesome and sufficient diet at seven cents per ration."

Throughout the first half of the century, agents were hired around the commonwealth and paid 5 percent commissions solely to sell penitentiary goods. Two enterprising Staunton sellers, Abraham and Silas Smith, submitted an invoice on June 26, 1811, listing numerous orders for such articles as bolts of cotton cloth, dozens of pairs of shoes, horse collars and nails totaling $402.97 for the month, making their cut $20.14. Another agent named F. Follet opened a store on Old Street in Petersburg in late July 1820. Cash only, no credit.

AARON BURR AND BRITISH PRISONERS OF WAR

On March 24, 1807, a stagecoach carrying the penitentiary's most distinguished prisoner, former vice president Aaron Burr, arrived under heavy security at Richmond's Eagle Tavern. Burr was captured in Natchez, Mississippi, and charged with treason against the United States by preparing an expedition against the colonies of Spain, a nation with whom the United States was at peace at the time. Burr claimed his intentions were honorable, that he wanted only to assist the United States "in case of war with Spain" to settle the Ouachita River Grant.

With the treason charge dismissed by Judge John Marshall, he claimed that there was sufficient evidence, however, to hold Burr on a second charge of providing means for an expedition against the territory of a nation at peace with the United States. Burr was released on $10,000 bail, and that night, he dined with Judge Marshall at defense lawyer John Wickham's house, which caused an uproar among Burr's detractors. Burr was held that night in a debtors' prison.

The next day, Burr was brought before the court, and one of his attorneys, Benjamin Botts (who would die with his wife four years later in the Richmond Theater fire), complained that the debtors' prison was a disgraceful, vermin-infested room that his client had to share with another couple. Burr was ordered on June 27 to a cell on the second floor of the penitentiary until his August 2 trial.

Burr was eventually found not guilty of both charges, so he left Richmond and a year later landed in Europe. There are no penitentiary or General Assembly records of his incarceration, other than a description in a letter he wrote to his daughter Theodosia on July 3, 1807. He cheerfully accepted his predicament to her, noting that "different servants have arrived with messages, notes and inquiries; bringing oranges, lemons, pineapples, cream butter…and some ordinary articles."

The consideration showed the former vice president, coupled with the inconsistent sentencing of less prestigious inmates, proved there were kinks in the still-new legal system to work out. For example, in 1809, Robert Gilmore was sentenced to life for horse stealing, while Richard Tomlinson's sentence for second-degree murder was eighteen years. Horse stealing was a major problem in Virginia—in fact, by 1816, it was the second most common reason for incarceration, behind grand larceny. Conversely, stealing a slave garnered four inmates sentences ranging from five to eight years.

Penitentiary regulations also allowed corporal punishment "of up to 39 lashes" inflicted by the keeper for such in-house crimes as "disobedience, profane cursing and swearing, indecent behavior, idleness and other breaches of duty and good order."

In September 1812, twenty-three prisoners petitioned Governor James Barbour to enlist in the army in exchange for pardons. "I have been [held] to this place for the term of twelve years…and at this time [am] willing to take up arms in the defense of my country," states a letter from a convict named Vaughn. "I hope and pray your honour that you will be pleased to grant me

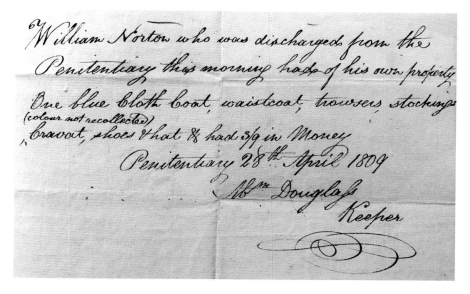

An inmate discharge slip, April 28, 1809. *Library of Virginia.*

an unfortunate prisoner the privilege of so doing which I promise faithfully to execute to the best of my will." There is no record that they were granted their requests.

Between April and November 1813, about thirty British prisoners of war—most all from a flotilla of the British ship *Victorious*—were captured along the Virginia coast and taken to the penitentiary. After only a few months, they were released back to their ship. There are no records of their presence in the penitentiary archives, but they are listed in a bound volume in the British Archives titled *The List of British Prisoners of War Captured by United States During War of 1812.*

POSTWAR IMPROVEMENTS

By 1815, the original penitentiary building was packed to overflowing; one twelve- by fourteen-foot cell intended for 4 inmates was jammed with 12. Recognizing the problem, the council recommended the construction of another barracks that would accommodate 120 inmates, along with a twelve-foot brick wall around the entire property.

26	Horse Stealing	4	22	.
18	Murder 2 Degree	2	14	-
8	Felony	3	4	
6	Voluntary Manslaughter	6		
6	Burglary	3		
5	Rape	1	4	
25	Grand Larceny	12	10	
3	Stabbing	1	2	
3	Petit Larceny	3		
1	Carr. Slaves out of Com	1		

A partial list of crimes and number of inmates admitted for each, 1814. *Library of Virginia.*

A small vegetable garden was started so that sick and invalid prisoners could "have a change of atmosphere" and get some exercise.

To also help relieve overcrowding, the council recommended that local jail terms and other unnamed forms of corporal punishment were more appropriate for "free Negroes and mulattoes." They also recommended that confinements in the penitentiary for terms less than two years should be abolished, with those convicts going to local jails.

By 1820, more and more prisoners were either finishing their sentences or being paroled or discharged, so the newly appointed board of directors, functioning as intermediaries between the governor and the superintendent, approved travel allowances of $0.08 per mile, not to exceed $30.00, to allow discharged and paroled prisoners to return to their home counties. Robert Pollard was thus given $5.84 to return to Stafford County, while Jefferson McClure was allowed $22.40 to return to Grayson County in Southwest Virginia.

QUESTIONS IF THE SYSTEM IS WORKING

In 1820, the penitentiary population varied from 184 to 200 prisoners, with their crimes at one point broken down as follows: manslaughter, 4 prisoners; second-degree murder, 19; rape, 7; stabbing, 7; burglary, 14; horse stealing, 47; stealing Negroes, 3; robbery, 5; grand larceny, 48; bigamy, 2; house burning, 2; smaller crimes, 26.

Problems lingered. Superintendent Samuel Parsons wrote a remarkable letter in his November 1821 annual report, stating that the overcrowding and difficulties of policing were having more of a detrimental than a curative effect on the convicts, causing, in his opinion, the grand experiment of penitentiary reformation to teeter on the edge of failure:

It has not, nor will it ever, answer the ostensible purpose of its institution, unless a change in the buildings and the laws can be affected. Although the internal police is good, and the convicts generally orderly and attentive to their business; still, it is doubtful many are reformed by the example; neither can it be seriously expected, when they are crowded in their lodging rooms, and those less versed in crimes are taught the act and mystery of vice.... They are turned loose on society more abandoned characters than when they are first received.

Also in 1821, Parsons admitted he had discovered a counterfeiting operation inside the penitentiary. One of the keepers reported to him that he found molds and several coins both on prisoners and hidden in different places around the buildings.

Parsons also addressed the sudden high mortality rate of the inmates, which had been climbing since the facility opened. In 1819, there were eleven deaths; in 1820, nine deaths; and in 1821, fifteen deaths. While the mortality could partly be explained by the proportional rising number of admissions, Parsons and the council agreed (as they had several years earlier) that it was mostly due to having no heat in the cells in winter.

Despite the heat problem, manufacturing thrived. On January 23, 1823, the penitentiary received a letter of commendation from a Henry Skipwith attesting to the quality of construction of a wagon built in the penitentiary workshops: "The timbers are of the very best kind, and the workmanship well executed. I have had the wagon now in use upwards of 12 months and must say that no man ever had a better one."

Fire!

In late January 1823, the council recommended that the shingle roof on the penitentiary be replaced by a slate roof because of the danger of fire. Ironically, on August 8 of that year, before a new roof could be added, there was a disastrous fire—the second of several in the history of the institution, and by far the worst.

The fire broke out around midnight in the workshop building and immediately grew in ferocity, damaging in varying degrees every building on the property. Fire engines rushed out, and a crowd of citizens were commandeered by Governor Pleasants to save the convicts, some of whom were trapped in their cells. Turnkeys who slept in barracks under the building were able to unlock the second-story cells, and those prisoners rushed through the open front gate, where Captain Bolling's public guard and unarmed citizens surrounded them to prevent escape.

Unfortunately, several of the lower cell doors remained locked, trapping the inmates inside. Somehow, several citizens from a nearby poor, mostly black neighborhood called "Penitentiary Bottom" were able to punch through the rear of the walls or cut the bars out of the windows to drag the inmates from what would have been a certain and horrific death.

One of the citizens assisting with freeing inmates was Gilbert Hunt, a slave who also assisted in saving a dozen women and Dr. J.B. McCaw in the 1811 Richmond Theater fire. A volunteer on the fire brigade, Hunt positioned himself while a fireman stood on his massive shoulders and helped cut through window bars to free prisoners, many of whom were wearing shackles made by Hunt in his downtown blacksmith shop.

All 242 inmates were removed and guided as a group to the capitol portico. They remained there until the next day, when the men were escorted to the armory and the twelve women to a barracks. There they were guarded around the clock by a special militia made up of citizens and the public guard. Not one escaped.

While most of the stone exterior of the original Latrobe building survived the fire relatively unscathed, most of the interior of the facility, except the kitchen and a few cells, lay in ruins. A news report claimed that "everything combustible throughout the whole of the other parts of the edifice, with but few exceptions, was entirely consumed."

Within a week, inmates were at work removing debris and preparing the facility for reconstruction. The cause of the fire was never found, although it was believed by some that one of the "trustys," or trusted prisoners not locked in a cell that night, may have set the fire in the shoe shop.

The fire was financially devastating to the commonwealth. In addition to the estimated $200,000 in damages to the structure and property, it was estimated that up to $10,000 in manufactured articles waiting to be delivered were destroyed. Also, there was an unknown amount lost in tools, machinery, raw materials and fixtures.

Total repairs and improvements to the buildings were finalized and ordered on March 9, 1824, with a cost estimated at just under $38,000.

Rebuilding Both Structure and Policy

As the trash and debris were removed, five underground cells were discovered sealed up with no doors or windows—an obvious construction mistake. They were divided, doors were cut in the walls and a passageway was built, proving ten much-needed temporary dungeon cells, intended only for short confinements. By the end of the year, a temporary roof was installed on the main building, doors were replaced and a brick floor was laid.

Many improvements were made to the buildings during the rebuilding. A small hospital was built on the top floor of the west wing, and a mess hall was carved out of the first floor. For some reason, the kitchen was moved to the cellar, which in later years proved problematic. The women's cell—formerly one large room—was divided into solitary cells, mainly to segregate white inmates from black.

All of the cells were divided into smaller spaces for sleeping and solitary confinement, and culverts to "take out the filth" were cut underneath them.

Prisoners began moving back in in mid-1824, and by November of that year, the completed rebuilding was seen as a "new start" for the penitentiary and the labor in confinement policy. The *Journal for the House of Delegates* for 1823–24 affirmed that

The penitentiary, about 1830. *Library of Virginia.*

the penitentiary system, as a substitute for that bloody and avengeful code which preceded it, originated in these generous feelings of philanthropy and humanity which so much enable the human heart; and constitute one of the distinct lines of separation between barbarous and enlightened age.... Capital punishment is certainly effectual enough, as to the delinquent himself. But would not a resort to other punishments, judiciously inflicted, prove sufficiently efficacious, without depriving the unhappy culprit of his life, and of the prospect of reformation and future usefulness?

The report went on to state that the General Assembly was satisfied with the effects of penitentiary punishment, that not only was it the most humane but also the wisest and most effectual system "ever yet adopted in any country." The report nevertheless expressed agreement that the penitentiary still had several problems to be addressed, including "subversive" unrestrained communication among inmates and frequent pardoning, described as a "sickly sympathy extended to those professing reformation under a cloak of religion."

The report also expressed disappointment that due to a lack of space, prisoners could not be isolated into individual cells to fulfill court-ordered solitary confinement sentences. "The Keepers [in New York and Pennsylvania] have found that when every other mode of discipline has proved insufficient to subdue and control the most incorrigible, a resort to solitary confinement and low diet [bread and water] has never failed to produce humility and obedience."

A report by the Virginia Senate in December 1823 listed twenty-two goals of the penitentiary for the coming years. These included restoring the damaged buildings and constructing two new ones, including more short-term solitary confinement cells and a well-ventilated and heated hospital; a seventeen-foot-high brick wall built around the property; twenty-four-hour outdoor oil lighting; slate roofs and sheet iron over the floors to minimize fire risk; a fire engine; several cisterns; and a convict-operated step wheel to raise water from the cisterns.

Finally, taking another cue from Auburn, silence was enforced. Any speaking among the male convicts not absolutely required for work would be punished by a leather ball gag in the mouth for twenty-four hours.

The "Problem" of Free Blacks

It had been ascertained in 1815 that Virginia's free blacks and mulattoes were better suited to incarceration in local jails or by corporal punishment, such as flogging, than sentenced to the penitentiary to prevent racial intermingling. By late 1823 all the way into the 1840s, the relationships between slaves and free blacks living in Richmond and Virginia caused much consternation among many members of the legislature. It started in a belief dating back to 1804 that the number of black slaves incarcerated in the penitentiary had become disproportionate to their number in society, drawing the cumbersome conclusion that free blacks were a bad influence on slaves and that existing criminal laws were entirely inadequate for a class as vicious as the "free Africans."

The prevailing reasoning was expressed by Governor Pleasants when he wrote in 1823 that "freedom to the negro is a curse, and his presence in our midst an evil of the most fearful magnitude." Free blacks, it was alleged, corrupted slaves; therefore, the free blacks were not worthy of living in more "civilized" society.

To deal with the free blacks and their perceived growing influence, a group of Richmond residents met on November 4, 1823, to form the Virginia Colonization Society, an arm of the American Colonization Society, with its purpose to encourage and provide monetary assistance to free blacks only (not slaves) to move to the west coast of Africa in a colony called Cape Mesurado. By 1847, Mesurado had become the nation of Liberia.

With the colonization effort in place, the law changed in 1825 with a much more insidious penalty: any free black convicted of any crime (except petty larceny) for which the prescribed punishment was two years or more would be punished not with a penitentiary sentence but by being whipped, sold and then transported as a slave. Thirty-five free blacks, including at least one black woman with a child, who were sold separately in 1827, were victims of this contemptible law.

Whether this was a blatant effort to push free blacks out of the country is speculative, but thankfully, public sentiment and Governor William Giles led the drive to repeal this admittedly barbaric edict on February 12, 1828. That year, penitentiary imprisonment was again made the punishment for free blacks, but five years was the minimum term for which a free black could be sentenced, whereas two years was the minimum for white prisoners.

Gilbert Hunt, the former slave who was freed for assisting in both the theater and penitentiary fires, moved to Mesurado under the colonization project in 1829. He returned to Richmond disappointed and campaigned to discourage blacks from going there. He was thus considered "a complete croaker" who was hurting the cause of colonization. Hunt nonetheless died a prosperous, free man in 1863 at age ninety.

JEFFERSON PASSES

In 1825, a new building containing workshops was finally completed and whitewashed with limestone, earning it the nickname the "white house." By December, a joint committee approved plans for a new sixty-five- by thirty-two-foot four-story building containing almost nothing but individual cells, with the exception of a bigger hospital on the fourth floor. The old hospital was divided into 12 cells, making a total of 192 cells on the property. "With this addition," stated an optimistic report in the 1826–27 *Journal of the House of Delegates*, "the system of solitude on days of rest, and at night, so long contemplated by the legislature, will be perfected."

With the rebuilding, the new construction and the growing manufacturing operations, the penitentiary soon became a magnet for tourists desiring to travel into the country to see the interior of this mysterious walled city and ogle at the drab inmates as they went about their daily duties. Between May and September 1827, there were 306 visitors to the penitentiary—so many that the directors proposed charging a fee and restricting visiting to only certain hours.

On July 4, 1827, the penitentiary lost its founding father and most vocal champion. Thomas Jefferson died at Monticello that day at 12:50 p.m., the very day and hour on which the Declaration of Independence was read fifty years before. News of his death did not reach Richmond until July 6, and the city (and country) sank into mourning.

As funeral arrangements were being made in Richmond for Jefferson, word reached the city that John Adams, the second U.S. president, had also died on July 4.

In the 1829 General Assembly session, an ecstatic Governor Giles informed the legislators that over the previous four years, only one white woman had been sentenced to the penitentiary. "How wonderful the fact," he bragged with gusto uncommon for the time, "that of a free white population of 660,000 souls, that only one white woman has been convicted of a Penitentiary offence within the last four years!!" Of course, white

A circa 1920s postcard, showing the "white house" in the center of the compound. *VCU James Branch Cabell Library Digital Collections, Special Collections and Archives.*

women had the lowest sentencing rates for similar crimes as compared to white males and blacks. White women were practically considered unable to commit serious crimes and certainly by virtue of their sex did not deserve harsh punishments when they did.

On the flip side of that boast, there were still three "persons of colour" convicted of crimes; therefore, according to the recently repealed Virginia law, they were grandfathered and still condemned to sale into slavery.

STENCH, CHOLERA AND MORE DEATH

Cholera is a bacterium found in contaminated water or food that causes extreme dysentery, fever, crippling abdominal cramping and frequently death. In 1832, an epidemic of it roared across the United States, starting in the New York area, traveling south and then west. On September 8, Richmond's first casualty was a black child about eleven years old who died only about five hours after showing symptoms. On September 18, the *Richmond Inquirer* newspaper noted that another victim, a fifty-five-year-old slave named Dorcas, exhibited "gross habits" and, prior to getting sick, did such unseemly things as eat "meat and cheese fried together."

At the time, cholera was considered a "poor person's" disease, believed caused by filthy personal habits and living conditions. Therefore, in Richmond, when blacks got sick it was reported as "the Cholera," but sick whites were reported just as having dysentery.

It is not difficult to see why cholera spread so rapidly: U.S. cities, including Richmond, were a filthy mess. With no landfills, sewers or trash pickup, garbage and human waste piled up in every corner and alley. Toxic byproducts of local slaughterhouses, tanneries and other manufacturing plants fouled the air and the James River. Privies, or outhouses—usually located between buildings and sometimes shared by a dozen families or more—were almost always overflowing. Horses and other scavenging livestock, including feral pigs, each dropped up to thirty pounds of uncollected manure per day in the streets.

At the penitentiary, when several convicts began getting sick with cholera in late September, it was believed the cause was the putrid sewage lagoon located by the canal below the facility. During the humid summer heat, the pool—filled with thirty-two years of decaying sewage—emitted a leaden cloud of "offensive miasma" that was carried from the breezes to the penitentiary, where it was trapped behind the huge brick wall and penetrated every cell, dungeon and workshop with a sickening stench. Even worse, the front of the prison was continually coated with mud, allowing the stench (and diseases) to linger well into the winter. A concerted effort to wash down cells with a mixture of tar and vinegar was implemented to check the spread after the first cases.

While the number of new prisoners admitted in the fiscal year 1833 was less than usual (forty-three total), fifty-one died that year alone, with about thirty-one deaths attributed to cholera and twenty to other causes, such as bilious fever, apoplexy, brain inflammation, dropsy and one suicide. Throughout Richmond, cholera spread virtually unchecked, with seventy to eighty new cases reported per day, forcing many residents to flee to rural areas. The epidemic paralyzed Richmond commerce until the latter part of October, when no new cases were reported in either Richmond or the penitentiary.

To help check further epidemics, Superintendent Charles S. Morgan submitted to Governor John Floyd just after the cholera outbreak a plan of improvement that included ventilating the outer walls with two large, well-secured windows and moving the north wall about one hundred feet out "so as to admit a greater space for the circulation of pure air."

SOLITARY, FOOD AND HEALTH CONCERNS

As meteors lit up the Richmond sky on November 13, 1833, the penitentiary issued new General Assembly–endorsed guidelines for solitary confinement. The new rules declared that solitary should be one-twelfth of the whole term and then served at intervals, not exceeding one month at a time. This was part of the adoption of one of three distinct plans of penitentiary economy and discipline, named for their prisons of origin—Richmond, Auburn or Cherry Hill (Philadelphia)—and outlined in the 1833–34 *Journal of the House of Delegates*.

The Richmond plan called for "isolation or solitude during nights and Sunday; labour in shops where the convicts are brought together; social intercourse prohibited, solitary confinement at intervals; a Bible, slate and pencil for each room and cell, and religious instructions permitted on Sunday but not provided for." This was slightly less strict than the Auburn plan and far more liberal than the austere Cherry Hill plan, which called for "isolation or solitude during the whole term; each convict allowed to labour in his room by himself, and religious instruction provided, with books, etc."

Morgan was considered a committed humanitarian, but one who advocated heavily for longer minimum penitentiary sentences. He thought that the best hope of moral reformation was centered on a term long enough to teach the habits of temperance and contrition and to learn an appropriate trade. Whereas in 1819 the minimum term for the penitentiary was lengthened from six months to two years, Morgan wanted to increase the minimum even more, to five years, since he believed that was how long it took to master a productive skill. Terms of less than five years, he believed, could be served in local jails.

Morgan also believed that long sentences of ten to seventeen years for crimes less than murder had a reverse effect, making prisoners stubborn, often desperate and unwilling to work. He thought that convicts became callous to moral and religious influences when subjected to extreme terms of imprisonment, making reformation even more difficult.

Morgan also believed the contract food rations system was riddled with problems. It was very cheap, awarded to the lowest bidder and with no regard to the nutritional values of the food provided. Penitentiary physician Dr. J.N. Broocks concurred, suggesting that the contracted, unchanging ration diet of the prisoners was furthering the spread of disease and producing many cases of scurvy.

Upon Broocks's recommendation, the system of contracting rations was abandoned in 1834 in favor of a physician-supervised diet. Then, in 1839, the superintendent was authorized to tailor individual diets for prisoners' specific requirements, with the rations purchased by the general agent.

These changes, coupled with enlarging the vegetable garden to four acres and the temporary draining of the sewage lagoon by the James River Construction Company in 1838, considerably improved the health and living conditions of the inmates.

IMPROVEMENTS AND SETBACKS UNDER CHARLES MORGAN

In 1833, sociologist, political theorist and historian Alex de Tocqueville published a devastating report on American prisons after touring America with Gustave de Beaumont. He called the Virginia Penitentiary "one of the bad prisons in the United States" and pointed out that the superintendent received an exorbitant salary of $2,000 annually. In contrast, the superintendent in Weathersfield, Connecticut, "one of the good prisons," received only $1,200 annually.

By 1840, Superintendent Charles Morgan was addressing de Tocqueville's criticisms. He made tremendous strides in the physical health of the convicted, and far fewer inmates died of overcrowding, malnutrition and filthy living conditions. From the penitentiary's opening in 1800 until 1824, a total of 1,366 inmates

De Tocqueville and de Beaumont's 1833 report on American prisons. *Wikimedia Commons.*

were admitted and 130 died, or about 1 in 10. But from January 1826 until December 1833, which included the period of the solitary confinements, the absence of a working hospital, unventilated exterior walls and the cholera epidemic, there were 200 deaths out of 615 received, resulting in a shocking death rate of 1 in 3. From January 1834 until 1839, which included the addition of a new hospital and the abolishment of long-term solitary, the penitentiary death rate improved to 1 in 12.

Morgan completely dedicated his life to the penitentiary. He supervised the construction of guard walkways built closer to the original building, as the old walks were too far away from the cells, where no talking or chiseling could be heard. In 1842, as the celebrated author Charles Dickens visited Richmond, Morgan personally designed a piping system to draw spring water to the facility. He also upgraded the original sewer system, supervised the installation of a steam engine to grind cornmeal and extended the manufacturing trades to include not just shoemakers and nailers but also carpenters, wheelwrights, blacksmiths, harness makers and weavers. Unlike Philadelphia, there is no evidence Dickens visited the Virginia Penitentiary.

Morgan also started a series of correspondence with superintendents in other states to share information and techniques in penitentiary management, a practice unheard of in the past.

For the first time, a few houses started springing up near the penitentiary, as blacks, Welsh and Irish immigrants took jobs at Tredegar Iron Works along the James River on the hill below the facility. Some of them jokingly noted that they were as far away from Richmond as they were from the Oregon territory, and since the acquisition of the far western American territories was in the news at the time, their settlement on the east side of Belvidere Street became known as Oregon.

The Penitentiary Becomes a Profitable Business

From 1816 to 1821, as manufacturing got up to speed and agents were hired around the state to sell penitentiary-made merchandise, the facility ran an annual financial deficit of about $8,800, to the continuing irritation of the General Assembly. The great fire of 1823 had been a huge setback, but the penitentiary clawed its way back, and from 1844 through 1848, sales of penitentiary-manufactured goods finally netted consistent annual profits of about $1,980.

In 1848, Morgan split the penitentiary manufacturing sector into five wards. Ward one consisted of shoe and harness making and tailoring. Ward two was heavier manufacture, including blacksmithing, axe making and grinding and millstone making. Ward three consisted of wool spinning, quilling, carding and twisting. Ward four was for wheel and wagon makers, carpenters, coopers and painters. Ward five was reserved for yard hands, nurses, runners, engineers and firemen, cooks and washers.

Then that same year, a change in penal code reduced the minimum penitentiary sentence from three years to one year, greatly impacting the pace and quality of manufacturing. A frustrated Morgan knew one year was hardly enough sentence for convicts to adequately learn a productive trade; thus, profits suddenly tumbled as convicts had not enough time to learn and make their labor productive. In fact, from 1849 to 1850, fifty-nine inmates were admitted, with 25 percent of that number admitted for one year and 50 percent admitted for three. The resulting gross manufacturing proceeds in 1850–51 dropped $5,000 from the previous year, and the profit dropped to an anemic $795.

Morgan deduced from these facts that crime was actually increasing under the amended laws and that short prison terms were less effective and the labor of the prisoners far less profitable. Penitentiary board president Robert G. Scott agreed, ominously writing in the 1851 *Annual Report of the Penitentiary Institution* that "the evil consequences, in a pecuniary point of view, of permitting any felon to be condemned for the short term of one year in the state prison, are already sensibly felt, and will be disastrously realized in the next two years."

Inmates, late 1840s. Virginia Cavalcade *magazine, June 1956.*

Scott, the board of directors and Superintendent Morgan therefore concurred that an increase in the minimum term of penitentiary confinement was the best fix, proposing at least three years for white persons and five for free blacks and mulattoes. The board put the best face possible on what was admittedly a barefaced move to increase profitability, verifying that while the reformation of offenders was of course the primary goal of the penitentiary system, there was nothing wrong with a self-sustaining or even profitable commercial operation. If the punishment could be "adjusted" to attain the primary initiative yet also refund the expenses of the establishment with deposits in the treasury, then the public interest was doubly supported.

Addressing the "Corrupting Influence" of Black Convicts

As generous, benevolent and business-minded as Morgan was, his compassion was still overshadowed by the racial biases of his time. By 1845, he had become alarmed by the high number of "free negroes" in the penitentiary—in fact, in that year the penitentiary received as many black inmates as white, with twenty of each.

Morgan believed white convicts were humiliated by having to serve time beside the "corrupting" influence of the black convicts. He believed that the penitentiary was no punishment to "degraded persons" of color, and since remanding free blacks to slavery had been outlawed in 1828, corporal punishment, such as "the stripes" (whipping) and other more brutal forms of retribution for sentences less than three years were better suited to the black race than longer-term confinement.

The presence of free blacks thus became an absurd contradiction; Morgan did not want more free blacks in his institution, but the laws were being twisted to make more free blacks prisoners there. According to the *House Journal of 1847–48*, there were many more chances for a free black to be sent to the penitentiary than for a white person. Two-thirds of the free blacks charged before the Hustings Court of Richmond were by laws that did not apply to whites. For example, it was made a criminal offense for a free black to remain in a city or county without proper registration, and it was a crime for a free black to be caught unemployed or just standing around.

This attitude was also exemplified in all its bigoted, xenophobic glory in an incendiary address presented in 1843 by Governor James McDowell, in which he wrote:

> *I must again call your attention to the painful and distressing fact, exhibited in our criminal statistics, that the free negroes, constituting about one twenty-fifth of our entire population, perpetrate about two fifths of the crimes of the state. Does not this establish the fact that the free negroes are disorderly and evil disposed persons, and as such dangerous to our peace and tranquility…and whose deportation is called for by the highest considerations of public duty?*
>
> *…Why is it that we do not allow them to be taught to read and write, to bear arms, to give evidence against a white man, to intermarry with whites, to vote, and to teach the word of God to their own race in public assemblies? It is because long experience has taught us that they are evil disposed and degraded, idlers, vagabonds and paupers.*

In 1850, the Virginia Colonization Society raised $10,925 and sent 107 free blacks to Liberia. The next year, it sent 141; then 171 in 1852 and 243 in 1853. The choice for free blacks was horribly clear: go to Liberia or risk arrest and imprisonment.

THE DEPRESSING INFLUENCE OF THE DEPRIVATION OF LIBERTY

In 1846, penitentiary physician Broocks noted an increase of diseases treated in the facility, with 282 admitted to the hospital and 100 placed on light work duty. None of those cases proved fatal, but according to him, the "depressing influence of the deprivation of liberty," coupled with insufficient exercise and that damn sewage pond, was a prolific source of disease and death in all prisons.

In response, that July the penitentiary adopted a plan where every prisoner bathed once every two weeks. While it is difficult to gauge the effectiveness of enforced bathing, in 1846–47, with a total population of 217 inmates, there were only two deaths from illness.

In the fiscal year 1850–51, the penitentiary saw a jump in the number of new inmates, specifically the number of slaves admitted. While the assembly had budgeted $40,000 for the transport of convicted prisoners to the facility, an unacceptable $43,103 was spent. With the number of convictions increasing, Superintendent Morgan tried to again make the case that the influence of inefficient punishments, such as shortened prison terms, weakened the true purpose of the penitentiary system.

"Misdemeanor and felony have of late years been so interwoven with each other, and the punishments generally of the latter been so much softened by analogy to the former, as hardly to be practical for any of the purposes originally designed," he wrote in the 1851 annual report. "They neither prevent crime, reform offenders, nor make compensation in any way to the community for the offences committed."

Morgan Is Censured

On February 10, 1854, a select committee was appointed to investigate a charge that Morgan had shown favoritism in petitioning a pardon of Samuel A. Smith for good behavior after serving only a fraction of his sentence for kidnapping slaves.

Smith was a model prisoner and was rumored to be giving information to Morgan regarding conversations overheard by him; thus, he was seen as a squealer to the other convicts. As a result, in April 1853, Smith was

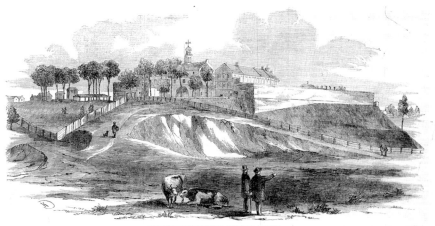

VIEW OF THE PENITENTIARY, RICHMOND, VIRGINIA.

The penitentiary, mid-1850s. *Library of Virginia.*

nearly killed by another prisoner named Jack Norvall, who stabbed him in the chest with a shoe knife concealed under his work apron. After a stint in the hospital, Smith made a full recovery.

Morgan did not deny Smith had been passing information to him but testified that it was not unusual for prisoners with long sentences to be recommended for pardon for unusual cooperation, good deeds or acts of heroism. He described a convict imprisoned for horse stealing being pardoned only twelve days after saving a guard from an axe attack. Then, in May 1850, a free black man serving a life sentence was also pardoned for telling a guard that a prisoner was hiding behind a pillar waiting to kill him.

Morgan closed his statement by stating, "Now…because I have had the temerity to do an act of simple justice to a prisoner, who had periled his life in obedience to my orders…if such be intended, I spurn the calumny with that contempt which every man who knows me, will testify it deserves."

The committee elected to drop the matter, and Morgan stayed on as superintendent.

ANOTHER FIRE

On December 7, 1855, around 8:00 p.m. a fire broke out behind a steam pipe in the wool carding room. The fire and choking smoke spread so fast that efforts to save panicking inmates took precedence over trying to save the shops, which were almost completely destroyed.

Morgan quickly ordered the cells opened and all available officers, guards and even Morgan's young son rushed from cell to cell, unlocking them, relieving the inmates from their "appalling conditions."

The shop roofs soon caved in, enabling the firefighters to extinguish the blaze. No one died, but there was one escape in the confusion: a Marshall, Virginia native named Elias Helms, who was serving five years for burglary.

Prior to the fire, the penitentiary was expecting its best manufacturing year yet, with General Agent John Spotts writing that "up to [the fire], the sales were unusually large, and we were flattered with the prospect of a heavy business during the year." The fire instead restricted total business to $45,421 when, under ordinary circumstances, it would have reached $70,000.

The wheelwrights were able to return to work almost immediately, as the majority of the damage was confined to the carpenters, axe makers and weavers' shops.

"The officers and guards belonging to the institution behaved with coolness, courage and activity," Morgan wrote in the 1855–56 annual report, "and many of the prisoners rendered every service in their power, and deserve much praise."

A Sudden Death and New Laws

In February 1858, just as the penitentiary seemed to operate more smoothly than it ever had, it was rocked by two major events. The first was the sudden death of Charles Morgan, after twenty-six years as superintendent.

The second blow was implementation of the law of 1857–58, which authorized the employment of free black and slave convicts on state public works. As a result, eighty-three black convicts, with sixty-eight of them highly skilled, were farmed out onto other jobs outside the walls of the penitentiary. This law answered several problems in the eyes of the legislature: it was a way for the state to pick up cheap labor while reducing penitentiary overcrowding and keeping the "corrupting influence" of the black prisoners away from the whites.

This was an early version of what would later become a convict lease system, which had already been adopted by other southern states. This devious law gave the courts unspoken permission to be more generous with penitentiary terms for free blacks and slaves, as evidenced by the explosion of the black convict population and their subsequent wholesale conscription to railroads, coal mines and quarries from 1858 well into the early 1900s.

With the law in place, by September 30, 1858, nine free blacks and four slaves were working on the North River Canal project; thirty-seven free blacks and eight slaves were working for the James River and Kanawha Company; four free blacks and twelve slaves were in the possession of Rosser and Lannis, contractors on the Covington and Ohio Railroad; and fifteen free blacks and seven slaves were employed building the Trans-Allegheny Lunatic Asylum. Later known as Weston State Hospital in Weston, West Virginia, this became the largest hand-cut stone masonry building in North America.

Unscrupulous contractors quickly discovered they could work the convicts with virtually no limits. In May 1859, seven convicts were returned to the penitentiary from the James River Company as "invalids" after being worked nearly to death. An extensive recovery followed, and by the end of the year, they were back at limited work inside the institution, too weak to go back out. According to scarce medical records, the seven of them amassed a total of 410 missed workdays.

This was a harbinger of much worse things to come, when the contractors began to institutionalize slavery under the banner of convict leasing.

As an unintended consequence, Acting Superintendent James Pendleton complained that in-house productivity was negatively impacted, not just by the law that took away his most skilled blacks but also because of the 121 convicts received, over half of them were in for a term of two years or less. Worse, less than 10 percent had any skills that could be used in the shops. Productivity inside the penitentiary plummeted.

Also in 1858, the penitentiary accepted five federal government prisoners, some with "long terms." Two other notable inmates admitted at this time were Captain William Bayliss, captain of the ship *Keziah*, who received a forty-year sentence for transporting slaves north. A white carpenter and abolitionist sympathizer named Samuel Smith, who built the crate for famous slavery escapee Henry "Box" Brown, was sentenced for assisting Brown and another slave in escaping Virginia. Brown spent several days nailed in the crate before arriving safely to an abolitionist in Philadelphia. Smith was convicted of boxing up two other slaves and received a sentence of eight years in the penitentiary. He was refused witnesses at his trial and was held for the first five months heavily chained in a small cell.

While conscripted black inmates endured slave-like working conditions outside the penitentiary, inside the institution dropsy, scurvy and scrofula were almost entirely eliminated by the addition of more healthy food (including salt fish for breakfast) and the construction of an inmate "bathing pool," with water warmed by steam pipes. In fact, physician Dr. William A. Patteson worried that while those measures added to the health of the prisoners, the penitentiary was at risk of becoming too comfortable. "It is a grave question," he wrote in his annual report, "whether, if the penitentiary is rendered a comfortable house of resort, it may fail of its intended effect on the convicts."

PREWAR ANXIETY

The 1860 penitentiary population was 264, composed of white convicts and only weak, elderly or infirm blacks, as the approximately 100 skilled and healthy blacks were employed outside for the rate of $100 annually.

A bill introduced in the General Assembly on January 6, 1860, to remove insane convicts from the penitentiary to the lunatic asylums was tabled by Representative Stuart, who suggested the transfer would have "an injurious effect" on the asylums, which received only civil cases, not criminal ones. Also that week, another Penitentiary Store opened at 27 Pearl Street in Richmond, selling "Negro clothing, shoes, wagons and carts, axes, crowbars, etc."

The first "three strikes you're out" bill also passed in 1860, which declared that any prisoner sentenced to the penitentiary for the third time (or for the third time by any other United States court) automatically must be sentenced for life. On March 13, 1895, this law almost sent Staunton man Joshua Stover to the penitentiary for life for stealing three pounds of bacon valued at thirty-eight cents. He had previously served two terms for larceny, but an appeal in September 1895 overturned the life sentence, and his original sentence of one year was upheld.

The prosperity enjoyed by the penitentiary, Richmond businesses and residents in 1859 vanished under the fog of impending secession from the Union, and anxiety replaced contentment almost overnight. Factories closed, throwing hundreds out of work. Service and retail business suffered, and banks suspended loans. Downtown was filled with the unemployed, as well as numerous vagrants who had arrived from the North. The winter of 1860 was unusually cold, and starvation became such a reality that a subscription rationing program had to be implemented to ensure food quantities.

By New Year 1861, the Commonwealth of Virginia's situation was so dire that Governor John Fletcher proclaimed January 4, 1861, as a day of fasting and prayer, as both the commonwealth and the penitentiary prepared for war.

CHAPTER 3
CORPORAL PUNISHMENTS

It is not only the prisoners who grow coarse and hardened from corporal punishment, but those as well who perpetrate the act or are present to witness it.
—Anton Chekhov, Russian playwright and short story writer

THE BALL AND CHAIN

A very heavy iron ball, with a roughly four-foot-long chain, was riveted and welded to the prisoner's ankle and worn twenty-four hours a day. In later years, a leg piece made of a bar of iron was welded on to the ankle band, with the leg piece spiked at the lower end. When adjusted on the prisoner, the spiked end extended about two inches beyond the leg, and if the convict attempted to walk fast or run, the spike stuck into the ground and threw him on his face. This was also called the "ball and spike."

Convicts Robert Davis and John Young displaying the ball and chain at the Goochland State Farm. Richmond Times-Dispatch, *undated clip.*

THE IRON MASK

This was a welded steel frame, resembling a baseball mask, but made large enough to cover the convict's entire head and chest. Other than being heavy and uncomfortable, it allegedly did not inflict any special pain but was used mainly for humiliation. While penitentiary administration claimed its use was discontinued in the 1890s, it was formally abolished in 1919.

THE CROSS (OR CRUCIFIXION)

The prisoner was laid out in a cell on his back spread-eagled on the floor and locked at both wrists and ankles by iron rings in the floor. Sometimes a brick or other object was placed under the prisoner's lower back, intensifying his pain and discomfort. He was kept in this position from one to six days, depending on the infraction. He was usually released for bread and water at meal times and sometimes put back in his own cell at night. This punishment was witnessed by Collis Lovely, special agent for the Missouri Department of Labor. His 1905 report on the condition of penal institutions in the United States included a similar description of this practice. Like the iron mask, its use was not discontinued until 1919.

FLOGGING ("THE STRIPES")

This was the most common form of corporal punishment and one that endured until 1946, and possibly longer. Women were cuffed to posts and lashed over their bare shoulders, while men were lashed over the back and gluteal region with a six-foot-long, one-and-a-half-inch-wide leather strap. Dr. Charles Carrington charged in 1919 that sometimes the guard dragged the whip across the gritty floor, picking up dirt, making the lash bite more deeply and making the scars slower to heal.

Some reasons for receiving the stripes, according to the 1896–1905 Penitentiary Punishment ledger, included disobedience (ten lashes), refusing to work or doing "bad work" (fifteen lashes), breaking line (ten lashes), "having a newspaper" (ten lashes), "singing after hours" (ten lashes), buggery or sodomy (twenty-five lashes) and extreme insubordination (the maximum

Richmond Times-Dispatch, August 8, 1913. *Chroniclingamerica.gov.*

thirty-nine lashes). From February 1901 until October 1902, a prisoner named James Johnson was flogged on twenty-two separate occasions, for infractions ranging from bad work (nine lashes) to "eating in cell" (seventeen lashes) to insubordination (thirty-nine lashes). On January 14, 1899, a woman, Eliza Hicks, received twenty stripes for fighting.

The maximum number of thirty-nine stripes hearkens from ancient Talmudic law. The original biblical maximum of forty lashes (according to Deuteronomy 25:3) was reduced to thirty-nine (Makkot 22a), "lest an additional one be done accidentally, and the negative commandment forbidding more than 40 to be given would be transgressed."

This was the only form of corporal punishment the penitentiary freely admitted using.

The Barrel

The prisoner was placed over a barrel, with his head between a guard's knees; another guard held his feet while a third inflicted the punishment with a leather strap. Thirty-nine blows across bare buttocks was the limit prescribed by regulations, but realistically convicts receive from 12 to 15 lashes.
—*Assistant Superintendent of the Virginia road camps D.P. Edwards describing the barrel punishment at the State Farm, quoted in the* Capitol Daily News, *St. Louis, Missouri, March 1, 1946*

A variation of the stripes, this punishment was used as late as 1946, when a lawsuit led to the practice being outlawed. It is not clear how often this practice was administered; penitentiary punishment records do not differentiate flogging over a barrel or at a post.

This is the alleged origin of the term "having someone over a barrel."

The Ball Gag

This was a leather ball attached to an iron headpiece that fit in the prisoner's mouth to stop him or her from talking. It was heavily used in the early days of the penitentiary, when absolute silence was to be maintained. The use of any type of ball gag was not permanently outlawed until after the 1968 sit-down strike.

The Rack

Also known as "hanging up," the rack was simply a bar set slightly above eye level, with the convict's wrists handcuffed to it. Sometimes the bar was set just high enough that the convict's toes were barely on the ground. The rack was supposedly discontinued when its use was made public in 1946.

SOLITARY CONFINEMENT ON BREAD AND WATER

This punishment was sometimes administered in the original dark dungeon cells for days or weeks on end. Prisoners generally received four slices of bread two times per day. In later years, the prisoner would receive two days of bread and then one day of normal meals. The prisoner's physical and mental health had to be monitored by the physician, as such a diet could be extremely dangerous over extended periods. Bread and water punishment was discontinued in the reforms of 1973.

These punishments were rightfully decried as "barbaric" and "hunnish," but some punishments in other southern states were far worse. The "water cure," prevalent in Florida and Georgia, was an early form of waterboarding. The prisoner was clamped into a tub, his mouth was pried and held open with a stick and a high-pressure jet of water was sprayed into it. Prisoners reportedly sometimes "swelled up like toads" from this torture.

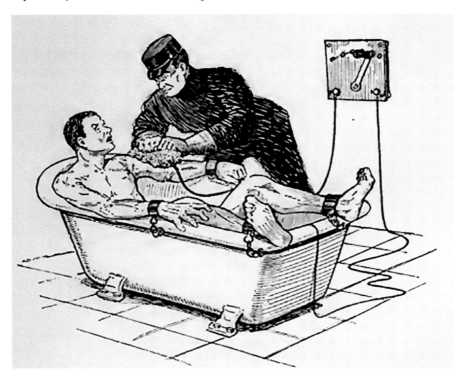

The "Humming-Bird" punishment. *From* The Crime of Criminals, *1910.*

The "Humming-Bird" was a torture used mainly in Ohio, where the prisoner was placed in a steel tub with an electrode attached to his wrist or ankle. The second electrode was attached to a wet sponge, which the guard wiped up and down the prisoner's limbs, causing them to convulse wildly.

The most horrible punishment was dubbed the "Tucker Telephone" and was used at the Tucker State Farm in Arkansas as late as the 1960s. An old crank telephone was stripped, and one wire was attached to the prisoner's ankle and the second to his genitals. The guard would then "make a call" by turning the crank, causing extraordinary pain and frequently permanent tissue damage and sterility.

There is no indication that any of these were ever used in Virginia.

CHAPTER 4

"BITE AND BE DAMNED"

THE PENITENTIARY AND THE AMERICAN CIVIL WAR

On April 12, 1861, at 4:30 a.m., Confederate troops from Charleston, under General P.G.T. Beauregard, opened fire on Union garrisons at Fort Sumter, South Carolina, triggering the Civil War. Two months later, on July 1, as the Virginia Penitentiary manufacturing shops produced cloth for Confederate uniforms, the fourth fire in the history of the institution broke out, badly damaging not just the cloth but also the carpentry, axe-making, spinning and weaving operations.

While convicts began feverishly fighting the fire, and as Richmond fire brigades and a contingent of foot cavalry under Thomas "Stonewall" Jackson were called out to assist, a torrential rainstorm extinguished the flames, preventing them from spreading. The $8,000 estimated damage included almost all weaving looms and the uniforms already sewn together, striking an admittedly small but symbolic blow to the Southern cause.

One prisoner, Joseph Davis, who was eleven years into an eighteen-year sentence for manslaughter, was granted a pardon for his bravery in helping suppress the fire.

After the fire, the efficacy of the entire institution came under another fire, this time from some members of the General Assembly, and a special committee was formed to study the resolution and offer solutions.

The committee maintained that by 1862, the penitentiary had "rested as an incubus on the state treasury, through injudicious management: and whereas, through serious defects in our criminal code, its inmates have increased so rapidly that the building is entirely inadequate to its uses, whether in regard to security, comfort or profitable employment." They insisted that since the city of Richmond had extended to the property, its values were greatly enhanced as to "amply remunerate the state for its removal to some more appropriate site, as well as abate it as a nuisance."

But the war made them promptly forget moving.

War Conditions inside the Pen

The political climate and the war were creating adverse conditions within the wall. Crime around Virginia was skyrocketing, and the penitentiary under Superintendent Charles Blue began swelling with convictions. Many Union prisoners of war were also sent to the penitentiary because of a shortage of places to put them. A shortage of raw materials resulted in many of the manufacturing shops being either closed or operated on reduced hours, so most of the inmates remained locked up at least twenty-three hours a day, with the smallest cells intended for one or two containing a half dozen or in some cases more, "endangering their lives, and permanently injuring their health." The most able-bodied of the three-hundred-plus convicts, including free blacks and slaves, were farmed out to the blast furnaces, including nearby Tredegar Iron Works, to manufacture pig iron for the war effort. A few of the remaining convicts, according to the 1863 *Journal of the House of Delegates*, were "in feeble health, and employed in light duties about the penitentiary and Public Square."

The report also took note of the diminished quality of the newly processed inmates. "Convicts consist of worthless, diseased, depraved and lazy characters," it continued, "fished up as it were from the worst form of society, without trades, unwilling to learn, skulk from duty and at every point possible destroyed materials."

Confined in the penitentiary during this time was Richard "Dick" Turner, the former Libby Prison soldier who was held under extra security on the charge of mistreating Federal prisoners. Next to Turner was the mysterious military "prisoner no. 5," who had his own personal guard and whose identity was never disclosed.

In 1929, Turner's son William Dandridge Turner wrote of visiting his father at the infamous penitentiary during the war:

The first morning that we reached the penitentiary I felt awed and strange. We drove through streets that I had never heard of or seen before, some with low squatty wood houses, some with no houses at all. We went down into the bottom…and presently we reached a little hill, and as we ascended a great big brick building hid all the sky. Just before you reached the penitentiary there was a sudden and steep rise, and there was gravel in the roadway, and it was wider in front of the gate; and a great big double iron gate was set back in an alcove. These iron gates would clang and sound so lonesome when they opened and shut.

EVACUATION AND ESCAPE

On April 3, 1865, when the Confederates set fire to the city in the face of advancing Union troops, the penitentiary guard abandoned the institution, leaving Superintendent Colin Bass and a skeleton crew of administrators to attempt to maintain a semblance of order. Soon, however, they also gave up and left. Bass carried many reports and records with him, which were never recovered.

The penitentiary inmates, abandoned by their guards and left on their own far from the downtown fire, rioted, ransacked and set fire to two of their own buildings. The hospital and the main administration building facing the river, including the superintendent's office, were destroyed, as were any remaining records.

Although it was rumored that Union troops let the penitentiary inmates out, it is more commonly believed that the inmates made riggings from beds, sheets and tools, and within twenty-four hours, all 287 of them escaped (the *Richmond Whig* reported 350 escaped), taking not only an estimated seven thousand pairs of shoes with them but also anvils, tools, window sashes, blacksmith bellows and most anything else not bolted down.

The penitentiary, for the first time in its sixty-five-year history, was a ghost town.

Many of the prisoners went downtown to witness or more likely participate in the "carnival of fire and pillaging" resulting from the evacuation. An August 27, 1881 eyewitness account of the evacuation written by Louis Manarin and published in the *Philadelphia Weekly Times* reported:

[Citizens'] *efforts to obtain provisions, combined with the fear of the spreading fire, quickly turned the crowd of people (now reinforced by stragglers from the army and escaped prisoners from the penitentiary) into a pillaging mob....It was not long before the vessels* [by] *the river began to explode and the powder magazine went up in an earth-shattering roar, sending pieces of brick and glass flying in all directions. The explosions brought out more residents, and they too joined the mob.*

To help stem the anarchy, all Richmond prisons and prisoners were placed under military authority, with Captain J.M. Schoonmaker appointed commandant and J.B. Holmes appointed general superintendent of the penitentiary. While local police returned a few of the penitentiary escapees, on May 5, Lieutenant Lyman Hoysradt, of the Twentieth New York State Militia, was officially put in charge of catching and returning the fugitive prisoners. He held that position until July 12, when the penitentiary was placed back under civilian control. By November 1865, 160 prisoners had been recaptured and returned. It is unknown exactly how many of the original escapees were eventually returned, although many of them also turned themselves in.

CHAPTER 5

THE BLACK CODES
AND LEGALIZED SLAVERY

We punish a man who steals a loaf, but if he steals an entire railroad
we ask him home to dinner.
—*Chicago minister Reverend Dr. Wayland, circa 1900*

POSTWAR REORGANIZATION

On February 9, 1865, Virginia ratified the Thirteenth Amendment outlawing slavery. Although the amendment abolished the ownership of other human beings, it also increased state control over the lives of convicted criminals. This expansion was magnified even more by the blunt language of *Ruffin v. Commonwealth*, which decided in 1871 that convicted criminals are "for the time being a slave of the State…and his estate, if he has any, is administered like that of a dead man."

After the war, the penitentiary administrators were anxious to return to normal, but it was a daunting task. Many of the inmates were sick, infested with vermin, insubordinate or refused to return to work. All the useable beds, blankets and clothing had been stolen in the mass escape, leaving only the filthiest and most threadbare. Since no money was appropriated for replacements, Governor Francis H. Pierpont defrayed those expenses out of the contingency fund until it, too, was exhausted. All the tools in the shops were gone except for the heaviest machinery. Food was almost nonexistent, and almost all meals consisted of a ration of corn bread and cabbage.

The penitentiary in April 1865, just after the evacuation of Richmond. The roof on the center front building is missing due to a fire set by escaping inmates. *Library of Congress.*

By the late summer of 1865, steady progress had been made rounding up the escaped prisoners, repairing the fire damage, cultivating the garden and restarting the manufacturing operations. "Over these shops is the shoemaking department," the *Richmond Commercial Bulletin* reported in August 1865. "… The cheapness, durability and beauty of the work by these convicts, will favorably compare with any work done in the city."

The governor discovered at this time that the penitentiary storekeeper, whose job it was to receive cash sales proceeds, was making 8 percent on each transaction, making his salary the same as appeals court judges. "It is strange that this abuse has been so long continued," he wrote in his 1866 report to the General Assembly. He also proposed moving the superintendent's personal dwelling to outside the penitentiary walls to avoid a repeat of the riot of the previous year, when inmates were able to easily break in and destroy all the remaining records.

In February 1866, James Pendleton returned briefly as superintendent, and all of the manufacturing industries, including axe making, weaving and broom and wheelbarrow making, resumed full operations.

Considered an "intelligent, enterprising and practical man" by the local press, Pendleton adapted different meal plans for inmates according to activity, at a cost of about twelve cents per meal. The average daily ration to each inmate in active manufacturing consisted of roughly one and a half pounds of corn bread, one-quarter pound of pork or a half pound of beef three times a week, about a pint of coffee and every other day a gill of molasses. Soup was prepared three days per week, and on other days, tomatoes and cabbages in season were provided from the penitentiary garden.

The penitentiary averaged 260 prisoners per day in 1866, and many of the healthiest were again contracted out on public works projects, including the Covington and Healey Springs Turnpike, the Chesapeake and Ohio (C&O) and the Covington and Ohio Railroads, the James River and Kanawha Canal and the Clover Hill coal mines in Chesterfield County. A few were sent to cut wood on a farm owned by R.H. Anderson.

Since there was no such thing as personal identification cards, Pendleton introduced what he considered a more precise and methodical system of identifying prisoners, especially for those (particularly blacks) who would be assigned works projects. An early admittance ledger from 1865–66 shows the list of prisoners and information including date of admittance, crime, sentence, etc., with the final column labeled "Marks or other peculiar descriptions." This was a listing of either a tattoo, a badly healed injury or, most commonly on the black inmates, a scar and its specific location. Joseph Turner, for example, admitted on November 22, 1864, had "the figure of a female with the letters LCW underneath in india and red ink on right arm near elbow." Scott Mosely, admitted on December 24, 1866, had a "scar on lower right thigh."

On June 5, 1867, twenty-two-year-old John McCabe was admitted to serve two years for grand larceny. His identifying markings are described in the ledger as follows:

> *A representation of the crucifixion of Christ with three stars over the heart and a figure of a man standing by the cross with an uplifted spear on the left arm in india ink. On the right arm in india ink the figure of a woman with a U.S. flag waving in her right hand, also above the elbow on the same arm in india ink the figure of a naked woman both of these figures are touched off with red ink as well as india ink. Also a heart with a spear through it on the top of the right foot in india ink, on the left foot a star on the top in india ink. The coat of arms of the U.S. in the center of his breast in india and red ink. The figure of a woman on the right leg above the knee in india ink and red ink, on the left leg the coat of arms U.S. above the knee in india and red ink.*

Hundreds of admissions from this period are identified in this manner. Although the vast majority of white inmates had tattoos, blacks were identified almost exclusively with scars, either from a previous incident or allegedly administered with a small knife at the penitentiary by the gate warden on Pendleton's order if no marks could be found.

This method of identification was replaced in 1906 by the Bertillon system of anthropometric measurements and inmate photography.

The "Black Codes" and Convict #497

On November 16, 1866, the day President Andrew Johnson declared a "day of thanksgiving and praise," a nineteen-year-old black Prince George County man was admitted to the penitentiary. He was an Elizabeth City, New Jersey native and had been sentenced to a seemingly arbitrary ten-year sentence for housebreaking and larceny. The admittance ledger listed him as five feet, one inch and identified with "a small scar on left arm above elbow." He was convict #497, going by the name John Henry.

Henry was arrested and sentenced by a recently passed set of laws called "black codes," which were enacted in 1865 and 1866 by the legislatures of not just Virginia but also Mississippi, Alabama, Georgia, Louisiana, Florida, Tennessee and North Carolina. While the newly formed Freedmen's Bureau sought to assist newly freed slaves and free blacks in acclimating to society before the implementation of formal congressional Reconstruction, black codes fought stridently against them, attempting to maintain white supremacy by inhibiting the movement of freed slaves, preventing potential uprisings and ensuring cheap labor.

John Henry's penitentiary admittance record (bottom row), November 16, 1866. *Library of Virginia.*

In Virginia, the suspension of vagrancy laws on January 24, 1866, by General Alfred Terry made unemployment a crime, and (unemployed) blacks could be arrested merely on the suspicion they were about to do something illegal. They could be charged with larceny, for example, if caught empty-handed on someone else's property or for such absurd, even nonsensical "crimes" as "showing an air of satisfaction" about the end of the war. So-called Pig Laws unfairly penalized poor blacks for crimes such as stealing a farm animal.

If found guilty, the criminal could either go to the penitentiary or be forced into unregulated employment for up to three months on railroads, highways or other public works projects. This situation was made even worse by employers who illegally collaborated to depress wages, reducing those arrested to a condition of slavery in everything but name. It was an outrageous, no-win situation.

To compound the issue, Virginia had been placed under military rule, and the General Assembly doubled sentencing guidelines for many crimes that had primarily black convictions, since they were undoubtedly aware that fewer newly freed blacks had steady incomes and frequently resorted to theft. For example, grand larceny sentences doubled from one to five years to up to ten years. Many misdemeanors were bumped up to felonies. On January 9, 1867, the assembly further suppressed blacks by rejecting the Fourteenth Amendment, which guaranteed equal protection under the laws, by a vote of 74–1 in the House, and 24–0 in the Senate.

Under this artificially created crime wave, the mass arrests of young black men across Virginia swelled the penitentiary population far beyond capacity with inmates such as John Henry, who were convicted and given inordinately long sentences for such lower-level crimes as larceny, burglary and housebreaking and then stuffed into cramped, suffocating cells with rapists and murderers. The *Richmond Dispatch* noted on November 30, 1868, that there were already 419 blacks and 116 whites incarcerated in the penitentiary under the new codes.

In March 1867, postwar military Reconstruction in Virginia formally started under the authority of General John Schofield, who appointed a new governor, General Henry Horatio Wells. Temporary penitentiary superintendent James Pendleton stepped down, and Schofield appointed a new superintendent named Burnham Wardwell.

A former ice merchant and Union sympathizer during the war, Burnham Wardwell was no stranger to unjust persecutions, wrongful arrests or filthy prison conditions. Some of his ancestors had been hanged as witches and wizards during the Salem trials in 1692, and he himself had been a war prisoner in Richmond's Castle Thunder in 1862 for refusing to take a loyalty oath to the Confederacy when Richmond was placed under martial law.

After the war, this "radical republican" supported blacks' rights, drawing the ire of elite white Richmonders who circulated the rumor that as a former Union supporter he was in a secret society called the Ferrets, whose task was to "ferret out" former Confederates who sought public office.

Wardwell was said to be honored in May 1866 to serve on the first interracial jury in Virginia for the trial of Jefferson Davis for treason.

Jefferson Davis's and John Henry's trials, coincidentally, began on the same day but had starkly different outcomes. Henry, a black man, received ten years in the penitentiary for petty theft, while the white former Confederate president—charged with treason, piracy and the murder of five hundred soldiers at Andersonville Prison in Georgia—walked free.

Wardwell was dismayed at the condition of the penitentiary and the prisoners upon his arrival on April 1, 1868—the sixty-eighth anniversary of its opening. "When Mr. Wardwell took charge of the prison it was in a disgustingly filthy condition," reported the *Richmond Dispatch*. "The cells, beds (sacks filled with straw), blankets, clothes, and persons of the prisoners, were not only filthy in the extreme (many of them having no change of clothes and wearing the same for months), but the filth naturally generated loathsome parasites."

Accordingly, Wardwell set in motion a concerted plan of fumigation, disinfecting and painting. The wall of every cell was scraped and whitewashed, the yard was graded and the sewage trough was upgraded. Any clothes and bedding not completely rotten were boiled in salt water.

Surprised by rumors of prisoner mistreatment by guards and the presence of torture devices—including the lash, irons and even a covered hole in the floor that served as a solitary confinement chamber—Wardwell expressed concern to Governor Wells that these methods were inappropriate that late in the nineteenth century and sought to do away with them or at least minimize their use. He also fired former temporary warden James Pendleton, who, as receiving clerk, administered identifying scars to new admittances, and replaced most of the guards.

Personal prisoner hygiene was upgraded and enforced. Each inmate had to appear at least once per week in a clean shirt. A retired Quaker pastor was brought down from Philadelphia to conduct mandatory Sunday morning sermons and establish a day school on Sunday afternoons, with reading, writing and arithmetic lessons. In 1868, eighty-four convicts were converted to Christianity.

Wardwell also greatly expanded the convict work program, and between August 1868 and January 1869, he consigned about 230 convicts to the Covington and Ohio Railroad, whose contractor, Mason, Gooch and Hoge, was constructing a line through the Alleghany Mountains of West Virginia, connecting the East Coast with Kentucky, Ohio and points west.

> *One dies, get another.*
> *—unknown "southern man" referring to leasing convicts, at the National Conference of Charities in Louisville, Kentucky, 1883*

Despite the freedoms guaranteed by the Emancipation Proclamation, railroad construction was also considered by some to be no more than slavery under the guise of contract labor. After the Civil War, slaves were freed without any provision for their welfare. Many had no jobs and few skills and were unable to even read the law that freed them. With the black codes sending more and more of them to prison, many southern states began adopting what became known as the convict lease system.

With the convict lease system, the richest men in the country—the white railroad barons—were given free rein to exploit and work to death the poorest and most disenfranchised in the country: the uneducated black convicts. Convict leasing thus became a sadistic limbo between slavery and freedom. The white leaderships of many southern states still contended that blacks needed to be kept "in their place" and that as free men, they worked best as they did as slaves: in groups, under the eyes of brutal overseers, in conditions equally debasing.

Virginia never adopted the full-blown institutionalized leasing program as did other southern states. Alabama first leased convicts in 1846, and from 1867 to 1874, reports showed that over one-third of the convicts died annually constructing railroads. Florida's particularly deadly leasing system (chronicled in J.C. Powell's 1891 book, *The American Siberia, or Fourteen Years' Experience in a Southern Convict Camp*) began during the Civil War and Georgia's notorious chain gangs soon afterward.

Still, the work in Virginia was so miserable and back-breaking, and the living conditions so squalid, that on October 6, 1868, twenty-five black convicts being transported west, facing fourteen-hour days hammering rock in the tunnels, took their chances near Gordonsville. They overpowered the single guard, opened the door of the baggage car and jumped from

Leased convicts in Florida, 1915. *Wikimedia Commons.*

the train going thirty miles per hour. One was instantly killed, and another was struck and killed by an Orange and Alexandria train following closely behind. According to the *Richmond Dispatch*, three were seriously wounded and "not expected to survive." Nineteen escaped, and it is not known if they were ever recovered.

Mass escapes such as this forced Governor Wells to amend the state's contract with Mason, Gooch and Hoge and other contractors to ensure the return of convicts or pay the expenses of recapturing if escaped. According to the terms, contractors would have to pay $100 for every leased convict not returned to the penitentiary, dead or alive, for whatever reason. Contractors thus could not claim a convict had died when he in fact escaped and was not caught.

On October 8, 1869, both houses of Virginia's General Assembly ratified both the Fourteenth and Fifteenth Amendments, about a year after they became law. The vote in the House of Delegates on the Fourteenth Amendment was 126–6; 21 of the 23 black members of the House of Delegates were present and voted for it. It passed the Senate 36–4. Convicts toiling in the mountains of West Virginia most likely never received this news that would have no impact on their own lives.

Convict height was always listed for those assigned to work on the railroads, as shorter convicts were a better size to work inside the tunnels. Thus, sixty-year-old, five-foot-two-inch William Palmer was better suited for tunnel work than thirty-nine-year-old, six-foot-two-inch Richard Kelly. Advanced age was also not a factor in determining who went to the railroads. On June 19, 1869, a six-foot-two-inch Henrico "mulatto" named John Robinson, serving the requisite black code sentence of ten years for burglary, was shipped under contract at age seventy-eight. At his height, he would more likely be a trackliner or a "mucker," cleaning up blasted rock and debris.

On December 1, 1869, the diminutive John Henry, along with fourteen other inmates, left Richmond to work on the Chesapeake and Ohio Railroad's Lewis and Big Bend Tunnels in the brand-new state of West Virginia. Most were probably given unskilled jobs, such as mucking and loading broken rock into cars and then dumping them into ravines, before graduating to more dangerous work drilling holes for explosives and mining rock for bridges. In Henry's case, he most likely went inside the tunnels.

And it was around this time that the legend of John Henry was born.

STEEL DRIVIN' MAN

The legend of John Henry seems to be less about a single man than a metaphor that shares his name, created by those convict tunnel drillers, muckers and trackliners eager to create a folk hero in their filthy and demoralizing surroundings.

Throughout history, every grueling industry had a larger-than-life champion who performed amazing feats of strength while promising hope and freedom to more mortal workers. For example, the tree cutters in the Northwest created Paul Bunyan, and the cowboys of the American West created Pecos Bill. Sailors told tales of the mighty Stormalong, who fought a Kraken in the northern seas and created the white cliffs of Dover.

Whether this particular John Henry from Prince George County was the man or even just the spark that created the legendary railroad folk hero who single-handedly beat modern technology is hypothetical, but it seems more likely that the name evolved to represent the hundreds of black convicts who gave their lives in labor on these railroads between 1869 and 1879. The legend paints a heroic image of a single, giant, muscled black man dying with a nine-pound hammer in his hand after beating a steam drill, but in actuality, convicts died less spectacularly of accidents, cave-ins, scurvy or silicosis, acquired from breathing sandstone dust between nitroglycerin blasts inside the tunnels.

A statue of John Henry near Talcott, West Virginia. *Wikimedia Commons.*

Scott Reynolds Nelson writes in his 2006 book *John Henry: The Untold Story of an American Legend* that

> *John Henry became the man whose hammer started large-scale mining in West Virginia, as well as the man who died while Reconstruction was ending: a Moses who gave the South the Promised Land of the West, but could not live to see it.... The song of John Henry became a boastful story that nonetheless suggested the gnawing fear that all trackliners faced: of becoming too slow or too old to work again. Trackliners had to be mighty men and so made John Henry in their own image.*

Bad Air and Falling Rock

Some of [the convicts are] *whipped on the works unmercifully every day.... There is twelve buried in this county and seven out of the twelve*

died all the way from ten minutes to twenty four hours after coming in off the works.
—letter from Abingdon resident James Harrison to penitentiary superintendent Lynn describing cruelty to convicts on the Abingdon railroad, circa 1871

Throughout the 1870s, about 10 percent of the convicts sent to the railroads and the granite quarry died, either on the job or after returning to the penitentiary. The quarry workers died mainly from accidents, malaria and pneumonia, while the railroad workers slowly suffocated to death from silicosis. The penitentiary physician's reports from those years trumpeted that prisoner mortality was always down, since he did not count those deaths that occurred under the contract system. He could also excuse the high number of cases of consumption (lung disease) treated in the hospital, as they were attributable to railroad work and were no fault of the penitentiary. Physician M. Walker made sure to point out that in July and August 1875, "malarial diseases were alarmingly prevalent at 'Granite,'" but not in Richmond.

As noted, the terms of the contract between the penitentiary and the C&O Railroad stipulated the convicts had to be returned or the contractor paid a $100-per-man fine. If a convict died on the job, his corpse was shipped back to be counted and avoid the fine and then buried in an unmarked grave on penitentiary property, years before a formal cemetery was created. Between 1870 and 1873, about one hundred convicts came back dead or dying, with another twenty-five dying by 1875, not of heroic feats of strength but of pulmonary-related disease.

Thus, it is unknown exactly when or where the real John Henry, the five-foot-one-inch young black convict, actually died. His admittance ledger states he was "transferred," with no other remarks. His name is also missing from the 1875 penitentiary hospital ledger, indicating he may have died around 1872 at the Lewis Tunnel (where the rock was mostly sandstone) or on the train back to Richmond.

One variation of the legend states that after death, Henry was taken to the "white house," which was mistakenly interpreted for many years as the White House in Washington, D.C. It was actually the whitewashed center building in the Virginia Penitentiary complex.

"According to the Thirteenth Amendment, people born as slaves in the pre-war South were supposed to die free in the post-war world," writes Dr. Peter Wallenstein in the 2016 *Louisiana Law Review*. "That supposition did not, however, fit the case of John Henry. Instead, born a free man in the

North before the Civil War, he fell into slavery in the South soon after the war ended and died there a slave."

In a chilling testament to the severity of the work and atrocious health risks, by 1880, there were almost no convict railroad workers left alive to tell of their experience on the mountain railroads between 1866 and 1879. Thus, starting in 1881, a whole new crop of workers went to work on those lines with little to no knowledge of what their predecessors endured and what ultimately waited for them.

A Brief Stab at Reform

In 1870, the New York Prison Society, which later became the National Prison Association, held a national conference in Cincinnati, Ohio. The conference freshly embraced the early reforms championed by Jefferson, the French and the Quakers, stressing the ideals of prisoner rehabilitation, society's responsibility for reformation and the need for religious, educational and industrial training. They even suggested a prisoner merit system.

While it is unknown if anyone from Richmond attended this conference, conditions inside the penitentiary from 1871 to 1876 under Superintendent George Strother remained slightly more hospitable for those mostly white inmates not contracted out, despite the widespread overcrowding. A September 30, 1871 census shows 395 inmates inside, with 433 contracted out on the railroads. This included 152 white men, 4 white women, 63 black women and 609 black men, for a total population of 828. The black codes were fulfilling their sinister quotas.

"I would again call the attention of the General Assembly to the necessity of enlarging the penitentiary by increasing the number of cells, and heating the same by steampipes [sic]," Strother implored in his 1871 report to the General Assembly. "If the 433 convicts at work on the railroad should be returned here, there would be no place to put them."

Exacerbating the problem was the temporary return of fifty inmates infected with scurvy from a contractor in Millboro, West Virginia. They had to be crammed into a hospital intended for twelve.

Of the 395 convicts retained inside the penitentiary that decade, 90 were employed as yard hands, laborers and water carriers, reflecting the lack of employable skills that so galled the accountants and the General Assemblymen. About 63 were employed as shoe and boot makers, with the

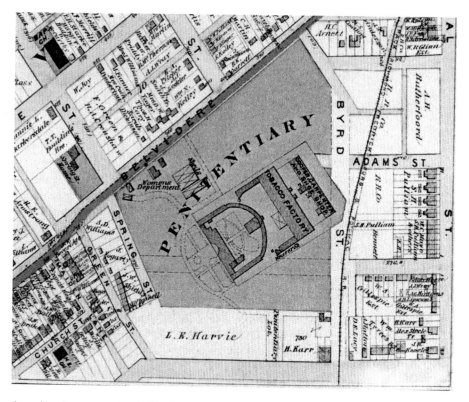

A penitentiary map, circa 1879, showing Latrobe's original building, manufacturing shops and "women's department." *Author's collection.*

remaining divided between wheel makers, coopers (barrel makers), weavers and blacksmiths. An additional 53 were listed as too sick or too feeble to work. Up until this time, female prisoners did no work, but Strother decided they could be put to use, so 20 were employed in the weaving shop, 31 with clothes making and 12 washing them. Strother considered making them cooks but abandoned this idea.

Penitentiary physician M. Walker gave a detailed account of the illnesses treated from October 1872 through November 1873 and then suggested that because of the crowding situation, health expectations should remain low:

> *If we take into consideration the variety of agencies operating upon such a class of individuals in prison life (particularly the pernicious habit of self-abuse), and all the unavoidable evils attendant upon the confinement*

of a large body of persons in a limited space, establishing a predisposition to many diseases, and susceptibility to any, I think we may conclude that we have no right to expect the health of the institution to be better than it has been.

It is significant to note that the "pernicious habit of self-abuse" (or masturbation) noted by Dr. Walker was directly addressed in a more disturbing manner exactly thirty years later by his successor, Dr. Charles Carrington, who viewed the habit as a symptom of a much greater crisis.

There were three significant additions to the penitentiary complex between 1871 and 1875, and none too soon. The dilapidated condition of the facility was already spurring calls to shut it down and move it farther away from Richmond. In fact, a legislative committee was appointed to find a new site, but plans fell by the wayside.

A new workshop building was constructed for about $8,400 on plans drawn by General W. Newberry, superintendent of public buildings. The three-story building was 236 feet long and 40 feet wide, with power and heat supplied by two thirty-horsepower boilers. Since the state was so broke, the foundation for this structure was built of recycled stone collected by inmates after the demolition of the old Virginia Courthouse. The former workshop building was converted into a kitchen on the first floor and a dining hall on the second. After seventy-three years of operation, the inmates did not have to carry food back to their cells to eat it.

The second addition was a two-story women's building, built for $1,300 with convict labor, that better separated the women from the men without any added expense.

The black codes were in full, destructive force in 1874–75, and a table published by the *Journal of the House of Delegates* from that year displayed the disparities of arrests between whites and blacks for certain crimes. For example, 12 black men were sent to the penitentiary that year for attempted rape, but not a single white man; 81 blacks were admitted for grand larceny, while only 15 whites were admitted for the same. Similarly, 82 blacks were sentenced for housebreaking versus only 7 whites; 40 blacks were sentenced for burglary, compared to 4 whites. All told, in that year, 307 blacks and 69 whites were admitted to the penitentiary, including many under the age of eighteen.

Eighteen Square Feet and a Cemetery

In 1876–77, several hundred of the leased convicts spilled back into the penitentiary for various reasons—either their contracts were up or they were too sick, diseased or exhausted to work anymore. The penitentiary population swelled to 1,250, and the supervisor's report stated that each man was allotted only eighteen square feet—enough room for a six- by three-foot bed. A projection of 2,000 inmates by 1880 would reduce that to twelve square feet per inmate, creating "standing room only" and "disastrous consequences."

It seemed the black codes were *too* efficient. In fact, the penitentiary was so overcrowded that inmates were gladly furnished to the James River Company to repair flood damage. This eased the crowding and gave the idle inmates something to do.

Also in 1877, Superintendent Strother was directed by the General Assembly to purchase a piece of ground to be used formally as a penitentiary cemetery, apparently since so many inmates were coming back mortally ill from the lease program. Unable to find a suitable ground for the money allotted, the board elected to use as a cemetery the property on the northeast side of the penitentiary complex beside the Richmond, Fredericksburg and Petersburg (RF&P) Railroad.

Another Fire and a New Contractor

The penitentiary experienced another fire on November 15, 1878, which completely destroyed the shoe manufacturing shops at a huge loss of about $33,600. The fire incited such a panic among the inmates that the military had to be called out to help restore order. Afterward, temporary wood buildings were erected and used until permanent ones were completed in the fall of 1879. The new building was about 40 feet by 221 feet and was three stories high. In June 1879, half of this new building was taken by Larus Brothers Tobacco, which employed about one hundred convicts processing plug and twist chewing tobacco. They paid the facility an annual fee for the space and about forty cents per day per convict.

There were flashes of hope and compassion in those years. Silas Beach, a prisoner sentenced in July 1874 to fifteen years in the penitentiary for murder, was pardoned on November 17, 1880, for his heroic actions during the fire. "He exerted himself very greatly, and rendered most valuable assistance in saving the public property," wrote Governor Kemper in the pardon.

CHANGES IN THE CONVICT LEASE SYSTEM

By 1881, new superintendent Sam C. Williams determined that the current form of convict lease system, in which the lessee or contractor paid a set price to the state and then retained total control over the lives and job duties of the convicts, had failed as a reformative measure. Abuses were rampant in this system that threw inmates all together in the same types of work, in the same abhorrent surroundings regardless of their crimes or sentences and left discipline up to the whims of the contractor and their sadistic, poorly trained guards. In addition to working the convicts to death, this method also seemed to harden the softer and younger convicts and, upon their release, sent them unprepared into society, where they quickly got into trouble. Recidivism skyrocketed.

Correctly calling the old system "barbarous in the extreme," Williams suggested changing the Virginia system to one where each convict was sent into a job best suited for his strength and temperament, where his labor was regulated by officers of the institution and discipline was strictly the responsibility of the state, not the contractor. "The dictates of humanity," Williams continued, "if no other consideration prevailed, should be sufficient to silence any effort to establish this system of prison management in Virginia."

Critics maintained that the proposed changes were instituted solely for financial reasons and had little to do with the welfare of the convicts; thus, the board disregarded Williams's suggestions and instead forced a full-blown lease system, as adopted by states such as Georgia and Louisiana. In fact, the board stated in the September 30, 1881 report, "[We are] pleased to discover, for the first time, that the general agent has reached the conclusion that the best way to make it [the prison] self-sustaining would be to lease the convict labor." George W. Cable wrote in *The Silent South* that "there seems to be reason to fear that this narrow view is carrying sentiment downward toward the Lease System itself."

By appearances, it would seem that way. In 1880–81, there were seven contractors actively leasing inmates both inside the penitentiary and out. Those inside the penitentiary included Joseph Davis & Company, shoe manufacturer (employing 285 convicts); S.G. Fairbanks, Cooperage manufacture (45 convicts); Larus Brothers Tobacco (89 convicts); and Weisenfeld and Company, a clothing manufacturer that employed 67 female inmates.

Outside contractors were all railroads, including Mason, Shanahan & Hoge of the Richmond and Alleghany Railroad (240 convicts), the Bristol

Coal and Iron Railroad (44 convicts) and Danville and New River Railroads (38 convicts). The Richmond and Clifton Forge Railroad Company was retained to provide transportation to all convicts in and out of Richmond. It also paid the expenses of prisons, medical facilities, kitchens and quarters for the inmates all along its line. By 1883, it was determined that these tweaks saved the state over $50,000 per year, especially in medical expenses.

DEATH AND FEUDING

Despite the fine-tuning, things seemed to go from bad to worse for the convicts. Between October 1880 and July 1881, twenty convicts died on the Richmond and Alleghany Railroad of various diseases, including dropsy, bronchitis, sunstroke and pneumonia. Eight alone died of dysentery and gastrointestinal problems, then three additional inmates died at the penitentiary of disease contracted on the railroad. Then, on August 9, 1881, nine more inmates—all black men between the ages of seventeen and forty-one—were crushed when a bank of earth collapsed on top of them. Physician M. Walker barely noted the tragedy, concluding in his report that "from the other railroads where prisoners were employed we have had good reports through the whole year."

Second, according to Superintendent Williams, penitentiary fiscal management prior to his arrival had been abysmal, and he was going to fix it. He claimed to find "wholly fictitious" earnings reports and that instead of the $90,000 reported as profits derived from manufacturing from 1875 to 1879, not one dollar of profit was actually realized to the state during that period. On the contrary, he maintained that large sums of money were actually lost during those four years.

After much arguing and finger-pointing between him, the board and penitentiary general agent Winfield Scott, Williams instituted numerous policy changes with only informal consultation with the penitentiary board of directors and no input from the General Assembly or his own staff. Agent Scott, appalled at Williams's despotic behavior and by what he perceived to be unethical and even illegal acts and lapses, responded by filing sixteen charges of malfeasance against his boss. These included improper bidding for contractors, the mismanagement of the wheelwright shop and even such personal offenses as the superintendent's consumption of penitentiary food and the purchase of carpets by him for his home with state money.

In their 1881 report to the governor and the assembly, the board addressed each charge, concluding, "The Board deems it simple justice to the Superintendent to say, that considering the obscurity and the conflicting character of the legislation governing the Penitentiary, it is a matter of surprise that he has not committed more mistakes, and that he has been able to make his administration a financial success by making the Penitentiary a self-supporting Institution." The governor concurred. Williams kept his job.

In 1883, a minister, Colonel W.P. Munford, celebrated fifteen straight years of volunteer duty conducting Sunday school without ever missing a single Sunday. During that tenure, Munford exercised a remarkable use of resources: out of his own pocket, and with what he could beg or borrow, he built and furnished the Sunday school and library and even somehow convinced the convicts to pool their measly earnings to buy an organ.

From 1882 to 1883, there were forty-seven convict deaths, with all but eleven occurring on the railroads (although many deaths in the penitentiary hospital were from the same diseases, indicating they may have gotten ill on the railroads and then quickly been shipped back to die in Richmond). Most deaths were from pneumonia, double pneumonia and pleuro-pneumonia, but there was one death from accidental injuries, two were shot trying to escape and two died from typhoid fever. One man, William Scott, died in the penitentiary hospital of "old age"—at age fifty-nine.

The main reason for the appalling and rapidly increasing number of railroad deaths was undoubtedly not just from the grueling labor but also the revolting living conditions the convicts endured under contractors who

Number	Name	Color	Age	Length of Time Confined		Date of Death	Disease or Cause of Death	Where Died
				Years	Months			
1	Scipio, Sie	Black	22		3	October 21, 1882	Meningitis	Valley railroad.
2	Stancil, George	"	40		5	November 2, 1882	Billious fever	Penitentiary hospital.
3	Brooks, Thomas	"	52	7	3	November 1, 1882	Accidental injuries	Valley railroad.
4	Jackson, William	"	20		1	November 28, 1882	Typho-malarial fever	Penitentiary hospital.
5	Lewis, Edward	"	19		½	November 30, 1882	Organic disease of the heart	Valley railroad.
6	Williams, Walker	"	51	1	1	January 13, 1883	Pneumonia	
7	Word, Henry	"	21		6	February 1, 1883	Pleuro-pneumonia	" "
8	Gardner, Jacob	"	50	3	4	February 4, 1883	Consumption	" "
9	Scott, William	"	59		8	February 6, 1883	Old age	Penitentiary hospital.
10	Aldridge, John	"	20	1	1	February 12, 1883	Bronchitis	" "
11	Bailey, Arthur	"	30	3	4	February 15, 1883	Pneumonitis	Valley railroad.
12	Williams, Edmund	"	37	1	6	February 25, 1883	Pleuro-pneumonia	" "
13	Whitman, Frank	"	18	4	9	February 25, 1883	Hypertrophy of the heart	" "
14	Baker, Charles	"	20	1	6	March 11, 1883	Typhoid pneumonia	Richm'd & Alleghany railroad.
15	Kain, Lee	"	21		5	March 21, 1883	Pneumonia	" "
16	Adams, Bradshaw	"	22	1		March 28, 1883	Pneumonia	" "
17	Turner, Hiram	"	26		9	March 24, 1883	Pneumonia	" "
18	Edwards, George	"	31	4	9	March 13, 1883	Double pneumonia	" "
19	Lewis, John	"	35		4	March 26, 1883	Pleuro-pneumonia	" "
20	Dickson, Cornelius	"	21	3		March 31, 1883	Pleuro-pneumonia	Valley railroad.
21	Bailey, Robert	"	22	1	10	April 1, 1883	Typhoid fever	" "
22	Waddleton, Martin	"	21		7	April 4, 1883	Heart disease	" "
23	Dinwiddie, William	"	54	4	1	April 9, 1883	Pneumonia	" "
24	Brent, James	"	31	4	1	April 7, 1883	Pneumonia	Bristol Coal & Iron railroad.
25	Johnson, Floyd	"	21		9	April 12, 1883	Pneumonia	Richm'd & Alleghany railroad.
26	Bacciguloupe, Angelo	White	42	3	3	May 8, 1883	Cholera morbus	Penitentiary hospital.
27	Dade, William	Black	28	2	11	May 9, 1883	Typhoid pneumonia	Richm'd & Alleghany railroad.
28	Hubbard, Phillip	"	68	2	9	May 14, 1883	Congestion of the lungs	Danville & New River railroad.
29	Gordon, Willie	"	56	40	5	May 20, 1883	Pneumonia	" "

A partial list of deaths in the penitentiary and convict lease camps in 1882–83. *1883* Journal of the House of Delegates.

simply didn't care. "Wherever I found the lease system in the South, I found convicts in a hopeless state of slavery, more cruel and inhuman than chattel slavery ever was during the last half of the last century," wrote Collis Lovely, the special agent in the Missouri Department of Labor who was investigating prison conditions in a series that appeared in the July–October 1905 editions of the *Shoe Makers Journal*. "The lessee has no interest in the convict except to secure the largest amount of labor in a given time."

There are not only nonexistent records but also no reporting of the actual conditions of the railroad work camps in Virginia and West Virginia from the late 1850s into the mid-1880s, for good reason—the *Richmond Whig* newspaper was owned by the Norfolk and Western Railroad and the *Richmond Inquirer* was owned by the Southern Railway, making it unlikely they would publicize atrocious working conditions promulgated by their own bosses. The city's black newspaper, the fiercely independent *Richmond Planet*, periodically reported atrocities occurring in other state railway camps but none involving convicts from the penitentiary in Richmond.

It may be presumed, however, that these camps varied little from similar camps dotting the American South. The sleeping apartments (prisons) were usually three loosely constructed box-type houses into which the prisoners were crowded together. The beds were made of rough wood in a continuous row, with a narrow board separating each one. The bedding consisted of straw-filled burlap "ticks" with two cotton blankets. The convicts sometimes slept two in a bed, naked or in their work clothes. Sodomy prevailed in some of the camps, "and the little boys were the sufferers," according to an investigative committee in the Tennessee camps.

The convicts' clothing was changed once a week and, when washed, was distributed indiscriminately, without regard to size, with no man getting the same clothing he had before.

Railroads tried to keep food costs to between four and eight cents per meal. Breakfast consisted of a coffee substitute, thin soup and corn bread. Lunch was usually a chunk of hog meat (sowbelly or fatback) and corn bread. Supper was cow peas or dried beans and corn bread.

Earthquake and Fire Again

On August 31, 1886, at about 10:00 p.m., a severe earthquake that destroyed Charleston, South Carolina, also rattled Richmond for almost a minute.

The shaking caused panic among the residents but especially inside the penitentiary, alarming many inmates to the point that many managed to free themselves from their cells and rush the main gate. There was a great scare but little to no damage from the quake.

In February 1888, under Superintendent Moses, fire again struck the penitentiary. This time, the shoe shop was destroyed, depriving the state of about $40,000 in revenue. By the end of that year, however, the damage had been repaired and 245 male convicts were back at work for the Davis Shoe Company, with 28 females in the women's shoes department. Also that year, 386 convicts were employed by four different railroads, with the Roanoke and Southern employing the most with 131. In 1888, 22 convicts died on those railroads, while 7 convicts died in the hospital.

Penitentiary physician Dr. J.C. Watson delivered a frank explanation for the high number of deaths in his report to the General Assembly, explaining that the state had been called during the winter months to furnish the different railroad companies a much larger number of convicts than usual. "And especially would I mention the treatment and manner in which these men were handled by those in charge," he wrote of their management in the hands of heartless, poorly trained guards. "Ordering these men, as must be done, directly from cells and workshops, exposing them thus totally unprepared to the vicissitudes of camp life, coupled with this sudden and unaccustomed hard labor, must necessarily and seriously impair the health and strength of many." The railroad had to proceed; the General Assembly yawned at Watson's warning.

Fortunately, the coming decade would cast more light on the Virginia penal system, and solutions to the overwhelming problems would finally be considered—including the daunting challenge of what to do about children inside the penitentiary.

CHAPTER 6
"LET THE CHILDREN SUFFER"

As there is no separation between prisoners convicted of different grades of crime, the boy from twelve to twenty years of age, who enters the prison for the first time, knowing little of crime and having no acquaintance with criminals, may find himself in the company of a man, possibly in a cell with three or four such, who have spent their lives in crime, and have no desire or purpose of changing their course.
—report of the general agent of the penitentiary to the board, 1883

On October 1, 1875, inmate Thomas Nowlin died of third-degree burns suffered when he fell into a tub of boiling coffee in the penitentiary kitchen.

Thomas was ten years old.

Virginia law once dictated that children as young as nine who committed certain crimes were sent, as Nowlin, to the penitentiary to serve sentences as full-blown inmates. There was no juvenile detention, reform schools or other options for these young lawbreakers, even though since before 1860 over a dozen states had initiated such reformatories. Most all ages were tried and sentenced as adults by Virginia's indifferent corrections system, and it appears little consideration was given to shortened sentences due to age. Corporal punishments, such as the ball and chain, were used even on the youngest inmates if necessary.

While there were a few instances of juveniles committing more serious crimes, such as arson and even manslaughter, most were convicted of

"The children scavengers" in Richmond, 1891. Frank Leslie's Illustrated Newspaper, *November 1891.*

nonviolent felonies such as vagrancy, housebreaking, larceny and burglary. These were not career criminals; they were almost always troubled, desperately poor or mentally disabled kids committing isolated incidents, many times at the behest of adults. A prisoner admittance register for 1873, for example, lists Emma Warren, a fourteen-year-old black girl from Mecklenburg County sentenced to six years for "jail burning." She was identified by "two front teeth broke off" and her "unkempt appearance." Her court record indicates she was attempting to free a parent from the county jail.

A nine-year-old Richmond boy named Jasper Washington was convicted in Hustings Court of stealing a horse and surrey and then sentenced in October 1896 to three years. In September 1898, the youth escaped from the Henrico work farm but was quickly recaptured. He was eventually released on May 22, 1899—a penitentiary veteran at age twelve.

Like Tom Nowlin, Jeff Connally was a ten-year-old black Halifax County youth who was sentenced on April 15, 1873, to five years for manslaughter. On November 13, Connally's situation got a lot worse when he was contracted out with thirty-five adult convicts to Mason, Gooch and Hoge to labor on the Valley Railroad. At fifty-one inches, he was an ideal height for working in the tunnels. At night, he was chained to several adults in the barracks. Fortunately for this child, his sentence was commuted sometime in 1875.

As evidenced by Connally, juvenile inmates were not exempt from being farmed out on grueling and often deadly public works projects to labor side by side with adults. On June 19, 1868, thirteen-year-old Thomas Buck, a black youth from Southampton County serving a ten-year sentence for grand larceny, was sent to work twelve-hour days as a "clay picker" for the Old Dominion Granite Company (ODGC). Twelve-year-old Richmond boy Marcellus Lowlen labored for two years there. Fifteen-year-old Sam Carter worked for four years at ODGC before he was discharged on May 17, 1872.

Located in Chesterfield, the ODGC started using convict labor at the suggestion of former Union Railroad engineer Herman Haupt, who formed an alliance with the quarry to transport the convict-mined granite for a reduced rate aboard his trains on the Richmond and Danville Railroad. These back-door deals at the expense of convict (and child) labor were typical of the times. At its peak, the quarry employed about 275 convicts and paid the penitentiary twenty-five cents per day for each. Shelter was provided in nearby unheated shanties.

On April 16, 1875, ODGC specifically requested "boys and infirm convicts" to work at an unspecified job. Penitentiary superintendent Strother responded by sending thirteen-year-old James Crocker, who was serving an eighteen-month sentence for unlawful shooting; ten-year-old William Davis, serving three years for larceny; and John Smith, a disabled eighteen-year-old serving ten years for malicious assault. They were accompanied by fifty-year-old Pittsylvania County man Morton Witcher, who was serving a fifteen-year sentence for homicide. On February 23, 1876, Crocker's work partner, thirty-nine-year-old Joe Bird, died after having both legs crushed by a massive block of granite at the quarry, underscoring the relentless worksite danger to which those young convicts were exposed.

There was an occasional motion of sympathy toward wayward youths by the penitentiary and Governor James Kemper in particular. On September 22, 1876, six black teenagers, all under the age of sixteen, were conditionally pardoned after serving hard labor for three months of a five-year sentence for burglary of a Wythe County hotel. Apparently hungry, they all broke into the hotel dining room and "took sundry edibles, which they consumed on the spot."

"Their offence was in the nature of an impulsive and frolicsome freak of boyhood," stated the governor's reason for the pardon, "wanting in some of the essential elements of burglary, yet not altogether free from such wickedness as deserves punishment."

Before being discharged from the penitentiary, each received thirty-nine lashes across their bare backs.

By September 30, 1881, there were incarcerated at the penitentiary three eleven-year-olds, three twelve-year-olds, eight thirteen-year-olds, twelve fourteen-year-olds and twenty-three fifteen-year-olds. All were black males with the exception of one eleven-year-old.

"Swaddled in Stripes"

There was another group of children in the penitentiary who were not convicts, but children of convicts, living under the same wretched, overcrowded conditions. The presence of newborns and children under the age of five was prescribed by informal codes until Virginia Penitentiary statute 4124 was formally instituted in 1887 and then amended in 1902. It ominously stipulated that "an infant accompanying a convict mother to the penitentiary, or born after her imprisonment therein, shall be returned, on attaining the age of four years, to the county or city from which the mother came, to be disposed of as the County Court of said county…may order."

The situation was seriously flawed and the rule erratically upheld. Fathers had little to no rights to their children, so the law forbid the very young from living alone outside the penitentiary with their fathers or with certain relatives. They were rarely discharged by their fourth birthday, as the law left them nowhere to go. There are several instances of children ages five years and six months still living inside the wall with their mothers.

These very young children were almost always black, since black mothers and pregnant black women were incarcerated far more regularly than pregnant white women, who usually got a pass from sympathetic judges and prosecutors unless they were particularly poor, "coarse" or their crime particularly heinous. For example, Maria Dabney, a black woman, was in her final days of pregnancy when she was admitted on April 6, 1876, for stealing. Her son James was born only seven days later.

Like the juvenile convicts, most of these women were not career criminals but desperately poor women driven to crime by circumstance.

Mary Morst was pregnant with twins when sentenced to the penitentiary for murdering her husband in 1912. She gave birth to Joseph and Martha, who years later were transferred to an orphanage. Joseph died in 1990 and Martha in 2008. *Library of Virginia.*

But as the post–Civil War black female convict population grew, the births increased and added to the overcrowding in the women's ward. On October 1, 1879, there were twelve black children under five years of age in the penitentiary. One child, Joseph K. Thornton, was five years, seven months on that date.

The penitentiary administration knew for years it had a children problem but had no clue how to address it in the face of a circular law, no reform programs and a recalcitrant General Assembly. Penitentiary physician W.A. Patteson reported to the assembly in 1858 that there had been four recent births, declaring, "These infants are not proper inmates of the prison, and as soon as they can be weaned from their parents, those of them who are free shall be removed therefrom."

The presence of four children of slave convicts in 1863 was of particular concern to Governor Letcher, who wrote, "[The children]...have committed no crime, and humanity requires that some disposition be made of them that will remove them from the institution." Letcher's "humane" recommendation in those pre-emancipation days was that the children be taken from their mothers and sold as property.

Of particular concern are certain births recorded inside the penitentiary that occurred long after the mother was admitted. Robert Douglas, a black male, was born on January 1, 1874, in the penitentiary hospital. His mother, Phillis Douglas, was admitted on August 11, 1869—five years earlier. On July 2, 1878, George Washington Deford was born to Martha Deford, who was admitted to the penitentiary six years earlier, on August 10, 1872.

With conjugal visits by males explicitly forbidden and separation of male inmates from women strictly enforced, the pregnancies of these women would be nothing short of biblical if not for the lurking presence of unscrupulous male guards who were notorious throughout the South for their brutal and misogynistic treatment of female prisoners. With no female matron until the early 1880s to advocate for the women, it may be assumed those babies were most likely the product of rape.

Many of the babies born in the penitentiary prior to 1900 were stillborn or died shortly after birth, mainly due to the inadequate nutrition of their mothers and the absence of prenatal care. One little unnamed boy born on February 5, 1879, died about twelve hours after birth. One set of twins, described on the hospital ledger as "small and emaciated," died within two days. There is no record of any of their burials.

It is academic to consider if the public would be so accepting of this situation had they been aware of the true conditions for these children, but it seems that due mainly to ingrained prison-based racism, they chose to ignore the problem and just accept the deceits spoon-fed to them by the local media. In the December 14, 1902 edition of the *Richmond Dispatch*, a white reporter writing under the initials R.C.H. composed an almost glowing description of a scene he personally witnessed on a visit to the penitentiary, informing the city's "gentle readers" that conditions were really not so bad for children born or living inside the wall:

> *Playing about on the pavement of the cell house where the women sleep were two little pickaninnies aged 18 months and three years. They are the only children in the penitentiary, and can stay there until they are five years old. They are allowed to run about in the yard, where the laundry is hung out, and seem as much at home as if they were around the old cabin door on the farm. They stared in wonder at the visitors as they passed through, entirely unmindful of their habitation and nativity. They seemed to be as well cared*

for as the average little darkey, and doubtless are a source of comfort to the women whose lives are spent in the confines of narrow cells.

According to the penitentiary report of 1902–03, these two "pickaninnies" were Henrietta Carrington Yates, daughter of Maria Yates, and Junius Raymond Dodson, son of the notorious Lizzie Dodson, who was serving a life term for her third conviction after famously escaping on Christmas Eve 1900.

"Conceived in sin and swaddled in stripes," the babies and young children who managed to make it to their fifth birthdays were an invisible class of prison society. Penitentiary records list their names, births and their mothers' names, but there is no record of their lives, care, education (if any) or disposition from the facility. After being taken from their mothers, it is unknown in all but a scarce few cases where they went or with whom they lived. A note on a 1902 physician's report states that three-year-old Maria Braxton, for example, was adopted by her grandmother on May 30 of that year. For the rest, one year they are listed on penitentiary reports, the next year they are not. They simply vanish.

Into the 1880s, governors and legislators continued to voice toothless apprehensions of the very real threat to both these offspring and the juvenile inmates in the general population of being corrupted (and much worse) by older and frequently more vicious inmates, but time and again, they failed to act on those concerns. Some assemblymen even insisted that for many of Richmond's notorious "street urchins," having a roof over their head and three meals a day inside the notorious penitentiary or toiling in chains in granite quarries and railroad tunnels was a more beneficial lifestyle than begging and scrounging through trash in the city's filthy streets.

Thus, Virginia continued its reprehensible treatment of children as the juvenile penitentiary population continued to grow. A general agent's

TABLE E.

Children Remaining in Penitentiary September 30, 1905

Number.	Name of Child.	Date of Birth.	Place of Birth.	Color.	Sex.	Name of Mother.	Mother Admitted.
1	Junius Raymond Dodson	September 2, 1901	Fairfax County	Colored	Male	Lizzie Dodson, 4092	November 30, 1901
2	Julia Lee Dabney	April, 1904	Fluvanna County	Colored	Female	Anna Dabney, 5762	January 12, 1905
3	Elizabeth Howard	March 17, 1905	Penitentiary	Colored	Female	Maggie Howard	February 3, 1905

Rosa Johnson, daughter of Eliza Johnson, 4702, born November, 1904, in Charlottesville, Va., died February 5, 1905.
Theo. Roosevelt Lewis, son of Queen Lewis, 5365, born November 8, 1904, in Penitentiary, died April 2, 1905.

A physician's report showing two deaths and three surviving children in the penitentiary in 1905, including Junius Dodson, age four. *1905* Journal of the General Assembly.

report to the General Assembly in 1883 stated that on September 30 of that year, there were 140 inmates between eleven and twenty-one years of age serving sentences of one year or more. "These young criminals are thrown in the cells at night, on Sundays and holidays, with hardened and habitual criminals of the most dangerous class," the report warned in almost customary boilerplate that, once again, would be ignored by the General Assembly. "If these young men have not belonged to the criminal class and enter the prison with the determination that this term shall be their last, they are disheartened and degraded by the association."

To the penitentiary's credit, this particular report recommended that the assembly establish for those prisoners under age eighteen a separate department, or reformatory, away from the adult prisoners, with detached workshops for the use of those young convicts who were not career criminals but who committed isolated punishable offenses. In such a department, the report concluded, the first aim should be to "employ the inmates at trades which would require hard labor and develop skill." Education was never mentioned, but it was a noble beginning. "To redeem these youths should be considered as one of the first needs of the Penitentiary."

Again, the assembly failed to act on this recommendation, but it did elect to appropriate funds to construct a new women's prison inside the facility to better keep the females separated from the men (although not necessarily the guards) and to help provide better care for the youngest children inside. Designed after New York's King County Prison, the new female unit was completed in 1884.

From Behind the Iron Bars

A decade later, a woman identified only as "O.L." of the Woman's Christian Temperance Union (WCTU), after visiting the penitentiary and city jails in Richmond, Culpeper and Lynchburg, stressed in a letter in the January 16, 1897 edition of *The Reformer* magazine that there was an immediate need in the commonwealth for a reformatory especially for "colored youths."

"Virginia, mother of states and statesman," she wrote, "has not yet learned the wisdom of practicing preventive methods, but waits for the offence to be committed, the way being kept open for the hapless child to fall into the pitfall of crime, and then provides punishment which, in most cases, leaves him worse in the last state than in the first."

O.L. wrote of visiting a fourteen-year-old boy in the penitentiary, "a little vagabond, who had become a nuisance in his neighborhood," who was sent there for five years for horse stealing. She described a girl, age twelve, who looked as if she were not over age ten, illustrating her as "a little ginger-cake colored thing, with very nice manners and a soft musical voice," who "scanned me curiously through the iron bars." After a few kind words and noticing there was nothing in her cell other than a straw mattress and a bucket, the writer promised to take her some quilt pieces so that she could "have something to do while in jail." This girl was most likely Roberta Jones, inmate no. 15006, who was admitted on August 15, 1896, to serve a two-year term for housebreaking. She was discharged on May 15, 1898.

O.L. also spoke of visiting a "sturdy boy" about age twelve, who had stabbed another boy with a knife in a fight over a game of marbles, "cutting his appetite out of him." She emphasized presciently that a child like this would eventually end up in the gallows if at such a young age he could not get the help he needed.

She closed her letter by stating, "Sometimes it seems to me that our community, while professing Christianity, has taken for its motto the words 'Let the children suffer,' instead of the saying of the founder of our faith, 'Suffer the little children to come unto me.'"

By 1900, the fact that over seventy-eight penitentiary inmates were still under eighteen years of age, all packed into cells with adults, proved the legislature was not serious about keeping children out, keeping them safe or reforming them in any way. The assembly did, according to the October 21, 1900 edition of the *Richmond Dispatch*, vote that session to allot funds to continue caring for "poor, aged, and enfeebled" Confederate veterans.

In 1902, the penitentiary admitted 157 inmates between the ages of ten and twenty, and in 1904, it received 127 between eleven and twenty. Effie Morton, a black girl twelve years of age, was sentenced for three years for setting her employer's house on fire after an argument. Ten-year-old Willie Smith was admitted in September 1896 to serve two years for housebreaking. He was released in 1897 and then was re-admitted on April 17, 1900, for stealing. He was sentenced to one year, with the requisite five more years added for the second offense. When he was eventually discharged on September 15, 1905, at age nineteen, he had already spent one-third of his young life in the penitentiary.

From Imprisoning to Executing:
The Slippery Slope

Harry Sitlington was sixteen years old when he was sentenced to death for the murder of Fannie Brown in Rockbridge County in 1910. Barely five feet tall and one hundred pounds, he was electrocuted in December, just after turning seventeen. The *Richmond Times* noted, "The boy had a criminal look and seemed not to realize the enormity of his crime." *Library of Virginia.*

By 1912, there were fewer juveniles under the age of sixteen sentenced for property crimes, but as late as 1915, Virginia was still imprisoning and, worse, had graduated to executing sixteen- and seventeen-year-olds—some even for non-capital crimes, such as attempted assault—proving again that fundamentally very little had changed in attitudes toward children from what Thomas Jefferson described as the "brutal and archaic" laws of colonial times.

In 1918, the General Assembly amended code 4124 again, stating that in the absence of any family members, a child whose mother was imprisoned could, upon reaching age four, be committed to the State Board of Charities. This was a respite for the babies born inside the penitentiary but did nothing to alleviate the suffering of the juvenile inmates.

Records are unclear as to when the practice of incarcerating young children finally stopped, although it was the reforms of the 1920s that made life easier for Virginia's law-breaking juveniles. The ball and chain for children was discontinued in 1920, but solitary confinements in "brigs" at the State Farm continued. These solitary cells had no beds, no mattresses and no chairs, leaving children to sleep on the concrete floor under one blanket for up to two weeks at a time. Legislation that created the Board of Public Welfare and a juvenile court in Richmond in 1922 specified that "all delinquent children intended to be placed in a state institution shall be committed to the State Board of Public Welfare."

Births inside the penitentiary dropped sharply in the early 1930s. Only one little girl, Madeline Johnson, was born there on August 9, 1926, and three more girls were born there between December 1930 and February 1931.

Thomas Nowlin, the little boy who was scalded to death, was "mulatto," four feet, seven inches in height and from Roanoke. He was admitted on

No.	NAMES.	COLOR.		AGE.		LENGTH OF TIME IN PRISON.		DATE OF DEATH.	DISEASE OR CAUSE OF DEATH.	REMARKS.
		White.	Black.	Years.	Mos.	Years.	Mos.			
1	Nowlin, Thomas....	....	Black..	10	6	....	5½	Oct. 1st, 1875....	....	This boy fell into a tub of boiling coffee and died on the 5th day after.

A physician's report on the death of ten-year-old Thomas Nowlin. *1875* Journal of the House of Delegates.

April 20, 1875—two weeks after his tenth birthday—to serve a four-year sentence for setting fire to a tobacco barn. On September 25, he was a little over five months into his sentence when he fell into the boiling coffee while working as a sweeper in the kitchen. He survived for five excruciating days in the penitentiary hospital before he died of his burns. His burial place is unknown.

CHAPTER 7

PUBLIC AWARENESS AND STATE FARMS

The only drawback to my delightful visit to Richmond was the knowledge I obtained about the horrible condition of the cells in the penitentiary, and the dreadful scenes I witnessed in the city jail, which linger in my mind.
—*"O.L.,"* The Reformer *magazine, 1897*

YE VISITED ME

Prison conditions across the American South were suddenly under scrutiny after the 1891 publication of J.C. Powell's *The American Siberia: or, Fourteen Years' Experience in a Southern Convict Camp*, which was an unflinching exposé of the barbaric Florida chain gangs. Its publication was rapidly followed by more revelations of the abuses of the Georgia chain gangs and of cruelties toward convicts in Louisiana and Tennessee. Books like *The Crime of Crimes* by Clarissa Olds Keeler and the Prison Reform League's *Crime and Criminals* raised public awareness of the state of America's southern convicts but apparently did little to increase public compassion toward them. Considering the majority of prisoners in those states were blacks convicted of crimes against whites, they were perhaps deemed not as worthy of white sympathies.

Virginia's penal system fared better in the media when compared to those horrifying gulags of the Deep South, but it did not completely escape study. A private inspection in 1896 and published in 1904 under the title

The Convict System Unmasked stated, in part, "The [Virginia] institution is ably managed from a financial point of view: otherwise it is a disgrace to humanity, a blot upon the escutcheon of the State. The old structure is in the main [building], antiquated, stuffy-cells, overladen with foul air, sanitary arrangements of the crudest character, the prisoners crowded… many cells infested with vermin, the condition beggars description."

The Reformer magazine also sent a reporter through many Virginia prisons in 1895, offering a report focusing more on the disproportionate number of blacks and children contained therein. "How pitiful seemed the condition of the wretched criminals," the anonymous writer opined, "some of them children in years, when one contrasted such pictures with that of the well-to-do classes assembling so often in the churches when the Gospel taught by him who said, 'I was in prison and ye visited me.'"

Those who visited "the wretched criminals" often found food and lodging at one of many Oregon Hill homes across Belvidere Street. Many of those offering comfort and housing were immigrants who had witnessed horrific treatments of their own families in their homelands.

STATE FARM

We doubt if there is any prison in any English-speaking land where the cells are as overcrowded as are those in the Virginia Penitentiary.
—*"A Disgrace,"* Richmond Dispatch, *September 15, 1897*

In addition to the shameful living conditions, the Virginia General Assembly was aghast at the $61,888 annual cost of feeding, clothing and guarding that many prisoners within the penitentiary walls. Superintendent Moses's term, however, was drawing to a close, and it appeared the problem again was going to get pushed to the back burner. It wasn't until Superintendent Bushrod Washington Lynn was appointed that he and Virginia's secretary of agriculture, Colonel Thomas Whitehead, floated the idea of creating a State Farm, where selected convicts could work farm labor and relieve some of the overcrowding at the penitentiary. Whitehead insisted to the Board of Agriculture that the farm would not only be self-sustaining but could even earn a profit.

In fact, the commonwealth saw the experimental farm serving the dual purpose of not just providing crops to other state institutions but also serving as a sanitarium for sick and terminally ill convicts to get them out of the city. In January 1893, the General Assembly inspected three properties and then the following January authorized the superintendent $16,000 to purchase a farm twenty-six miles west of Richmond. They erected necessary buildings, cells and stockades for "the care and employment of convicts unfit for service in the penitentiary, or who for sanitary or other reasons should be removed there from." Within one year, there were two hundred convicts there, many of them ill and unable to work.

Not everyone was a fan of the farm. The *Alexandria Gazette* asked, "How much better would it be for the state and everybody in it if the convicts were employed in the work of improving the country roads? But legislators are too much engaged with other things to bother themselves about the improvement of roads."

Superintendent Lynn, however, was listening to his critics, and in 1895, he proposed that felony convictions of one year or less should, at the behest of the judge or jury, be either sentenced to the penitentiary, sent to their local city or county jail or farmed out on road work. He saw this as fixing numerous problems, including relieving overcrowding at the penitentiary, getting much-needed road work done and reducing the exorbitant costs of transporting short-timers to Richmond from outlying counties.

By 1895, as the State Farm struggled financially, the penitentiary itself became profitable. "We are now on a solid business basis," wrote Superintendent Lynn in the 1894 annual report. "Our contracts run for a long period of time, and with no adverse or unwise legislation to destroy our industries we shall not only be self-sustaining, but be able to pay into the treasury of the State a handsome sum each year."

But a problem arose: critics of penitentiary manufacturing maintained that it was unfair to private industry to have to compete with convict labor, which produced goods at a much cheaper cost. The penitentiary, in turn, argued that convicts languishing in "enforced idleness" would result in a loss to the state of at least $150,000 annually, which was out of the question.

The debate was deflected by the General Assembly to roads and bridges. "With good thoroughfares and strong and durable bridges, instead of the miserable makeshifts now in use all over the commonwealth, there would be an improvement...that would, in a short time...add largely to the taxable wealth of the State," the January 22, 1896 *Roanoke Times* agreed in returning convicts to public works projects. "Flourishing villages would spring up...and substantial school houses, commodious places of worship and homes of elegance and comfort would be the rule in the rural districts where they are now the exception."

The fact that the penitentiary was finally turning a profit was irresistible to the legislature, and the manufacturing concerns remained unchanged.

A MUTINY IS QUELLED, THEN THE STATE FARM BLOSSOMS

To be confined at the farm, a convict had to fit at least one of four criteria: (1) be from county jails and suffering from tuberculosis, syphilis or other "loathsome diseases"; (2) be crippled, disabled or wounded as to be unfit for work at the penitentiary; (3) be an "idiot, imbecile or a juvenile" for whom the law had not yet provided a home; or (4) have contracted a disease inside the penitentiary.

In May 1896, Governor O'Farrell visited the farm and was duly impressed. Tobacco was being cultivated on 150 acres, corn on 400 acres, oats on 200 acres and 150 acres in peas and beans. During his visit, many convicts appealed to his honor for clemency, including a "small number of negro boys."

Exactly one year later, however, a mutiny nearly broke out. Riddick Christmas, a black convict, approached guard Hudgins after dinner, ostensibly to ask a favor. He spit tobacco juice in Hudgins's eyes and grabbed his rifle. At that moment, several convicts watching broke for freedom. Another guard named Quales saw the altercation and the fleeing convicts and fired twice at Christmas, hitting him in the shoulder and the ankle. The shooting stopped the escape attempts of all except James Mallory, who was later recaptured.

In 1898, there were fifty-two diseases and injuries treated at the farm, with consumption and dysentery by far the most common. There were twelve deaths, with more than half from consumption. One fourteen-year-old named W.H. Jordan "took sick at farm" with lung congestion and died. A seventy-two-year-old named Thomas Griffin was listed as "received in a debilitated state" at the farm and died of chronic diarrhea.

Under Superintendent Helms, the conditional pardon system was instituted. Under this system, any convict, after serving half of his or her sentence and being a model prisoner, could apply for a conditional pardon. The program was considered successful; out of the 495 convicts pardoned by 1902, only 7 had been returned to the penitentiary.

With the farm still unprofitable, the board recommended in 1904 that the penitentiary and the State Farm have separate supervisors. Over the next several years, several construction projects were initiated, including the building of consumptive and tubercular wards, a well, a cattle barn and a huge concrete silo. From 1908 to 1912, a new brick steam-heated cellblock was added that at the time was the most modern prison building in the United States.

In 1906, many convicts were finally put to work building roads with the passage of the Withers-Lassiter Good Roads Law, which placed construction of all Virginia roadways under the control of the penitentiary superintendent. Three camps opened that year, employing almost 200 convicts, and after two more years, six camps were established constructing roads in eight counties. Road crew duty was confined to felons sentenced five years or less, so of the 344 convicts employed in these camps, 246 were from the penitentiary and the rest from local jails.

There were inevitable objections to the plan. The sight of predominantly black chain gangs in striped uniforms toiling along the roadway was supposedly insulting to white travelers, who felt it improperly introduced their children to the concept of (black) crime and punishment.

Regardless, soon there were thirty-three road crew camps around Virginia, from Warrenton to Wytheville, each costing the state only about seventy cents per day in operating costs. For recreation, some camps had radios or even Victrola record players. Many had baseball teams, and religious services were conducted under the supervision of Reverend R.V. Lancaster.

On November 26, 1910, the penitentiary inmates got some entertainment of their own when barnstorming pilot John Moisant took off from the fairgrounds in a Bleriot monoplane, which the previous year had been flown across the English Channel by its inventor, Louis Bleriot. Moisant made a few passes over the penitentiary at the request of the *Times-Dispatch*, giving the star-struck inmates their first look at a real airplane.

In 1914, a lime grinding plant started operation in Staunton to provide low-cost limestone to valley farmers and builders. It employed about fifty convicts.

In 1915, the farm turned a profit of $19,928, and in 1919, the profit was $66,473. Clearly, with the farm, the lime plant and the road camps, Virginia's penal system had found a winning combination.

But back at the penitentiary, something very horrifying had unfolded.

CHAPTER 8

EUGENICS COVER-UP

In our enlightened age, let us put a stop to this hideous reproduction of criminals and sterilize the criminal grandson for the good it will do in the coming years.
—*Dr. Charles V. Carrington, Virginia Penitentiary physician, in an address to the American Prison Association, Richmond, Virginia, 1908*

Dr. Charles Venable Carrington had impeccable medical credentials. A Charlotte County native, he was accepted into the University of Virginia medical program in 1885 and was a member of the Chi Phi fraternity. After his 1889 graduation, he became resident physician at Richmond's St. Luke's Hospital, working for Dr. Hunter McGuire. He was associate professor of clinical surgery at the University College of Medicine at Richmond and visiting surgeon at the Magdalene home and the United States military recruiting station.

Dr. Carrington was also a respected figure in Richmond society, attending all the right social events with his beautiful wife, the former Avis Walker, and their daughter, Frances. He was soon appointed both staff surgeon for Governor Tyler and part-time assistant physician at the Virginia Penitentiary in 1898 under fellow UVa graduate Dr. Benjamin Harrison, whose father was nephew of the late president.

Dr. Harrison became sick with typhoid fever after serving as penitentiary physician for seven years. He took a leave of absence on August 20, 1900, and then died on September 11. Governor Tyler appointed Dr. Carrington penitentiary physician on September 15.

Dr. Charles V. Carrington. *From* Men of Mark in Virginia, *1909.*

A New Doctor in Town

Within one week of his appointment, Carrington had to prepare a report for the 1900 *Annual Reports of Officers, Boards and Institutions for the Commonwealth of Virginia*. "My observations thus far enable me to state that the general health of the inmates is good," he wrote, "…but [I could] write volumes upon the horrors of the badly ventilated, filthy cells and the inhumanity of crowding men in them." He, however, had much praise for the women's matron, Mrs. Page, and the excellent health standards maintained by her in the women's ward.

The filthy and overcrowded conditions in the men's cells continuously challenged Carrington's medical acumen. In a March 26, 1901 speech at the Hotel Jefferson to the Virginia Academy of Medicine and Surgery, he decried the Virginia legislature's decision to pack the criminally insane with the healthy "like so many sardines" to reduce costs to the state mental hospitals. Cell number 135, for example, which was twenty-two feet by twenty-five feet and built for a maximum capacity of 8, contained 32 inmates. The smallest cells, designed for 1 or 2 inmates, held 4. Altogether, the nearly 1,300 inmates were jammed into 192 cells, "as thick as cattle."

Doctors and health professionals in the audience were mortified to hear that the penitentiary at that time had no formal kitchen or mess hall, and meals were still being prepared as they had been fifty years earlier in what Carrington described as "a former filthy dungeon." He told them that prisoners ate their frequently cold food in their cells with their hands. In older cells without sewage disposal pipes, the toilet buckets still had to be carried out and dumped in the trough to the open-air lagoon. Sleep was almost impossible, "with beds alive with bugs which have resisted efforts to destroy them."

Despite the horrible conditions he described, his 1901–02 report to the General Assembly was much more upbeat, noting that the all-important death rate during that year was only 17.25 per 1,000. "Two of these deaths occurred within fifty days after the men were received; they contracted the diseases resulting in their death on the outside," he wrote, adding it was no fault of the penitentiary. He also reported a 16 percent drop in patients treated in the hospital, and the number of inmates suffering from "the itch" was down 50 percent. Also, a dentist, Dr. E.W. Bowles, DDS, started making regular visits, resulting in "added comfort to the men." Seven hundred inmates had teeth extracted that year. Of course, the death rate was so low because the sickest men were sent to the State Farm, where the death rates were 45.5 per 1,000.

But while Carrington heavily criticized most departments of the penitentiary, reiterating the "villainous health surroundings, abominable kitchen, infamous sewage system and no dining room," he profusely thanked the assembly for the finely equipped operating room, where he could repair hernias, suture amputated fingers and perform other surgeries as needed. "This liberality on your part has resulted in the cure of two cases of almost pronounced permanent disability and given me untold comfort in the knowledge that I was thoroughly equipped for any emergency that might arise."

But the following year, that "finely equipped operating room" would become the scene of something far more sinister than hernia repair.

"I Sterilized Him"

On March 5, 1897, a black Tazewell man named Hiram Steele was picked up for transportation to the penitentiary to serve a ten-year sentence for second-degree murder. Considered "cruelly deranged," he attacked another prisoner to whom he was handcuffed when he was brought out of the Tazewell jail, beating and biting the man viciously. On the train to Richmond, Steele threw a fit and tried to bite other passengers. Once in Richmond, the erratic man bounced between the penitentiary and Central State Hospital near Petersburg for four years because no one wanted to be responsible for him.

In 1901, Steele escaped from Central State not once but twice, was recaptured both times and sent back to the penitentiary. While there, Carrington took a special interest in the unbalanced and violent prisoner. "This poor creature was most dangerously homicidal, and was the wildest, fiercest, most consistent masturbator I have ever seen; as strong as a bull, as

Hiram Steele, involuntarily sterilized in September 1902. *Library of Virginia.*

cunning as a hyena, and more ferocious and quite as dangerous as a Bengal tiger," he reported in the December 24, 1909 issue of the *Virginia Medical Monthly* of the mentally disabled Steele.

He had an idea. Conflating homicidal impulses with sexual derangement, Carrington in September 1902 took Steele into his finely appointed hospital. "I determined to tame [Steele], and under general anesthesia, I sterilized him," Carrington reported to the Virginia Medical Society. "Improvement with him was reasonably rapid, both physically and mentally."

Thus, Carrington instituted, with no precedent, no oversight and no administrative authority, a prototype program of involuntary institutional sterilization a full twenty-two years before the 1924 passage of Virginia's Eugenics Bill No. 96, to "provide for the sexual sterilization of inmates of or patients in State Institutions." He firmly believed that sterilization was the only thing that would calm the irrational and homicidal Hiram Steele.

"The punitive side of our dealings with criminals is always to the front," Carrington wrote in the *Journal of Prison Discipline.* "Punish him is the first proposition. Lock him up. These are our Christianizing reformative measures, splendid in their way, but for the habitual criminal there must be some powerful deterrent remedy, and sterilization is undoubtedly that remedy."

But the procedure Carrington actually performed on Steele is suspect. The penitentiary hospital ledger and quotes from addresses to medical groups indicate that Carrington may not have performed a simple vasectomy on the sexually deranged prisoner to "calm him down" and stop him from masturbating. In fact, Steele's hospital ledger entry shows the original procedure "Testectomy" (a form of castration) redacted in ink and the term "Vasectomy" written in Carrington's distinctive script beside it.

This is the case with every sterilization procedure Carrington performed. Records show "Vasectomy" (or his term "Dementia Vasectomy" in four cases) as the procedure. He also described textbook vasectomy processes at conferences as his established protocol.

Vasectomy, however, was well known at that time to not interfere with sex drive or the sensation of orgasm. In 1913, Cincinnati physician Dr. Benjamin Ricketts stated in the *Medical Review of Reviews* that "vasectomy sterilizes a man without the slightest impairment of his sexual desire or pleasure." This description does not match the results Carrington described; of Steele's post-operative behavior, Carrington wrote, "Now he is a sleek, fat, docile, intelligent fellow—a trusty about the yard—cured by sterilization."

HOUSE BILL No. 96

A BILL

To provide for the sexual sterilization of inmates of or patients in State institutions in certain cases, and to repeal an act entitled an act to provide for the sexual sterilization of inmates of State institutions in certain cases, approved March 20, 1924.

Patron—Mr. Watts.

Reported from Committee on Asylums and Prisons.

Whereas, both the health of the individual and the wel-

2 fare of society may be promoted in certain cases by the

3 sterilization of defectives under careful safeguard and by

4 competent and conscientious authority; and,

5 Whereas, such sterilization may be effected in males

6 by the operation of vasectomy and in females by the opera-

7 tion of salpingectomy, both of which said operations may

8 be performed without serious pain or substantial danger

9 to the life of the patient; and,

10 Whereas, the Commonwealth has in custodial care and

11 is supporting in various State *eleemosynary* institutions

Right: Virginia's Eugenics Bill, 1924. *Author's collection.*

Below: The 1902 penitentiary surgical ledger. Hiram Steele's "Testectomy" is redacted, and "Vasectomy" is substituted. *Library of Virginia.*

HOSPITAL, VIRGINIA PENITENTIARY.

NAMES	NUMBER	ADMITTED	DISEASE	DISCHARGED			REMARKS
J. E. P. Peddick	2		Lithæmia				
Robert Trainham			Debility	10	1	02	
Jas. P. Blanton			Debility	11	3	02	
Lewis Washington			Haute Hepatitis	11	28	02	
Jos. Moon			Bilious Spell	11	20	02	
Gus Ford			Bilious Spell	11	6	02	
Henry Lewis			Jaundice & Gastritis	11	10	02	
Jack Walker			Bronchitis & Pneumonia	10	30	02	
Paulus Nicholas			Hydrocele	10	18	1902	
Hy. Steele		Vasectomy					
J. C. Ramsey	1	11 1 02	Debility	10	20	02	

107

Carrington also overstated Steele's long-term results; Steele was, in fact, declared insane two months after his surgery and sent back to Central State for at least six years. He was discharged in June 1910 and supposedly moved to West Virginia.

Carrington's reputed second case in 1908 was an unnamed "debased little negro, a degenerate with a heinous record as a masturbator and sodomist." Carrington went on to claim that sterilization cured the man of his vicious habits, and by 1909, he was "a strapping, healthy-looking young buck."

Carrington also specified that "when [this inmate] completes his sentence and leaves, he cannot reproduce his species"—a chilling reference to an even more immoral turn his involuntary prisoner sterilization program was taking.

THE BREEDING MUST BE STOPPED

Justice Oliver Wendell Holmes famously remarked in the 1927 Virginia eugenics case *Buck v. Bell* that "three generations of imbeciles were enough," referring to the Buck family and his contention that mental disability, or "feeble-mindedness," was hereditary and needed to be halted prior to the third generation of infection.

Dr. Carrington, remarking with no documentation that an alarming number of "feeble-minded" inmates also had fathers and grandfathers who had been incarcerated, believed similarly that three generations of criminals were more than enough. "Certain families in Virginia have been regularly represented on our prison rolls for the past fifty years," he wrote in the January 1909 edition of the *Journal of Prison Discipline and Philanthropy* without citing one example. "And will go on unless the breeding is stopped."

Therefore, between 1905 and 1908, Carrington became an advocate of the involuntary sterilization of both male and female prisoners not just to prevent sodomy and deranged masturbation (and what he believed to be the ensuing crime) but also to prevent their procreation and stop the inherited criminal lineage of "confirmed criminals, idiots, imbeciles and rapists."

In his 1908 paper "Sterilization of Habitual Criminals," Carrington bulldozed down the slippery slope, writing, "I am unreservedly of the opinion that in this enlightened age, this hideous reproduction of criminals, from father to son and to grandson, should be stopped; and it will be in time, if doctors of Virginia will awaken to the importance of this proposition as a crime preventer." He claimed that with his proposal, "crime and degeneracy" in fifty years would be decreased by at least 50 percent.

"SOLVING THE NEGRO PROBLEM"

Other Virginia doctors began embracing Carrington's ominous proposition. On June 28, 1910, Dr. Bernard Barrow, a racist, perversely paternalistic Buckingham County physician, told the Southside Virginia Medical Association in Petersburg that blacks were genetically unable to subsist in polite white society. "The negro, as a savage race, cannot solve his social and sanitary problems, and he should not be blamed for it; it is a responsibility which rests on the shoulders of the stronger race—the white man."

He went on to say:

> *If the good therapeutic results claimed by Dr. Sharp, of Indianapolis; Dr. Belfield, of Chicago, and even the limited experience of Dr. Carrington, of Richmond, be forthcoming there is little doubt that we physicians of the South will begin this work in a general way within a short time, while it will be so popular among this defective class of negroes that within a few generations its effect will be so far-reaching that it will go a long way towards solving the negro problem by eliminating the vicious, criminally inclined, disease-bearing portion of the race.*

Barrow maintained that as of February of that year, he had sterilized five black men. Although he claimed to get consent from each one and supposedly told them the procedure was reversible, it is unknown if any of the men truly understood the procedure or what that "consent" actually entailed.

Unskilled, poorly educated black penitentiary prisoners with no legal rights had gone from being slaves, to "black code" victims, to railroad slave laborers and finally to unwitting medical experiments for these early University of Virginia–educated socialist utopians. Carrington and others like him saw modern medicine finally merging with social justice, with the penitentiary and other prisons providing plenty of "lab rats" on which to ply their brand of reproductive hygiene. They frequently trotted out Richard Dugdale's 1895 research on New York's Jukes family to bolster their contentions that they were not just university qualified but also virtually divinely appointed to stop criminally degenerate and feeble-minded families from passing along defective genetics.

"All of us know that in many instances the criminal inherits his instincts," Carrington said to the Prison Physician's Association on November 18, 1908. "Now, if the grandfather had been sterilized, what a lot of crime and suffering would have been prevented."

Mosco Savage, involuntarily sterilized in October 1909. *Library of Virginia.*

Carrington in October 1909 sterilized his one known white patient (although he later claimed two others), a man named Mosco Savage, "one of the worst prisoners as I had ever seen." After his "dementia vasectomy," Savage "just laid in his bunk all day." He was later diagnosed as feeble-minded and transferred to Western State Hospital in Staunton.

After sterilizing Frank Baylor in December 1909, Dr. Carrington sterilized Chris Hayes, Richard Mills and Morris Scott all on January 17, 1910. Hayes was twenty-three years old when he was sterilized and was transferred to Central State a few months later. He died of tuberculosis in 1921 at the State Farm. Mills was serving a sixteen-year sentence for murder and, after a stay at Central State, was discharged from the penitentiary in 1921. Scott, who was serving a two-year term for housebreaking, had no previous relatives at the penitentiary and was not described as a sodomist or a habitual masturbator, so it is not known why exactly he was selected for sterilization. Perhaps by then no reason was needed.

A Legislative Setback

Emboldened by his unimpeded progress, in late January 1910, Carrington sought legal validation for his theories and sent to General Assembly Speaker Richard Byrd a bill he drafted advocating the sterilization of "vicious, diseased or depraved" felons "convicted of the more atrocious measures against morality" and designed to "save future generations from a race of criminals and degenerates."

Bill 298, "To prevent procreation by confirmed criminals, idiots, imbeciles and rapists," was a hard sell in the General Assembly. It was vague and overly broad, and it made the identification of institutionalized "idiots and imbeciles" compulsory by an appointed physician, who could recommend sterilization with no hearing, no family consent and no patient advocacy.

Though similar legislation had already been enacted in Utah, Indiana, Connecticut and California, medical authorities and criminologists disagreed on its efficacy. In 1910, the American Bar Association, for example, denounced sterilization as "offensive, barbaric and objectionable because of the lack of safeguards for the victim."

Bill 298 passed the Senate but was defeated in the House on February 18, 1910. "Dr. Stephenson (sponsor) made an earnest fight for his bill," stated the *Richmond Times-Dispatch*, "but did not convince the members that Virginia was ready for this sort of legislation."

William Carter, involuntarily sterilized in November 1910. *Library of Virginia.*

Carrington was infuriated by the setback, telling the Virginia Medical Society in 1912 that "the whole effort came to naught, when some unintentional ignoramus would rise from his seat in the hall of our Legislature and discourse on 'the inalienable rights of a man to reproduce his species,' never caring for a moment how vitiated and tainted that special species was, or how much sorrow and suffering, misery and expense resulted from the propogation [*sic*] of that vicious strain in the human family."

When informed of the defeat, Western State Hospital director Joseph DeJarnette, considered Virginia's father of compulsory sterilization and eugenics, ominously declared, "When [the House] voted against it, I really felt they ought to have been sterilized as unfit."

Scoffing at the legislative setback, Carrington resumed his illegal surgeries the very next month. He sterilized Marshall Robinson and William Bonner and then sent them to Central State shortly thereafter. William Carter and Joe White were both sterilized on November 23, 1910, after their second convictions.

Dr. Carrington's penchant for exaggeration—from describing hangings that he never witnessed, to the surgical procedures he may or may not have performed, to the long-term results of those procedures he described but did not observe, even exaggerating his years of service as penitentiary physician—casts doubt on the exact number of sterilizations and the type of surgeries he actually performed. He sometimes claimed twelve vasectomies, but the hospital admission ledger from October 1902 to June 28, 1933, lists only ten. Then, in the March 10, 1910 edition of the *Virginia Medical Semi-Monthly*, he wrote, "I have sterilized some 20-odd cases by vasectomy during the past 12 years," which would have made his first sterilization in 1898. In each case, he claimed that "masturbation has ceased [and] the patients have invariably improved mentally and physically."

WAS DR. CARRINGTON "DISCOVERED"?

Then, something happened. In July 1911, just as he was up for reappointment, Carrington inexplicably reported inmate mistreatment at the Thacker Boot and Shoe Company, a penitentiary contractor, to the *Richmond Times-Dispatch* rather than to his boss, Superintendent J.B. Wood. He also claimed prisoners were being retained past their parole dates in order to keep working for Thacker, who he said had "a malign influence" on the superintendent.

While there are no records to support it, it is possible someone (perhaps Wood) discovered Carrington was illegally castrating prisoners and then fraudulently recording the operations as medically necessary vasectomies. Threatened with exposure, Carrington may have gone to the media about the mistreatments to ensure Wood's—and ultimately the board's—silence. Whether this is exactly the case is speculative, but what is known is that Carrington—the golden boy of prison medicine who had been reappointed unanimously twice—was suddenly and inexplicably a pariah with the Penitentiary Board, and his third reappointment was in serious doubt.

Subsequent events support this assumption. In September 1911, Governor Horace Mann nominated his own nephew, Dr. Herbert Mann, for consideration by the board as the new penitentiary physician. Governor Mann then made a revealing comment regarding Carrington in the September 30, 1911 *Times-Dispatch*: "[I] assumed that if the Penitentiary Board did not re-elect Dr. Carrington it would be *because they had knowledge of facts which in their judgment would make it for the interest of the State that they should not do so*" (italics added).

While it is also theoretical to assume that the illegal castrations Carrington performed inside the penitentiary were all or part of the "facts" hinted at by Governor Mann, it is curious to note that according to the Library of Virginia in Richmond, which retains all the archives of the Virginia Penitentiary, none of Dr. Carrington's penitentiary records or personal papers from 1900 to 1911 can be located; therefore, no details of the operations can be verified.

(In a presentation to the forty-third annual session of the Medical Society of Virginia in Norfolk on October 22, 1912, Carrington said, "My penitentiary data should be more complete, but, owing to the hostility of the parties now in control of the penitentiary, I have been refused the privilege of copying the data of my work along these lines whilst I was surgeon—these people going so far as to refuse all data on 'anything Dr. Carrington had done.'")

On the very afternoon after the governor's curious comment, the Penitentiary Board unanimously elected Dr. Mann as the new physician for a four-year tenure starting January 1, 1912. "Had the conditions at the penitentiary been different," read an almost taunting statement by the board, "we would certainly have voted to retain the present surgeon; but knowing conditions as we do, we believe that the best interests of the penitentiary demand a change."

What "conditions" did they know?

Carrington was not going down without a fight. On October 3, he wrote a blistering article for the *Richmond Times-Dispatch* outlining prisoner mistreatment and the suffocating influence of the governor on the board to remove him and install his nephew. Carrington again charged the Thacker Boot and Shoe Company with corruption and prisoner abuse.

"The board is more or less of a political body, and has little if any, practical hand in the routine work of the prison," Carrington blustered, "and yet they do not hesitate without charge or complaint to turn out a man of twelve years' experience in favor of the nephew of the Governor who appoints them." A request by Carrington for an investigation by the State Board of Charities and Corrections into his dismissal was denied.

The article triggered a vicious back-and-forth series of letters between him and the board. On October 9, the board demanded in writing to know which convicts, by name, had been mistreated by guards and by the Thacker Company. They also asked that if Carrington knew convicts had been mistreated in the past, as he indicated, why had he not reported that abuse?

Carrington tersely responded that every instance of brutal treatment he had observed since becoming physician had been reported by him in writing to the superintendent and to the board. An examination of all correspondence, however, showed that the last report of cruelty made by the doctor was in July 1902. Reports made from 1907 to 1909 by Carrington were all very complimentary of the prisoner management, with no hint of mistreatment.

"Punishment is as necessary as food and water," Carrington had written to the board in October 1907, "[and] I have no hesitation in saying that during the last few years punishments have been administered with equity, firmness and justice."

In a response to the governor's questions regarding corporal punishments and paroles, the board noted that it was impossible for a prisoner to be held past his parole date, despite Carrington's claims, and that punishments only by "the stripes (whipping) was allowed, and only very judiciously applied."

Fanning the flames of mistreatment rumors was a former prisoner, Charles A. Morganfield, who had been released from the penitentiary in early January 1911 after serving fifteen years of an eighteen-year sentence for train robbery. He was on the lecture circuit within days of his release, delivering a speech entitled "Fifteen Years in Hell" that revealed ugly "inner workings of this modern day bastille."

Regardless of the scurrilous pronouncements of Morganfield, who was viewed by many as more of a carnival barker with a chip on his shoulder than an authority on incarceration methods, Carrington was promptly removed from office after the October 3 publication of his exposé on prison conditions, despite the fact that he had two months of service left before Dr. Mann took over, on January 1.

Still scrapping, Carrington appealed his termination to the Richmond Circuit Court, and on December 6, Judge R. Carter Scott, by peremptory mandamus, reinstated him as physician. But when Carrington returned to the penitentiary the next day, Superintendent Wood met him at the front gate and, despite the judge's directive, notified him that he had been ordered by the board to refuse him admittance. As a final insult, he closed and locked the doors in Carrington's face.

Wood had good reason to keep Carrington out. Board member Luther Scherer told the *Times-Dispatch* that "if Major Wood, superintendent of the penitentiary, allows Dr. Charles V. Carrington to enter the walls of that institution in any other capacity than that of a private citizen, Major Wood will have failed to comply with the instructions given him by the board of directors and will himself be fired from office before night."

Giving Prisoner Mistreatment a Bad Name

After the penitentiary debacle, Carrington settled into private practice, rarely making headlines but maintaining an interest in eugenics and racial purity. On October 21, 1913, he gave a speech entitled "Eugenic Marriages" to the State Medical Society in Lynchburg, in which he praised the state asylums and the efforts of Dr. Joseph DeJarnette, Dr. Aubrey Strode and Dr. Albert Priddy for establishing the Virginia Colony for the Epileptic and Feeble-Minded near Lynchburg.

In April 1919, the State Board of Charities and Corrections called in numerous former guards and inmates to answer charges leveled by the Prisoner's Relief Society of Washington, D.C., that the penitentiary was a "torture chamber" and that it was "the most mismanaged prison in America."

Dr. Carrington was refused admission to this hearing and was doubly incensed when he heard it was going to be closed to the public. When his appeal to Governor Davis for open sessions was denied, he responded with a long article for several Virginia newspapers detailing "gruesome" cruelties administered against prisoners by guards at the facility. These included more benign punishments such as cutting privileges or eliminating "good" time to more brutal and dehumanizing punishments, such as the ball and chain, the iron mask and the barrel.

Virginia newspapers that ran Carrington's article were astonished that such "Hunnish" punishments were still being dispensed inside the penitentiary. "That a man should be stripped, held across a barrel by four brutal men, and lashed by a still more brutal bully, with a heavy leather thong, and a woman tied and lashed over bare shoulders is horrifying, disgraceful, degrading and heathenish," howled an infuriated editorial in the April 18, 1919 edition of the *Clinch Valley News*.

It seems incongruous that professional people were shocked by whippings and solitary confinement yet still maintained that involuntary sterilization, with no consent and no family input, was wholly acceptable. Dr. Carrington and others like him were perfectly comfortable with prisoner mistreatment only when it was performed clandestinely by qualified gentlemen inside surgical rooms, not like those brutes with whips and barrels who gave prisoner mistreatment a bad name.

In 1919, after becoming immaterial to Virginia corrections and after a serious operation for a duodenal ulcer, Dr. Charles Carrington faded from public view. He witnessed the passage of Virginia's Racial Integrity Act in 1924 with no public comment before he died of a heart attack at his home on 932 Park Avenue in Richmond on July 22, 1927, taking his penitentiary secrets with him. He and his wife, Avis, who died on April 13, 1929, are buried in Hollywood Cemetery in Richmond.

CHAPTER 9
THE ELECTRIC CHAIR AND NOTABLE PENITENTIARY ELECTROCUTIONS

Eve, a negro slave woman belonging to Peter Montague, late of Orange county, Virginia, had, on August 19th, 1745, poisoned Mr. Montague, [and he died] December 27th. Eve was led to the bar under the custody of the sheriff, and put her on trial for his murder. She pleaded not guilty.... The court decided that she was guilty of the murder, and it was determined that she should be drawn upon a hurdle to the place of execution, and be burnt [at the stake].... The sentence was probably executed on the high hills of Orange county, adjacent to the old courthouse, and the smoke of the burning of Eve was visible over a large extent of country.
—Dr. A.G. Grinnan, "The Burning of Eve in Virginia" (one of only three legal burnings at the stake recorded in America), Virginia Historical Magazine, *June 1896*

CARNIVALS OF DEATH

While burning at the stake was considered repulsive even by colonial Virginia standards, it was long believed by nineteenth-century lawmakers that public hangings had virtue and that they were instructive lessons with a beneficial influence and were a deterrent to crime, especially to the black communities, where a disproportionate number were carried out.

But up until after the Civil War, Virginia's predominantly white General Assembly became more and more concerned that these increasingly public and predominantly black executions were becoming infused with an

The penitentiary electric chair. *Beth Myers Yamamoto.*

evangelical fervor that more resembled fundamentalist tent revivals than executions. Facing imminent death, the prisoner for the first time in his life held a commanding moment in a previously difficult and anonymous life. He was seen almost as a prophet; his words spoken at the gallows—sometimes for an hour or more—had an authority never carried before, despite the fact that he (or she) had been convicted of a major crime. Onlookers took off from work, and the very presence of Jesus would be displayed in them by shouting, swaying and even screaming. In the Deep South, cotton picking would sometimes be suspended up to three days. Vendors hawked watermelon, lemonade and patent medicine.

There is little evidence to conclude that the crowds gathered to condemn the crimes of the prisoner. On the contrary, the widespread prejudices in the judicial process, from arrest to conviction to execution, were more likely to induce southern blacks to recognize a condemned prisoner more as a martyr, and their purpose was more to share the prisoner's future "in the promised land" rather than condemn any past transgressions.

An 1879 law prohibiting public hangings (sometimes called "carnivals of death" because of their party atmosphere) had little to no effect on limiting

Augusta County gallows, circa 1900. The surrounding brick wall was added to comply with the 1879 law prohibiting public executions. *Augusta County Sheriff's Office.*

crowds, as it only dictated that hangings had to be inside enclosures and made no provisions for those who could see over these enclosures or climb on top of them. It wasn't until 1908, when the General Assembly voted to switch from hanging to the electric chair in the basement of the penitentiary, that they effectively ended public executions for good.

The end of public executions became a bizarre paradox of civility and racism; they were considered a victory for progressive reformers desiring a more civilized form of capital punishment but also for Jim Crow segregationists who wanted to eliminate any and all forms of black influence and stop large crowds of blacks from congregating and partying in public.

Regardless, the law did little to slow down executions. In the 1880s and 1890s, the South, including Virginia, executed approximately three times more prisoners (relative to the region's population) than other states. The reasons are numerous, including the fact that the South applied capital punishment to more crimes and found more reasons to execute blacks. Hangings were common for blacks for such crimes as highway robbery, certain grand larcenies and attempted assault against whites, especially white women.

Despite the privacy law, people still gathered to watch hangings well into the twentieth century. In 1902, about one thousand Wise County residents watched George Robinson get hanged twice for murdering his wife (after the rope broke the first time). The July 13, 1906 *Newport News Daily Press* reported that two hundred people, including many children, lined the wall of the Newport News City Jail to witness the hanging of Andrew Davenport for murder.

EXTRA BRUTAL: DEATH BY ELECTROCUTION

On August 6, 1890, in New York's Auburn Prison, convicted murderer William Kemmler became the first American to be executed in the electric chair. It did not go well. After the first eighteen-second, 1,800-volt cycle, a half dozen physicians felt for a pulse. No sooner had they all confidently pronounced him dead than Kemmler started coming back to life. After a few minutes, a second two-minute cycle was applied, with no success. The dynamo was again turned on, this time for four agonizing minutes. Witnesses were revolted. Smoke poured from Kemmler's twitching mouth, and the odor of burning flesh and hair smothered the small room. A press representative named Bain threw up. "The scene was most horrible," said C.R. Huntley, the prison electrician. "No one can depict in words the apparent horrible sufferings of that poor devil."

Not everyone was cynical. Dr. Carlos McDonald emerged from the execution and said, "I think the execution was a success. It is true the first application of the electric current did not extinguish the life of the subject, but it is quite evident he experienced no suffering and died without a pain."

The autopsy showed a severe burn at the base of Kemmler's spine the size of a man's hand (the location of the second electrode). The muscles were reportedly "baked clear to the bone." The scalp was burned away, and Kemmler's brain "was baked."

After the execution, the witnesses were led to a hotel for a light breakfast.

Virginia's Electric Chair: Inspiring Terror "in the Heart of the Superstitious African"

Virginia legislators showed no interest in embracing the electric chair until early February 1908, when an advertisement from the Adams Electric Company of Trenton, New Jersey, was passed among the representatives. It described the improved "Electrocuting Plant," which showed much improvement over the early haphazard, homemade rig used in New York. The ad also assured that all the equipment used in the construction of this electrocuting device was designed with great care and that the makers "guarantee absolute reliability."

Henrico delegate Charles W. Throckmorton apparently took a keen interest in the ad. When Bill No. 398—"An Act to Establish a Permanent Place in the State Penitentiary at Richmond, VA for the Execution of State Felons upon Whom the Death Penalty Has Been Imposed"—was introduced, he added an amendment to change the method of execution from the gallows to the electric chair. Another amendment offered by Page County senator C. Parks provided that the body of the executed criminal be returned to relatives only upon payment of transportation; otherwise, the body would go to the dissecting lab at the Medical College of Virginia.

This bill passed 60–19. It was signed by Governor Claude Swanson on March 16, 1908, and became law on July 1.

Newspapers around the commonwealth were near unanimous in their approval of the new law, which they saw as effectively shutting down the party atmospheres and long speeches attending executions in the black communities. The move from public hanging to basement electrocution forced the condemned to pay for their crimes not before large praying, singing and chanting crowds of peers but before small, somber white audiences of jurors and prison authorities.

The October 14, 1908 edition of the *Richmond Times-Dispatch* contended:

> *The publicity, the excitement and the general hurrah-and-holiday air attending the old-time hanging were a positive allurement to the negro.... The electric execution wholly does away with that. The time set for turning on the death current is unannounced, the public is rigorously eluded, and the whole affair is conducted with secrecy and mystery, well calculated to inspire terror in the heart of the superstitious African....We have a very strong hope that the privacy and mystery of the execution of the death sentence will tend to make the law more terrible and to diminish crime.*

CONSTRUCTION ON THE CHEAP

The new execution law only appropriated $1,000 to convert capital punishment over to the electric chair, an amount considered by the media as entirely inadequate. "Arrangements now are being made for the purchase of the necessary apparatus which will cost $6,500," reported the April 12, 1908 *Richmond Dispatch*. "Doubtless a commonwealth can buy electric chairs on credit," the editorial continued, somewhat sarcastically, "or it may be that the Governor will arrange for the deferred payments."

With the price of brand-new chairs out of reach, Governor Swanson and Penitentiary Superintendent Evan Morgan instead directed inmates to build a custom oak chair in the penitentiary wood shop, using a picture of the chair used at New York's Sing Sing Prison for a model. The penitentiary also constructed nine detention cells and three extra rooms at a cost of nearly $7,000.

In 1910, a state official in Canton, China, wrote to the Montgomery Ward Company of Chicago inquiring about buying an electric chair, apparently under the impression that they could be purchased by mail order. Montgomery Ward politely referred the official to Superintendent Morgan at the penitentiary. Morgan wrote back with the offer to install a fully operating electric chair plant for $3,000, plus travel expenses back and forth to China. There is no record of him actually going to China.

Under the new statute, newspapers were prohibited from publishing details, photographs, illustrations or films of actual electrocutions. There was originally no legal recourse for violation, but still the press observed the law "for the wholesome effect it will unquestionably have in Virginia."

> *Evidence of innocence is irrelevant.*
> —*former Virginia attorney general Mary Sue Terry, circa 1991, in responding to an appeal to introduce new evidence after the twenty-one-day rule regarding death row prisoner Joseph Giarratano's potential innocence*

WILLIAM FINNEY: SPARED ELECTROCUTION FOR BEING AN "IDIOT"

William Finney, a black man convicted of assaulting a young white girl in Franklin County in July 1908, was the first prisoner to be sentenced to death in the new electric chair, but he dodged the new punishment.

In Roanoke for safekeeping against lynch mobs, Finney was visited by a sheriff, several attorneys and a doctor, who all petitioned Governor Swanson to commute the death sentence, as they concurred from Finney's manner and appearance that he was an "idiot." In fact, the judge who presided at the trial, the prosecuting attorney and many reputable Franklin County residents all sent letters to the governor explaining that Finney "seemed to be entirely lacking in any mental power."

On October 9, Finney's sentence was commuted to life imprisonment, and he was transferred to the penitentiary. In 1914, he was transferred to Central State Hospital for the remainder of his life.

HENRY SMITH: FIRST ELECTROCUTION IN VIRGINIA

Henry Smith, the first Virginian to die in the electric chair, October 1908. *Library of Virginia.*

The first execution under the new statute that substituted electrocution for hanging took place on October 13, 1908, in the penitentiary basement. Henry Smith, also known as Oscar Perry, a black Portsmouth man convicted of rape and robbery, was Virginia's 1,041st person to be executed since 1608.

Smith, age twenty-two, was a previous penitentiary convict and described by the news media as "below average in sense, but pleasant-faced and seemingly docile." On August 11, 1908, this "pleasant-faced" man robbed, raped and then beat "into a state of insensibility" a seventy-five-year-old white Portsmouth woman, Catherine Powell.

As the crime was occurring, a young grocery delivery boy named Pope approached the house, and he testified that he heard the voice of a woman praying for mercy. He also said that Mrs. Powell then called to him from an upstairs window to "catch that negro." Running around to the back of the house, Pope saw Smith run from the back door.

Smith and an alleged accomplice, William "Brack" King, were arrested and held in the Portsmouth Jail. A few days later, fourteen men unsuccessfully stormed the jail in an attempt to lynch the prisoners. Ten of the fourteen, including two black men, were charged with rioting and fined $100 each with sixty days in jail.

At the September 8 trial, Smith pleaded not guilty, but Mrs. Powell positively identified him in describing the attack. Smith was found guilty of first-degree assault, and after being sent back twice by Judge Bain, the jury agreed on the death penalty.

On September 30, Smith allegedly made a full and complete confession of the rape from his cell, saying that he alone was responsible and exonerating "Brack" King, who was later acquitted on the basis of Smith's confession.

On October 1, Smith was taken to the penitentiary's death row, where he did nothing but sleep and eat. "I never saw a condemned man with such an appetite," a penitentiary officer told a *Roanoke Evening News* reporter on October 6. "The negro does not seem to be worrying about what is going to happen to him Tuesday."

Just days prior to the execution, Superintendent Morgan received a handwritten note from Smith's mother thanking him in advance for turning the body over to her after the electrocution: "I was very glad to know that I can get my boy's body by paying all expenses and furnishing coffin so I will come up after him Tuesday. Yours truly, [signed] Pampey Smith."

On October 13, the day of execution, Smith was accompanied by the Reverend W.H. Dean, pastor of Leigh Street Methodist Church, and Mr. S.C. Burrell of the Colored Young Men's Christian Association in prayer and singing hymns. Smith was pronounced dead less than ten minutes after leaving his cell at 7:20 a.m.

While no details of the electrocution were provided by prison authorities per the new law, penitentiary physician Charles Carrington praised the new policy and the chair's performance, writing in the 1908 *Report of the Virginia Penitentiary*:

> [It was a] *swift, sure, solemn and awe-inspiring mode of punishment, and to my mind is infinitely more humane than hanging....When you eliminate the psalm-singing-forgiving-your-enemies that usually, I am told, preceded a hanging, and in its stead institute a solemn, very swift mode of inflicting the death penalty, you have taken a step which will in time be powerfully deterrent on the criminal classes.*

An autopsy performed by Dr. Carrington revealed the right side of Smith's heart had burst due to violent muscular contractions.

Winston Green: Executed for Maybe Touching a White Girl

Winston Green, a mentally disabled seventeen-year-old black youth, was put to death on October 30, 1908, at 7:30 a.m. for "attempted criminal assault" on twelve-year-old Alice Larsen, of Chestnut Hill.

On September 11, Larsen and two friends were driving a small buggy in Chesterfield County between Dry Bridge and Hallsboro when a young black man stepped in the road, stopped them, grabbed their horse and ordered Larsen out of the wagon. It is unclear what happened as she got out; the September 27 *Richmond Times-Dispatch* reported that Green only "ordered the girl to get out" but did not touch her. The October 31 *Newport News Daily Press* reported the "young negro…demanded that she alight, seizing the horse and stopping

Winston Green. *Library of Virginia.*

the vehicle." Only the October 30 *Brooklyn Daily Eagle* reported Green as "attacking a young white girl." Whether he touched Larsen or not, Green ran into nearby woods when she began to scream.

After Larsen returned home and reported the incident to her father, word got out that she had been "assaulted" by a black man, and two posses of twenty-five men each were organized. Green was captured within a few hours. He was taken before a shaken Larsen, and she positively identified him.

Two weeks later, at a special term of the Chesterfield County Circuit Court, Green strenuously denied his guilt, but after his conviction of attempted criminal assault, "he made a complete confession." He was sentenced on September 20 to die in the electric chair.

The *Richmond Times-Dispatch* reported, "The youth had no legal counsel."

Green's case is especially haunting, as it highlights the assumptions of black male guilt in those pre-DNA, pre-fingerprinting days, when victim identification was the sole criteria for arrest and conviction. When Larsen was confronted in her front yard by twenty-five infuriated white men escorting a most likely terrified, beat-up, mentally disabled black man, she could have been too intimidated to admit to the angry posse that Green may *not* have been her "attacker." Thus, Green was tried and sentenced to

Richmond , Va., Octo. 26th 1908.

Dr. E.C.Fisher,

    1418 Park Ave.,

      Richmond, Va.,

Dear Sir:

    Please be at the Penitentiary at 7 A. M. Friday October 30th, to witness the electro-cution of Winston Green. Please regard this communication as confidential, especially as to the hour. Present this letter at the gate.

          Very respectfully,

k/j   Superintendent.

An invitation to witness the electrocution of Winston Green. *Library of Virginia.*

death without a lawyer based solely on the identification of a distraught twelve-year-old.

On October 18, Winston Green was taken to the penitentiary and placed in solitary confinement. His family was allowed to visit him to say goodbye the day before he died.

On the day of his execution, Green was accompanied in his walk to the death chamber by two local black ministers. He entered the chamber at 7:29 a.m., and after a few minutes, his body was removed from the chair and turned over to his father for burial.

Rather than speculate on the impropriety of the conviction and execution, the October 31 *Newport News Daily Press* instead boasted that "the infliction of the death penalty was a complete success....It could not have gone more satisfactory [*sic*]."

BENJAMIN GILBERT: FIRST WHITE MAN ELECTROCUTED IN VIRGINIA

Nineteen-year-old Benjamin Gilbert became Virginia's first white victim of the electric chair on March 29, 1909, after being convicted for the murder of his former girlfriend, Amanda Morse, on Norfolk's Campostella Bridge on July 23, 1908.

Benjamin Gilbert, the first white person executed in Virginia's electric chair. *Library of Virginia.*

On that night, Morse and several other young people were talking on the bridge when Gilbert approached and asked Morse if he could speak with her privately. When she refused, Gilbert pulled out a pistol and fired three times, hitting Morse twice in the back. Gilbert was held on the bridge until police arrived.

Gilbert's defense in the Corporation Court was general mental irresponsibility, depravity and hereditary insanity. When Judge Hanckel sentenced him to death, Gilbert replied, "It suits me."

Gilbert's parents spent all their money and mortgaged their home and belongings to raise money in appeals. Gilbert's lawyer, Daniel Coleman Jr., not only received no compensation but also supplemented out of pocket the money raised by Gilbert's parents in appeals for their condemned son. Five thousand signatures were gathered on a petition in Norfolk to commute the sentence to life imprisonment.

Governor Swanson considered the petitions for commutation but then announced that if he commuted Gilbert's sentence, he "could not allow another person to be electrocuted while I am Governor of Virginia."

Gilbert went to the electric chair praying for the welfare of his mother.

After the execution, Dr. J.P. Jackson of South Norfolk offered to revive Gilbert with a respirator he invented. The proposal had to be abandoned, however, because Jackson claimed too much time had elapsed between Gilbert's execution and his body's subsequent arrival in Norfolk. Dr. Jackson told the *Norfolk Ledger-Star* newspaper that if he could have had the respirator in Richmond, he would have conducted the process immediately after Gilbert's electrocution. The newspaper countered Dr. Jackson's proposal by stating that even if such an attempt proved successful, Gilbert would then have to be resentenced and electrocuted again.

Gilbert was buried in Norfolk's Cedar Grove Cemetery.

VIRGINIA CHRISTIAN: FIRST VIRGINIA WOMAN TO DIE IN THE CHAIR

Labor disputes between blacks and whites, which routinely bred frustration, suspicion, and anger on both sides of the color line, were sometimes fought out to bloody conclusions, thus weaving a thread of violence into southern labor relations.
—*William Fitzhugh Brundage,* Lynching in the New South: Georgia and Virginia 1880–1930, *1993*

Virginia Christian was the first juvenile female executed in the United States. *Library of Virginia.*

On August 16, 1912, the day after her seventeenth birthday (although her age is disputed), Virginia Christian of Elizabeth City County became the first juvenile female in America to be executed in the electric chair.

The *Newport News Daily Press* described Christian as "a full-blooded negress, with kinky hair done up in threads, with dark lusterless eyes and with splotches on the skin of her face. Her color was dark brown, and her figure was short, dumpy and squashy. She had some schooling, but her speech betrayed it. Her language was the same as the unlettered members of her race."

At the age of thirteen, Christian dropped out of Hampton's Whitter Training School to work as a laundress for Mrs. Ida Belote, age fifty-two, an esteemed middle-class widow and mother of eight children. Mrs. Belote was part of Hampton's white aristocracy by way of her father's prominence as the owner of a large grocery store.

On March 19, 1912, Mrs. Belote went to the Christian home at 326 Wine Street in Hampton to ask Virginia's mother if the girl could do some washing for her. Mrs. Christian, who was confined to a wheelchair, was hesitant because she knew Mrs. Belote frequently mistreated her daughter, but she told her she would send Virginia to her house when she returned.

Virginia went to Belote's house, and an argument ensued when Belote accused Christian of stealing a locket and a skirt (although Belote found the skirt). According to Christian, the physical altercation between herself and Belote was incited by this verbatim conversation published in the *Newport News Times-Herald*:

> *"Virgi, have you seen my gold locket? I can't seem to find it."*
> *"No, ma'am, I ain't seen no locket."*
> *"Are you sure you haven't seen it?"*
> *"Yes, ma'am, I ain't seen no locket."*
> *"You must have it, Virgi!"*
> *"I ain't seen nothing of no locket."*
> *"I want it back or I'll make trouble for you, Virgi."*
> *"If I did have your locket, you won't get it back! I quit! I don't want to work for you no mo."*

In anger, Belote threw a ceramic cuspidor (a spittoon) at Virginia, hitting her on the shoulder. It fell and broke, and then Mrs. Belote began throwing the broken pieces. Christian then rushed to protect herself, and the altercation escalated when Christian and Belote both ran for two broom handles used to prop up bedroom windows. Christian grabbed one of the broom handles and struck Belote on the forehead, knocking her to the floor. In an attempt to stifle Belote's screams, Christian stuffed a towel in the woman's mouth and, with the broom handle, forced it down her throat. The woman died of suffocation.

Christian dragged Mrs. Belote's body to a back room. She then returned home, busying herself with housework and saying nothing of the affair.

Eight-year-old Sadie and thirteen-year-old Harriet Belote later discovered their mother's bloody body on the floor. When Sheriff Curtis and Hampton police arrived at the Belote home, they found a trail of blood across the lower floor. Overturned furniture and the broken spittoon showed that there had been a horrific struggle.

Neighbors reported hearing no noise from the house, nor did they see anyone leave during the day.

Elizabeth City County coroner Dr. George Vanderslice arrived at the crime scene and reported on the condition of the body:

A bloody towel was rolled and stuffed tightly down the throat, pushing in the hair, pushing down the tongue, and inverting the lower lip. Bruises around the neck, a large cut and bruise, and black above and below one eye about the right eye, the left eye bruised swollen stuck together, finger marks around side of neck beneath the jaw and below the ear. In addition, there is a large cut three inches long down to the bone, just above the left ear.

Christian was immediately suspected. Police searched her home, and when they found a bloody waistcoat under her bed, they arrested and charged her with capital murder. During questioning (without legal counsel present), she admitted to hitting Belote but was shocked that the woman was dead. A pocketbook, ring and other valuables belonging to Mrs. Belote were reportedly found on Virginia after her arrest.

While confined in jail awaiting trial, she called her pastor, the Reverend J.W. Patterson, and subsequently made a full confession to him, Elder T.H. Shorts and Sheriff R.K. Curtis. The full text was printed verbatim and in plantation dialect a week later in the April 11 edition of the *Times-Herald* newspaper:

She [Mrs. Belote] *come to mammer's house dat morning an' say she want me to come an' do some washin'. When I come home mammer say miss Belote want me an' I went 'roun' to de house. I wen' in de back way an' when she see me she asked me about a gold locket she missed. I told her I ain't seen it an' don't know nuthin' about it. She also say sumthin' about a skirt but de main thing was the locket. She say "yes you got it an' if you don't bring it back, I'm goin' to have you put in jail."*

I got mad an' told her if I did have it, she wasn't goin' to git it back. Den she picked up de spittoon and hit me wit it an' it broke. They wuz two sticks in de room, broom handles. She run for one, an' I for de' other. I got my stick furst an' I hit her wit it 'side de hade and she fell down. She kep' hollerin' so I took a towel and stuffed it in her mouth. I helt it there twel she quit hollerin' and jes' groaned. I didn't mean to kill her an' I didn't know I had. I was mad when I hit her an' stuffed the towel in her mouth to keep her from hollerin'. I never meant to kill her. When I lef' she was groanin' and layin' on her back.

On April 1, a huge crowd gathered at the courtroom, trying to get in to the eight-day trial. Christian never took the stand on her own behalf; her black attorneys, Joseph Thomas Newsome and George Washington Fields, feared

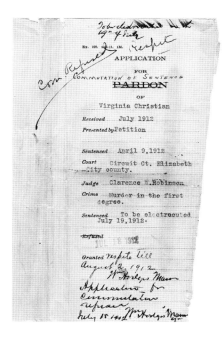

The commutation of Virginia Christian's death sentence was refused by Governor William Hodges Mann in July 1912. *Library of Virginia.*

her "uncouth appearance and her insolent way of describing the deed" could incite widespread violence against blacks. The media speculated without conducting a single interview that many Hampton middle-class blacks did not view Christian's crime as an act of self-defense against exploitative labor conditions and the white power structure but an embarrassing and disgraceful offense that called for swift justice. This was a common sentiment reported of black neighborhoods, from residents who feared recrimination or even lynch mobs for questioning white accusers and a justice system stacked against them.

For a first-degree murder conviction, premeditation had to be proven. The prosecution maintained that the time it took for Christian to force the towel five inches down Mrs. Belote's throat with the window stick was sufficient to constitute premeditation, which under Virginia law need only be of a few minutes' duration.

Despite a vigorous defense and a vote of confidence from Mrs. Belote's brother, Lewter Hobbs, to Governor Mann that justice would prevail, and with a lynch mob still looming in the background, the Elizabeth City County prosecutor fully intended to make an example out of Christian and used the case to show the local black community that the consequences of killing a white person (for whatever reason) were always going to be death. It was no surprise when the jury returned a verdict of guilty of first-degree murder after only twenty-three minutes of deliberation. Trial Judge Clarence W. Robinson sentenced her to death in the electric chair on the day after her seventeenth birthday in August 1912.

On July 24, 1912, former National Association of Colored Women (NACW) president Mary Church Terrell arrived at the governor's mansion in Richmond and presented Governor Mann with a petition with the names of over three hundred NACW members to commute the sentence of Virginia Christian. The petition stated, in part:

> The members of the National Association of Colored Women do most earnestly implore His Excellency to commute the sentence of Virginia Christian....The extreme youth of this girl, the lack of training during her childhood...justifies mercy for this unfortunate girl. We feel that the electrocution of this poor girl would be repugnant to the Christian womanhood and manhood of not only the United States but of the whole civilized world.

Soon afterward, the newly formed National Association for the Advancement of Colored People (NAACP) got involved in the Christian case, and even Richmond bank president Maggie Walker implored Governor Mann to commute Christian's sentence.

In early August, Virginia was sent to the penitentiary to await execution. Governor Mann declined to commute her sentence, despite a personal plea from Virginia's mother, Charlotte Christian, who wrote:

> My dear mr governor,
> Please for give me for Bowing low to write you a few lines: I am the mother of Virginiany Christian. I have been pairalized for mor then three years and I could not look after Gennie as I wants too. I know she dun an awful weaked thing when she kill Miss Belote and I hear that the people at the penetintry wants to kill her but I is praying night and day on my knees to God that he will soften your heart so that She may spend the rest of her days in prison. They say that the whole thing is in yours Hands and I know Governer if you will onely save my child who is little over sixteen years old God will Bless you for ever....If I was able to come to see you I could splain things to you better but I cant do nothing but pray to God and ask him to help you to simpithise with me and my truble
> I am your most umble subgeck,
> Charlotte Christian

Word of the case reached Chicago, and black and white social activists, business owners and politicians sent more than five hundred letters to the governor asking for mercy for the girl. E. Val Putnam, managing editor of the *Chicago Daily World* newspaper, showed up in person to see the governor and then wrote that "never before has there been such as impassioned appeal to save a young colored girl from being electrocuted in Virginia." Mr. W.J. Anderson, a Chicago lawyer nicknamed "Habeas Corpus" Anderson, also arrived on August 15 to plead the girl's case with the governor.

The governor remained unmoved, writing that "Christian's murder of her white employer, Ida Virginia Belote, was the most dastardly in the state's history and that Christian's execution is necessary to ensure public safety....I have therefore reluctantly reached the conclusion that there is nothing in the case which justifies executive clemency."

The fact that the governor reiterated the race of the victim as "white" supports his belief in the jury's supposition that the sentence for a black killing a white person must always be death.

Christian's execution was carried out on August 16. The night before, she wrote, "I know that I am getting no more than I deserve. I am prepared to answer for my sins, and I believe that the Lord has forgiven me. I fear that Mrs. Belote may not have been a Christian. I blame no one for my situation. I hope to meet Mrs. Belote in heaven. I thank all who have worked on my behalf."

On that final day, she was awakened just after 4:00 a.m. and given a breakfast of eggs, biscuits and coffee. She collapsed in her cell as the death warrant was being read but was able afterward to walk to the execution chamber on her own. Since she was the first female to go to the chair, the electrodes were attached to her head and forearm instead of to her leg in a somewhat bizarre act of southern propriety.

A reporter from the *Lima News* newspaper in Lima, Ohio, who witnessed the execution described what he saw:

> *Her face was absolutely calm. She gave a quick glance at the instrument of death, more in curiosity than in fear, lowered her eyes and stepped on the platform. A guard motioned her to be seated in the chair and the negress sank into her place. Three guards hurried forward, one adjusted the strap, another strapped the woman's form into the chair, and the other clasped on the headpiece. A moment later the body stiffened and twisted, a wisp of sickening smoke floated through the leather head piece.*

Christian's body was sent to the Charles H. Jones Funeral Home in Hampton with funds provided by Richmond and Chicago political activists. On August 18, 1912, her funeral was held at First Baptist Church.

"Virginia Christian is a sacrifice to society," wrote *The Crisis* magazine about the Christian case.

From the unfortunate girl's tragedy the great commonwealth, whose name by a bitter irony of fate she bears, should read its lesson. Why has not Virginia a reformatory for colored girls? Why has it not a law forbidding the execution of children of sixteen? How many more legalized murders must be committed before civilization receives an answer to these questions and grapples with those social conditions which produce Virginia Christians in a race which obtains neither nor fair play in so many states of this union?

HERBERT CAPLE: EXECUTED FOR ROBBING A WHITE MAN

In mid-February 1915, Herbert Caple, a black man, hailed a farmer named Fuller on a Sussex County road and asked for a ride. While riding, he hit Fuller on the head with some blunt object and then robbed him. Caple denied the charge, but Fuller identified him as his assailant.

On March 20, Caple was tried, convicted of highway robbery in the Sussex Circuit Court under Judge J.F. West and incredibly sentenced to death. In the same session, a white man named William Peters was convicted of beating and maiming a black man but was only fined twenty dollars. Caple was executed at the penitentiary on April 30.

After execution, Caple's body was claimed by the State Anatomical Board and sent to the dissecting room of the Medical College of Virginia.

ROBERT MAIS: TWENTY MINUTES IN THE CHAIR

Robert Howard Mais and Walter Legenza were leaders of a ruthless group known as the Tri-State Gang. Throughout the 1930s, this gang committed murders, hijackings and robberies in several eastern states. On June 1, 1934, Mais and Legenza were arrested in Baltimore and charged with the murder of a Richmond Federal Reserve Bank driver named E.M. Hubard. Legenza shot Hubard the instant the gang forced the truck's rear doors open, and the pair threw a pile of mail sacks into their car and fled. Later, they found out they had only bags and bags of cancelled checks.

Both were caught and extradited to Virginia, where they were convicted and received death sentences.

On September 29, Mais's mother brought the men a can of boned chicken with a gun hidden inside. In a dramatic escape, city jail officer William Toot

Killers' Bullets Fatal to Officer; Mrs. Mais Faces Accessory Count

*

Guard Loses Gallant Fight; Pistol Smuggling Inquiry Pushed

Police Officer William A. Toot, riddled with gangster bullets in the escape of Walter Legenza and Robert Mais from the city jail Saturday, died at Memorial Hospital at 6:45 o'clock last night.

His death, resulting from a gallant but futile attempt to halt the two desperadoes as they shot their way to freedom, was the second Richmond murder ascribed to the gangster pair, already convicted to die for the shooting of E. M. Huband here last March.

A warrant charging Mrs. Elizabeth Mais, 57-year-old mother of the younger of the two gunmen, with being an accessory before the murder of Policeman Toot will be sworn out if further investigation definitely establishes she smuggled guns to her son and Legenza, Commonwealth's Attorney T. Gray Haddon said last night.

Dies of Wounds

Policeman W. A. Toot

The death of Officer W.A. Toot. Richmond Dispatch, *September 30, 1934.*

was killed and two other officers were wounded. Wracked with guilt over the prisoners' escape and murder of his friend and co-worker, city night sergeant Richard Duke later took his own life.

In January 1935, Mais and Legenza were captured by the FBI in New York City. They were sent back to Virginia, guarded by a squad of nine handpicked officers.

Triggerman Walter Legenza, who had to be carried from his cell to the chair because both of his legs had been broken trying to escape from Philadelphia police, likened himself to Robin Hood and was "bitter, cynical and jeering" up until his moment of execution. He was the first white man to be sentenced to electrocution by a Richmond jury.

There was an unspecified malfunction with the electric chair during Mais's execution, and it reportedly took twenty minutes for him to die.

Amon J. Gusler: The Booby-Trap Slayer

Amon Gusler was a fifty-two-year-old mild-mannered maintenance electrician at the Bassett Furniture plant in Martinsville who went to the electric chair for rigging a dynamite booby trap for a co-worker because he was scared of reprisal after stealing a kiss from the victim's wife.

Gusler, a married father of three children and a loyal twenty-five-year employee, told the Henry County Circuit Court on July 13, 1946, that he had planned J. Russell Smith's death for months after he stole a kiss from Smith's wife after drinking heavily at a party two years earlier. Gusler said Smith was angry at him after that and once threatened to kill him or run him out of town for kissing his wife.

Amon J. Gusler. *Library of Virginia.*

One May morning, Gusler arrived early at the Bassett plant and rigged a three-stick dynamite charge under Smith's desk, wiring it to a switch through the electrical panel. Three months later, Smith discovered the switch, flipped it and was literally incinerated by an enormous detonation that also heavily damaged most of the plant.

Gusler claimed during a psychiatric hearing on November 26 that he had found a pipe bomb in his own office three weeks earlier and claimed that he believed Smith planted it.

Despite testimony from a psychiatrist that Gusler suffered from a paranoiac condition at the time, the Virginia Board of Pardons refused to commute his death sentence to life imprisonment. He was electrocuted on January 3, 1947. The witness form states Gusler "was seated at 7:33 a.m.; current on at 7:34; current off at 7:35. Dead at 7:39."

CHAIR "NO LONGER LEGITIMATE"

A moratorium was declared on executions after the electrocution of Carroll Garland on March 2, 1962. Corrections officials were concerned that the electric chair was no longer a legitimate way of administering Virginia's death penalty. An increasing possibility of malfunction after fifty-four years of use prompted a request to the state to appropriate $15,000 to modernize the chair. The proposal stalled, however, pending the outcome of a number of U.S. Supreme Court cases seeking to abolish the death penalty as "cruel and unusual punishment" and in violation of the Eighth Amendment. Consequently, a stay of execution was granted to fourteen death row inmates.

In June 1972, a Supreme Court decision, *Furman v. Georgia*, emphasized three inherent problems in state applications of the death penalty: that the death penalty had been inflicted in an arbitrary and irrational manner; that juries had excessive discretion in determining whether a life sentence or the death penalty should be imposed for certain criminal offenses; and that poor and black defendants were disproportionate recipients of the penalty.

Justices Thurgood Marshall and William J. Brennan Jr. asserted that the death penalty itself was unconstitutional, while the three other majority justices asserted that it was not the death penalty but the arbitrary application of it that was an unconstitutional violation of the Eighth Amendment's guarantee against "cruel and unusual punishment." Thus, the application of the penalty was left up to individual states.

In his address to a joint session of the 1974 General Assembly, newly elected governor Mills Godwin called for a resumption of the death penalty. He indicated (in seeming contradiction to the ambiguous Supreme Court decision regarding "excessive discretion") that a jury should have the option to impose the death sentence under three circumstances: conviction for murder of a law enforcement officer in the line of duty; conviction of murder in connection with rape and/or arson; and a second conviction for first-degree murder. Later, bills introduced in subsequent sessions further expanded the death penalty to include many other convictions.

Frank Coppola: "I'm Not Geared for Living"

Virginia executions resumed on August 10, 1982, with the electrocution of former Portsmouth policeman and Catholic seminarian Frank Coppola for the brutal April 22, 1978 murder of Muriel Hatchell.

The seventy-four-year-old electric chair was in bad shape in the summer of 1982. It had been boxed up in 1962 and left in A basement, which leaked whenever it rained. According to Jerry Givens, who was a member of the original 1982 death squad, the baseboard, leather straps and seat were rotted and mildewed, so they all had to be replaced. The squad rebuilt and repaired the chair for the execution of Coppola.

Like Gilmore in Utah, Coppola elected to fire his lawyers and stop appealing his sentence. "No one can relate to death, but people don't understand I have been on death row for four years," he wrote to Judge D. Dortch Warriner. "I'm not geared for living."

At 11:00 p.m. the night of the execution, Governor Charles Robb gave the order to Corrections Director Raymond Procunier to proceed. Coppola was then electrocuted at 11:27 p.m. According to Givens, Coppola's pants leg was not rolled up far enough, and it briefly caught on fire from the lower electrode.

LINWOOD BRILEY: "BURN, BRILEY, BURN"

Linwood Briley. *Author's collection.*

In October 1979, Detective Leroy Morgan was called to assist with the interrogation of Linwood Briley, one of a notorious gang of murderers who, along with his brothers James and Anthony and another named Duncan Meekins, terrorized Richmond for an entire year while they violently killed twelve people, and possibly as many as twenty. Their victims during that eight-month spree in 1978 and '79 were white, black, rich and poor. But no one knew at the time of the interrogation that the Brileys were responsible for killing popular DJ Johnny "Johnny G" Gallaher, whose body had been found on September 15 partially submerged in the James River. Morgan had taken Gallaher's death personally; they were good friends.

Upon arriving at the police station, the first thing Morgan noticed about Linwood Briley was a turquoise ring on his finger. His heart dropped—he recognized the ring as belonging to his friend Gallaher. Morgan had been with Gallaher when he bought it. "I'm not a violent person, but I sure could have…well, it wouldn't have taken much for me to have jumped him," Morgan told *Times-Dispatch* reporters Reed Williams and Bill McKelway in 2009.

Morgan's recognition of the ring helped solve Gallaher's murder. It also earned Linwood Briley the death penalty.

On October 12, 1984, a crowd of about five hundred demonstrators divided for and against capital punishment gathered outside the penitentiary to await Linwood Briley's execution. Among those holding a candlelight

Protestors at the execution of Linwood Briley, 1984. *David Stover.*

vigil protesting the death penalty on the east side of Belvidere Street was Nancy Gowen, whose seventy-six-year-old mother, Mary Gowen, had been brutally raped and murdered by the Briley gang. "I think it's something wrong with our system," she told a UPI reporter. "I don't think to murder someone for a murder committed is the answer."

On the west side of Belvidere, a pro-death crowd was twice as large and the mood decidedly different. A middle-aged man and a younger woman held homemade signs that read "Kill the negro!" Another nearby sign said "Fry 'em." Rednecks and beer guts mingled with mohawks and leather jackets in a loud, Confederate flag–fueled street party. Two teenage girls danced around in plastic shower caps, saying, "We've got Linwood hats" (both Brileys were

Children at the execution of Linwood Briley, 1984. *David Stover*.

wearing shower caps when they were caught in Philadelphia) as the crowd started chanting "Burn, Briley, Burn." One man told *ThroTTle* magazine writer Jeff Lindholm, "We think justice today is screwed. Nobody should get appeals. The Confederate flag was from back when we had segregation, not all this integration we have now."

One older woman told this writer that she had turned out all her lights and even unplugged her refrigerator at her Oregon Hill home so "more electricity could get to the penitentiary."

At 11:05 p.m., Linwood died, claiming he was innocent. Those in front of the penitentiary blew out their candles and removed their name tags, each bearing the name of a death row inmate and their victim(s).

Across the road, the several hundred supporters drunkenly shouted racial epithets, laughed and flipped the finger at the others before many left for a crab feast in Oregon Hill.

One young man looked over his shoulder at the rowdy crowd and said, "I'm losing a lot of friends tonight."

Wilbert Lee Evans: "Relieved by Death Watch"

On January 27, 1981, Alexandria City sheriff's deputy William Truesdale was shot with his own gun by Wilbert Lee Evans while leading Evans back to jail after a hearing in an adjacent courthouse. Imprisoned in North Carolina on an assault charge, Evans was in Alexandria to testify against another prisoner. During his brief freedom, Evans pointed the gun he had taken from Truesdale at an approaching officer and pulled the trigger, but the gun jammed. He was taken back into custody.

During sentencing after his trial, Alexandria commonwealth's attorney John Kloch argued for the death penalty, saying Evans posed a menace to society. To prove it, he showed records supposedly proving Evans had seven prior convictions, including assault on a police officer. Based on this new information, the jury recommended death.

The problem was most of those convictions never happened—and a memo from Kloch's assistant, written two months prior, showed Kloch knew full well at the time that only two of those seven convictions were true. Kloch later admitted that he knew at the time he introduced the records into evidence that at least two of them were false. Thus, Evans was sentenced to death partly on deliberately erroneous information.

On March 28, 1983, ten months after Evans's attorney Jonathan Shapiro called out the bogus records, the state admitted an error. Then-governor Charles Robb signed emergency legislation that same day allowing the state to resentence prisoners.

In September, a judge ruled that there was no willful misconduct by prosecutors or the attorney general's office. At a new trial in February 1984, Kloch—seemingly hell-bent on putting Evans to death—introduced brand-new evidence, including unsupported charges that Evans killed a man in 1978 in an argument. Once again, the jury sentenced Evans to death.

On May 31, 1984, while held at Mecklenburg Correctional Facility, Evans protected twelve guards and two nurses from a half dozen rampaging inmates during the largest death row escape in U.S. history. Despite several guards later claiming they owed their lives to Evans, the attorney general refused to believe he was no longer a menace to society. His clemency plea went to Governor L. Douglas Wilder, who campaigned as a death penalty supporter and refused to commute his sentence.

Fifteen days prior to execution, Evans was taken to the penitentiary to await electrocution. On October 16, he was transferred to an A basement holding cell for his final twenty-four hours. His penitentiary night shift area supervisor's report shows the utter banality of the remaining few hours of life before the electric chair. (Note: The following is a transcription of the actual handwritten report. Private names and phone numbers have been deleted.)

State Penitentiary, Richmond VA
Area Supervisor's Report
Date: 10-16-90   Time: 1800–0600   Watch: Night Shift

18:00 pm   Cpl CA Baum along with Cpls. T. Andrews & E. Botts relieved Cpls Mack, Martin & Rowe & assumed the duties of A Basement. All equipment appears accounted for. Temp 73°. Made a check of area. Received one inmate, W Evans, #124549 Cell #3.

18:19 pm   M__ D__, B__ S__ & Rev B__ J__, escorted by Major Turner entered A basement to see inmate Evans. Inmate Evans still talking on phone.

18:30 pm   Lt Campbell entered area.

18:44 pm   Call completed

18:49 pm   Made call to Jonathan Shapiro—attorney 202-___-____

18:55 pm   Phone call completed. Major Turner & Lt. Campbell departed area

19:12 pm   M__ D__, B__ S__ & Rev J__ departed area. Made call to H__ E__, 6__-____

19:17 pm   Inmate requested a cup of juice

19:25 pm   Nurse entered area.

19:31 pm   Nurse departed area. Made security call.

19:40 pm   Ms. Terrangi, deputy warden entered area with Lt. Campbell for check

19:43 pm   Ms. Terrangi & Lt. Campbell departed area.

19:53 pm   Rev. B__ entered A Basement to visit inmate Evans. Inmate on phone & sitting on bed.

19:56 pm   Completed phone call. Inmate requested a cup of juice.

19:58 pm   Made call to L__ B__ 2__-____

20:00 pm   Made security call. Inmate talking on phone.

20:48 pm   Call completed.

20:50 pm   Made call to B__ E__ 919-__-____

21:00 pm   Rev B__ departed area. Made security call. Inmate sitting on bed talking on phone

21:28 pm   Count cleared. Inmate talking on phone. Made security call.

21:45 pm   Call completed

21:46 pm   Made call to B__ S__ 3__-____. Inmate talking on phone & using the toilet

21:52 pm   Call completed. Made call to J__ H__. No answer.

21:58 pm   Made call to L__ N__ 202-__-____

22:00 pm   Made security call. Inmate Evans sitting on bed talking on phone.

22:05 pm   Call completed. Made call to J__ H__ 202-__-____ No answer.

22:28 pm   Call to J__ H__ 202-___-____. No answer. Made call to L__ E__ 301-___-___. Made security call. Inmate on bed talking on phone.

22:40 pm   Inmate requested apple.

22:50 pm   B__ S__ entered area to talk to inmate Evans. Call completed.

22:58 pm   Relieved by death watch.

Cpl CA Baum

CHAPTER 10

REFORM YEARS

1920-1940

VENEREAL DISEASE EPIDEMIC TRIGGERS
SWEEPING REFORMS

In June 1920, blood tests taken on all prisoners at the penitentiary as part of a medical program overhaul confirmed that 25 percent had syphilis. In addition, 2 were found with acute gonorrhea, and almost 10 percent more suffered with stricture and enlarged post-gonorrhea prostates. At the State Farm, penitentiary physician Dr. Leonard found that 33 percent of the 170 convicts examined also had syphilis, as did 14 percent of the 258 convicts in the road camps.

"These figures speak for themselves," stated the 1920 annual report to the General Assembly, "and the condition revealed alone justifies the action of your Excellency in forcing the adoption of better prison methods in Virginia." In April 1920, Governor Westmoreland Davis took the advice and for starters asked for the resignations of several of the penitentiary board members.

With the syphilis epidemic the catalyst, Virginia then embarked on a radical multi-year program of penal reform. Over the next two years, the entire program was overhauled from top to bottom, including: (1) a new system of institutional management and control; (2) an updated accounting and bookkeeping system; (3) a better-equipped medical and hospital system; (4) a system for better examining and mentally classifying the prisoners

The penitentiary, circa 1918. *VCU James Branch Cabell Library Digital Collections, Special Collections and Archives.*

(including the fingerprint method of identification); (5) the establishment of a system of elementary education and vocational training for the inmates; (6) an organized method of conducting religious and recreational activities; (7) the establishment of a state-use industrial system to replace the contract (lease) system; and (8) a closer working relationship between the penal institutions and other state agencies.

One of the first items of business was eliminating the old "monstrous and degrading" striped uniforms in favor of "prison brown." The horizontal black and white stripes had been standardized one hundred years earlier at New York's Auburn Prison to supposedly make it more difficult for inmates to escape unnoticed. Virginia was one of the last states to eliminate the striped uniforms.

Also, as a result of a 1919 investigation and exposé by Dr. E. Duddington, president of the Prisoners' Relief Society, and published in the magazine *The Delinquent*, two forms of corporal punishment, the "cross" and the "iron mask," were finally abolished in Virginia.

Conferences held at the penitentiary between the State Board of Health, the United States Public Health Service, the Medical College of Virginia and the Medical Society of Virginia approved extensive improvements to the penitentiary hospital and the hospital at the State Farm. Finding also that nearly every prison in America had libraries, the Board of Directors ordered by resolutions that prisoners in all state institutions be allowed to have "proper reading matter, including daily newspapers and periodicals."

The board learned that medical recordkeeping had been virtually nonexistent; therefore, new procedures were instituted. By September 1921, the penitentiary's medical department featured a hospital, interns and a dentist from the Medical College of Virginia. The next year, Dr. Nelson Turner, an eye, ear, nose and throat specialist, began weekly visits.

Rice M. Youell was elected penitentiary superintendent on May 15, 1922, after the resignation of James B. Wood. Youell served as superintendent until 1942, when he was selected as the first commissioner of corrections. In 1948, he was named director of the reorganized corrections division, a position he held until his retirement in 1960.

LATROBE'S BUILDING IS DEMOLISHED

By 1925, Benjamin Latrobe's original 125-year-old penitentiary building was terribly out of date and practically of no use, with only a small section able to contain any inmates. With money appropriated by the 1927 General Assembly, the original building was demolished and a new multipurpose building was completed by January 1, 1929, with many original materials. Finally, the penitentiary had a modern laundry, ice plant, cold storage, dining room, chapel, kitchen, hospital, shop and storeroom.

It was an ignominious end of an era and done with no consideration of the historical aspects of the original structure. This was a modern penitentiary, after all, with all the inherent risks and dangers, not a shrine to the fading ideals of a founding father and a semi-obscure eighteenth-century architect. The practical aspects of demolishing this artifact took precedence over any historical significance.

A plaque placed on an exterior wall of the replacement building stated (incorrectly), "The bricks used in the construction of these buildings were from the original penitentiary which was designed by Thomas Jefferson and erected on this site in the year 1797."

Business Practices Revised

In 1929, the federal Hawes-Cooper Bill addressed the supposedly unfair business practices of penitentiary-manufactured goods competing with those privately made. This bill stipulated that convict-produced goods could be sent to other states for sale providing they were taxed and sold the same and at competitive prices in those states as privately made goods. Penitentiaries were given five years to become compliant by January 19, 1934. Then, that year, the Virginia General Assembly passed legislation that specified that prison industries should only produce items needed by state agencies or political subdivisions.

By 1931, the contracts with the National Pants Company of Washington, D.C., and the Fiber Craft Chair Company of Kentucky had ended. The printing shop was in operation, as was the license tag division, which was saving thousands of dollars every year for the state.

Between 1920 and 1930, the prison population in Virginia ballooned from 1,494 to 2,722, an increase of 82 percent and sixteen times the rate of general population increase. By 1937, only six states and the District of Columbia had more incarcerated inmates per 100,000 of population than Virginia. Since 70 percent of those admissions were recidivists, a 1939 report concluded that Virginia was "teaching her offenders to be permanently criminal instead of permanently law-abiding."

School Days

As part of the reforms, the new Penitentiary Board stipulated that any "illiterate" convict who had never attended grades one through four attend at least two hours of mandatory school per week. Classrooms were remodeled, a full-time religious and educational director was hired and the first penitentiary school opened in October 1920, with two classes of fifteen white convicts each. The following year, a class started for black convicts. Soon, twenty-two classes were organized to handle the four hundred convicts assigned to classes based on their educational level. In 1922, classes were formed for the female convicts as well.

The program was considered a success; in 1943, one hundred convicts graduated at the fifth-grade level.

State Farm for Women

By 1930, several Virginia women's associations, along with the State Department of Public Welfare, realized a state farm for female convicts was needed to relieve overcrowding in the women's section of the penitentiary and to "rehabilitate and re-shape ill-defined life patterns through religious, academic, vocational, social and cultural education." In January 1932, the State Industrial Farm for Women opened on a plot of land at Goochland Court House, twenty-nine miles west of Richmond on the James River. Any woman, white or black, serving a minimum of sixty days could be transferred to the farm, which functioned as a part of the State Prison Board under Major Rice Youell and board president Walker Cottrell.

Under Superintendent Elizabeth Kates, a newspaper clipping of the facility may give the impression the farm was more like a women's Bible college than a prison, with none of the horrors experienced (and later exposed) at the men's farm a scant six miles away. "The State is giving these unfortunate women every opportunity to develop body and mind," stated the April 14, 1939 *Richmond Times-Dispatch*. "Good health is arranged for the first, through needed medical care, good food and regular hours. A receptive and creative mind is usually the response and it is at this time that the educational and vocational program is developed."

After seven years of operation, the farm received 1,523 inmates, with only 10 percent returned as recidivists. A statewide fundraising operation among church women raised about $10,000 to build a nondenominational chapel there.

In 1933, the total convict population, including those at the penitentiary, the State Farm, the Industrial Farm for Women, the lime grinding plant and the road crews, was 3,278. During that year, 1,911 new prisoners were admitted, an increase of 369 over the previous year. Of those, 1,093 were between the ages of fifteen and twenty-five. Twenty-nine escapees and 7 parole violators were returned; 22 prisoners escaped that year from the road crews.

One-third of all prisoners, or 592 total, admitted to the penitentiary that year were for housebreaking, which was attributed to the effects of the Great Depression. Also, 237 were admitted for grand larceny and 141 for store-breaking. In contrast, 31 were admitted for first-degree murder and 58 for second-degree. Of the new prisoners received, 12 percent had previously served terms at the penitentiary, and an astonishing 41 percent had done time in other correctional institutions somewhere in the United States.

In 1937, the State Prison Board established the Southampton State Farm for youthful and first-time offenders, three miles west of Drewryville. Composed of 2,837 acres, 604 were used primarily for cotton cultivation. In the fiscal year 1938–39, this farm held 122 male prisoners: 114 black and 8 white.

Finally, the system was addressing juvenile reformation.

In 1938, prison board chairman Walker Cottrell announced a $400,000 appropriation had been approved for a two-year building program on Spring Street. With all the improvements, work crews and state farms in operation, it seemed Virginia's penal system had shed its negative southern image and reputation and could finally be considered "progressive." But in the next decade, an escaped prisoner and an arrogant young Richmond lawyer would unmask a dark underbelly and push punitive regulations to their breaking points.

CHAPTER 11

THE CHARGE AGAINST FLOGGING

*Flogging is brutal and pagan—no Preacher or Sunday School Teacher
can Tell Me Differently.*
—Richmond attorney Howard Carwile,
WRNL radio speech transcript, February 24, 1946

In June 1940, an unnamed sixty-year-old man received a conditional pardon and was released from the penitentiary after serving over twelve years for statutory rape. Soon afterward, the man contacted Superintendent Major Rice Youell and told him he wished to be readmitted. According to him, life on the outside was far too troublesome, and he yearned for a life "free from worries" inside the walls of the "old state pen."

Youell explained he could not just take him back, so the man stole a cow—a felony in Virginia—and let himself be caught. He was tried in July and resentenced for an unknown period.

VIOLENCE BEGETS VIOLENCE

Despite all the "feel good" improvements of the previous two decades, few inmates in the 1940s found life in the penitentiary free from worries. In fact, the years 1941–51 were some of the most violent in the history of the facility, and the Commonwealth of Virginia endured years of terrible nationwide press as a result. Stabbings, beatings and sexual assaults by convicts and guards—at the penitentiary, the State Farm and in the road crews—reached record highs.

Then, in November 1945, a brash young Richmond lawyer (and serial Richmond newspaper letter-to-the-editor writer) named Howard Carwile was contacted by the sister of a State Farm inmate named Edward Wall, who described sadistic treatments committed against her brother. She wanted to know if anything could be done.

Carwile had quickly gained a reputation with some in central Virginia as a champion of the poor and those victimized by the state legal system but by others as a quarrelsome, obnoxious loudmouth. Calling himself "a man without a party, and a friend to the oppressed," Carwile had recently represented a young black woman who was detained in a basement holding cell at Richmond City Hall with her two-month-old baby, with the judge declaring the incarceration "won't hurt the baby." In 1945, Purple Heart recipient Alphaeus Robinson got pro bono representation from Carwile when he was locked up on a vagrancy charge and then left in jail for twelve days on bogus "suspicion of murder" charges. Carwile claimed his detention was a frame-up involving corrupt policemen.

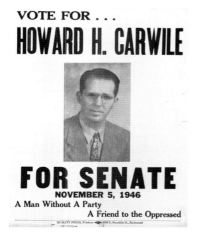

Howard Carwile for Senate, 1946. *VCU James Branch Cabell Library Digital Collections, Special Collections and Archives.*

One longtime Richmonder in 2016 described Carwile as the kind of man that if you asked him if it was raining, he would respond not with a yes or no but with a fifteen-minute oration on rain.

Carwile—who also happened to be an independent candidate for governor at the time—was all over the Wall case and demanded an immediate investigation into abuses by guards and State Farm officials. His untiring work two years later led to the passage of Virginia's first anti-flogging law.

"DIE AND PROVE IT"

By 1945, all prisons in northern states had long since abandoned the punishment of convict flogging, yet it was still considered appropriate not only in Virginia but in Georgia, Florida, North and South Carolina, Alabama, Mississippi and Louisiana as well.

Edward Wall's sister, Helen Kuntz, charged that her thirty-year-old brother, sentenced to a three-year term at the State Farm for bigamy, had not received medical attention while he and others endured brutal overwork, bloody beatings and cruel, immoral treatment by other convicts. After a visit to the farm, Carwile told Governor Colgate Darden that he had not only Wall but also sixty other convicts ready to testify of abuses and substandard living and work arrangements, and they wanted assurances that they would not be punished for doing so. He also requested a hearing before the Board of Corrections that would be open to the public. Darden agreed but kept the hearing closed.

Superintendent Rice Youell, a man as big and powerful as any pro football fullback, admitted prior to the hearing that he gave State Farm superintendent R.L. Royster permission to flog convicts as state law provided. According to Wall, on September 19, Royster, armed with a riot gun, oversaw the strap whipping of twelve men, including Wall, for refusing to work in a knee-deep muddy cornfield to stop rising floodwaters. Five of them were "put across the barrel." Wall also claimed he was struck in the head with a rifle butt, breaking three teeth. Carwile, as a result, designated Royster his main target in the investigation, charging that he was a sadist and unfit for his job.

Wall, on the other hand, was considered a "malingerer" at the farm and, according to officials, seemed to complain of a different malady almost every day. But it was not until Wall was eventually taken back to the penitentiary hospital that Dr. Asa Shield, neuropsychiatrist and advisor on nervous diseases there, admitted that he was not faking, claiming, "In his present condition, I don't think he's fit to do any work."

On November 10, a prisoner named R.C. Almond was released from the State Farm and, in an interview with the *Richmond News-Leader*, verified all of Wall's claims of mistreatment at the farm. Almond said that he slept in a bunk next to a prisoner named Robert Johnson, who was one of the convicts lashed thirty-nine times for refusing to work in the cornfield. He said Johnson was sunburned on his back yet was still beaten with a two-inch-wide strap, "making him bleed profusely." Johnson was rumored to have been taken to Medical College Hospital by another more sympathetic guard for treatment. Almond also told of a twenty-three-year-old convict named Dye who was kept in chains for eleven months. Later, Dye was found to be diabetic and was only given medical care after he wasted down to ninety-eight pounds.

A subcommittee chaired by Albert Bryan of Alexandria and State Senator A.E. Stevens was formed on November 14 to investigate the charges brought by Carwile. Then, a hearing conducted on November 20 before the State Board of Corrections branched into the airing of other charges, not just at the farm but at all units of the state penal system.

The cat was suddenly out of the bag. Seventeen-year-old State Farm inmate Ray Barden told of wearing shackles that cut into him until he bled and of being flogged and "hung up on a bar" (also known as "the rack") in a standing position with his arms at eye level and toes barely touching the floor.

A penitentiary parolee named Jesse Woodson testified that a road camp guard, Johnny Perry, told sick men to "die and prove it." Another road camp guard named W. Harvey allegedly kicked sick men in shackles and beat men in the face with blackjacks when they were "hung up" and unable to defend themselves.

Inmate Charles Stewart testified that sexual perversion at the penitentiary was more widespread and more pervasive than at any prison he had ever been held. When confronted with his prison record, which included sixteen escapes from eight different prisons, Stewart admitted, "I'm not trying to pretend I'm a good man, because I'm not."

Two other State Farm convicts testified that one prisoner, Kenneth Burroughs, was accused by the physician of malingering and sent to unload dirt from a cart. He subsequently fell desperately ill while being forced to work and died after being sent back to the penitentiary.

In all, twenty convicts reiterated similar stories of floggings with straps, spoiled and maggot-filled food, refusal of minimal medical care and the failures of the administration to stop the widespread sexual perversions practiced among some of the stronger, alpha-male inmates.

"After reading the reports in the *News-Leader* concerning the inhuman treatment of the prisoners at the State Farm of Virginia, I begin to wonder why our servicemen went abroad to relieve persons in the concentration camps," stated a 1945 letter to the editor of that newspaper signed "Worried Reader." "Seems to me the Gestapo could have taken lessons on this side."

Guards and administrators insisted that there was no abusive behavior by guards against inmates and that the inmates were fabricating charges against them. All told, fifty-five witnesses—guards and inmates—testified.

LIKE "HITLER PRESIDING AT HIS OWN TRIAL"

On December 17, the subcommittee submitted its twenty-five-page report, showing zero instances of unjust punishment or brutality against inmates. The worst charge was the association of young offenders with older, more hardened convicts. "We find temporary road camps give rise to objectionable although unavoidable conditions and practices, such as the chaining of prisoners at night to secure them, inadequate sanitary facilities, and unprogressive methods of punishment which could be eliminated in a system of permanent road camps," the report added.

The report also devoted considerable attention to the practice of flogging, which was authorized under state law but supposedly under limited conditions. The report reminded readers that a particular flogging in question, in which five men were held over a barrel and lashed over their bare buttocks and backs for insubordination, was attended by doctors both before and after the whippings.

The account—which likely infuriated Carwile more with each new paragraph—also stated that the form of punishments known as "hanging up" and "the rack" did not mean what the words implied. Prisoners were not suspended over the floor, it stated, but left in a standing position with their arms locked to a bar at eye level. Still, the *Richmond Times-Dispatch* took issue with this punishment, echoing Thomas Jefferson almost 150 years earlier by saying, "One does not have to be in favor of coddling prisoners to think that a medieval form of punishment as this has no place in an enlightened state."

The report glossed over the charges of sexual perversions, noting that such activities were "common," that they "exist in all institutions of this type" and were "far from widespread." Food was found to be "ample, wholesome and clean."

Carwile raged that the report "was as complete and thorough whitewashing as was ever perpetrated, and is the same as if Hitler were presiding at his own trial."

While all penal officials were exonerated by the report, any celebrating by them was cut short when, ironically, Virginia started getting dreadful national press after a prisoner named Lawrence Starling, who escaped from prison camp 24 at South Hill, was captured in Kansas City, Missouri.

An articulate spokesman with boyish Hollywood good looks, Starling described to a United Press International reporter a "bitter story of spread-eagle treatment, of shackles and lashings" at the Virginia camp. Now Virginia's penal system was pushed out of closed committee hearings and

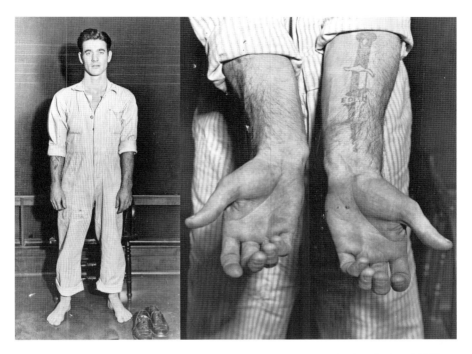

Lawrence Starling in Kansas City, Missouri, displaying bruises received at the South Hill work camp. *VCU James Branch Cabell Library Special Collections and Archives.*

into the national spotlight, especially after photos of Starling displaying his bruised wrists and feet circulated among the legislators. To the great embarrassment of Governor William Tuck, Missouri governor Phil Donnelly decried Virginia's methods as "medieval" and "barbaric."

Then lo and behold, just as the 1946 General Assembly session convened, House member Charles Phillips proposed an anti-flogging bill. Phillips's bill forbid the use of "whipping, flogging, or administration of any similar corporal punishment of, or to, any prisoner." During discussion, tensions erupted between Carwile and Tazewell representative Dr. Jack Witten, an opponent of the bill, forcing the bellowing Carwile to be bodily escorted from the chamber by Isle of Wight representative Andrew Stephens and bill clerk Wallace Clark. Carwile shouted that he objected to the "Nazism" of the proceedings and claimed his rights were being abused as he was hustled into the corridor and threatened with arrest.

He calmed down and later was allowed back in as long as he behaved, and the bill passed. It was signed by Governor Tuck on March 11 and became effective on June 18, 1946.

Corrections Superintendent Youell had strenuously opposed the bill and encouraged legislators to defeat it, claiming that the authority to administer corporal punishment needed to be left to the discretion of the farm and road camp supervisors until isolation cells could be constructed to contain the most unruly convicts. He later contradicted himself when he claimed that he actually ended the practice of flogging in February, two months ahead of the deadline but before the Phillips bill was even passed by the assembly.

"SERVILE NEWSPAPERS, SPINELESS PREACHERS AND SINISTER POLITICIANS"

Reports of horrific conditions in Virginia's prisons, farms and road camps did not stop with the passage of Phillips's bill, and reports trickled out into the spring and summer of 1946, all of them investigated by "Hollerin' Howard" Carwile. His reputation as a troublemaker and a "bad boy," however, caused many in the press and within the state capitol to no longer take him seriously.

"It is unfortunate that the name of Howard Carwile should be connected in any way to these investigations, for it will tend to make most people discount a good deal that is said," stated the *Danville Commercial Appeal*. "… It is probable that much good [in the prisons] could be done—by someone whose name is not synonymous with gross exaggeration."

Virginia's penal system, however, had an even worse reputation than Carwile. Almost every newspaper columnist in the state decried the unorthodox tactics of the loud and aggressive Richmond attorney but still took up the cause of abused prisoners, giving little to no credence to prison authorities who scrambled to discount the convicts' often outrageous claims. "There is not a word of truth to anything [convict] Starling said," State Farm superintendent Frank Smyth Jr. insisted of the assertions by the Missouri escapee, to deaf statewide ears.

With his inimitable applications of the English language and his love of adjectives, Carwile took his fight to the airwaves on February 2, 1946, on his fifteen-minute radio show on WRNL in Richmond, saying, among other things:

> *This fight to civilize the prison system of our state shall be won. Servile newspapers, spineless preachers and sinister politicians can delay victory, but all these fakers combined can never annihilate crusading zeal engendered by the righteousness of the cause….*

These officials have admitted the flogging, chaining and shackling of prisoners. Many lame excuses were offered to justify the admitted fact that an aged epileptic had been forced to carry a ball and chain on the State Farm....These officials, on cross-examination, confessed that a tuberculosis patient, with a collapsed lung, had been flogged and forced to do heavy work such as loading fertilizer....

The people of this state will not be duped by Major Youell's self-righteous, pseudo-scientific clap-trap about the lack of funds and modern facilities. Dark Age devices are never justified.

"$100,000 in Social Gain"

In September 1946, Youell told the *Washington Post* that the ban on flogging had resulted in increased disciplinary problems and estimated that the law was costing Virginia $50,000 in decreased prisoner labor. Men who may have been whipped or threatened to be whipped to make them work simply were not working, and the superintendents had little recourse in punishment toward them.

The next day, Delegate Charles Phillips answered Youell's contention by stating that his bill was worth "$100,000 in social gain" and certainly was going to improve Virginia's reputation nationwide.

Regardless of the effectiveness of the Phillips bill, it was Howard Carwile who took full credit. "Some people say that I am always tearing down, but never doing anything constructive," he said in a letter to the *Times-Dispatch* editor on July 28, 1946. "I ask these critics: who took the bloody lash off the backs of teenage boys in our prisons? Every fair-minded person in this commonwealth knows that my sensational exposure of the barbarities on the State Farm in Goochland County culminated in the passage of the anti-flogging bill."

The flogging bill did little to quell inmate-on-inmate penitentiary violence, which seemed to get worse as the decade wore on. In late 1946, eighteen-year old John Outerbridge was stabbed to death by Alfred Washington with a homemade knife in a dispute described by Superintendent Smyth as one of those "isolated" and non-widespread "sex perversion" cases.

On July 3, 1949, twenty-six-year-old inmate J. Spikes died in the yard of stab wounds in the heart. On September 22 of that same year, inmate Patterson Walker killed Howard Diggs in cell house A and Moses Williams in cell house B for "talking about him." Diggs died of dozens of stab wounds in the chest, neck, shoulder and abdomen. On January 1, 1951, inmate P. Walker snuck up behind G. Harrington and stabbed him multiple times in the chest. Harrington later died in the penitentiary hospital.

Yet as the press and the legislature decried inmate-on-inmate violence and the medieval act of flogging, Virginia prepared to electrocute five condemned men in one day.

CHAPTER 12

THE POWHATAN THIRTEEN TO THE MARTINSVILLE SEVEN

ASSEMBLY-LINE EXECUTION

"DECIDEDLY DEPRESSING"

On the night of February 12, 1909, between 8:00 and 9:00 p.m., John Brown, his son William, cousins Joe and Isham Taylor, Lewis Jenkins and three others arrived at the Powhatan County home of Mary Skipwith and Walter Johnson and knocked. When Johnson opened the door, Isham Taylor raised a shotgun loaded with No. 8 shot and fired point blank into the man's face.

With Johnson down, the men rushed into the house. Mrs. Skipwith came into the upper hall to investigate the gunshot, and one of the robbers crushed her head with an axe, killing her immediately. Her body was dragged to the lower floor, and the looting began. Everything of value was taken; even the portraits of Johnson's parents were torn from the walls. Jewelry, money and silver were taken and divided.

Joe and Isham Taylor worked as hearse drivers, and days later, in an almost unbelievable coincidence, they drove the hearses containing their two victims to the cemetery. John and William Brown also coincidentally dug their victims' graves. John Brown, in fact, became so nervous at the grave site when he found out who the bodies were that the grave lines had to be redrawn twice for him, raising suspicions.

The Taylor cousins, Lewis Jenkins and Robert Taylor were arrested soon after, and while confined in the Farmville jail, they confessed to the crime, implicating six others: John and William Brown, William Robinson,

Nannie Taylor and Emanuel and Charles Brown. In addition to those, three more were also arrested and questioned. This group become known as the Powhatan Thirteen.

Jenkins was the first to be tried. On the witness stand, he declared he wasn't at the scene of the crime that night but that a divine dream gave him full details of what had happened. He then perfectly described the entire crime, and his bizarre "confession" implicated all the others. After trials, five of the thirteen—Jenkins, Joe and Isham Taylor and John and William Brown—were sentenced to death. Isham Taylor's wife, Nannie, who was a lookout, was sentenced to five years in the penitentiary. The rest were all exonerated. Circuit Court Judge Hundley then ordered the five guilty men to the electric chair on the same day: April 30, 1909.

Hundley's decision was not well received. Governor Claude Swanson was against five electrocutions in one day, and penitentiary superintendent Morgan felt that such wholesale killing would make the "atmosphere of the prison decidedly depressing on the appointed day."

Yet preparations started. On March 27, Morgan sent a letter to Adams Electric Company, which originally wired the six-month-old electric chair, requesting extra components to have on hand for the unusually heavy load of upcoming electrocutions:

> Dear sirs; We have five subjects for the electric chair to be executed on the same day, April 30. Please quote me a price on extra helmet and leg electrode complete, and 2 extra helmet sponges. It is possible you are not familiar with all the types of negro heads and consequently it has not occurred to you that there could be much wide departure from the normal shape; therefore if it can be done, that the helmet be made as to be flexible to some extent at least. Our last experience demonstrated the necessity for such an arrangement, as the current dried out the sponge on each side of the head…and showered itself in sparks.

But even with the right equipment, Morgan and the penitentiary were not emotionally prepared for multiple executions. After giving up attempting to organize such a gruesome task, Morgan asked for a conference with Governor Swanson about the matter. They spoke, and then Morgan followed up with an explanatory letter dated April 12:

> You will recall the talk I had with you several days ago.…It is absolutely impossible to electrocute all of these men on the same date.

I would be glad to have you respite Joe and Isham Taylor until the 5th of May and Lewis Jenkins until the 7th of May. I am afraid to undertake the execution of more than two men on the same day.

The governor took Morgan's advice. On April 30, John Brown, age fifty-seven, and his son William, age thirty-three, were the first to die for the Powhatan murders. John Brown was strapped in the chair at 7:24 a.m., and after twelve minutes, the dead body of his son had also been removed. These were the first back-to-back electrocutions in the history of the penitentiary and the first father-and-son executions.

Joe and Isham Taylor died in the chair on May 5. The last of the Powhatan murderers to be executed was Lewis Jenkins, the "divine dreamer," who died just after 7:00 a.m. on May 7.

The Martinsville Seven: "Is Mercy in Virginia Dead?"

Forty-two years later, on February 2, 1951, five men—with four of them part of a notorious Martinsville rape case—were executed in one day. Obviously, the prospect of five electrocutions in one day no longer taxed the technical limitations of the execution apparatus, nor did it have the demoralizing effect on penitentiary personnel that it had in 1909. In the years between the Powhatan Thirteen and the Martinsville cases there were exactly 200 electrocutions at the penitentiary: 172 black, 28 white; 199 males, 1 female. Perhaps the imbruting effect of so many executions just made everyone more comfortable with (or more numb to) the process.

The "Martinsville Seven" case remains a stain on Virginia penological history. On the evening of January 8, 1949, a woman named Ruby Stroud Floyd accused seven black men of raping her "14 or 15 times" while she walked through an African American neighborhood in Martinsville to collect six dollars owed by a woman for a suit and a pair of shoes. Floyd did not know the area, so she stopped at the home of Dan Gilmer to ask directions to the house. Gilmer urged her to return home since it was getting dark, and on Saturday night the locals "like to celebrate and have a nice time." Mrs. Floyd insisted on continuing, however, and asked eleven-year-old Charlie Martin, the son of a woman she knew, to help her.

VOL. 60, NO. 207   N.E.A. Service   MARTINSVILLE, VIRGINIA,

The Virginia Supreme Court of Appeals today agreed to review the cases of seven Martinsville Negroes sentenced to death for rape. The seven are, left to right, Booker T. Millner, Frank Hairston, Jr., Howard Lee Hairston, Joe Henry Hampton, John Clabon Taylor, Francis DeSales Grayson, and James Luther Hairston.

The Martinsville Seven. *Undated clip,* Martinsville Bulletin.

Floyd was then allegedly grabbed by four men who paid Charlie Martin a quarter to leave. She testified that they dragged and attacked her near a secluded train track, where they were joined by three more.

After the rapes, police quickly arrested Booker T. Millner and Frank Hairston Jr. Soon John Taylor, James L. Hairston, Howard Lee Hairston, Francis D. Grayson and James Henry Hampton were also arrested. They became known as the Martinsville Seven.

All these men were between eighteen and twenty years of age (except for Grayson, a World War II veteran who was thirty-seven) and worked as laborers in local furniture factories. All the men were also from what was called "East Martinsville," a "colored" side of town looked on less favorably than the whiter "West Martinsville," but none of them had serious criminal backgrounds. Hampton had earlier received a suspended sentence for grand larceny, Millner had been fined for public drunkenness and Taylor had been arrested for "fornication" in 1944.

Floyd immediately identified Grayson and Hampton as her rapists, but since the attack happened at night, she could not positively identify the others. After being questioned by local police, however, several other defendants eventually confessed to either being present or "aiding and abetting" the assault. By April, all seven men faced rape charges.

A "Mob of a Thousand Men"

The Reverend Robert Anderson, pastor of Fifth Baptist Church and spiritual minister to John Taylor, told the *Afro-American* newspaper that he was told by at least two of the defendants of improper conduct by the Martinsville police during questioning. They claimed they were seated in a chair and surrounded by several officers. One officer allegedly held a nightstick over their heads, telling them that if they did not admit guilt, they would be beaten to death. Several of the men were told by police that their companions had already confessed and implicated them, and if they did not also confess they would be handed over to a "mob of a thousand men waiting outside to [lynch] you." Anderson was unsuccessful in getting this information to Governor John S. Battle.

Prior to the trials, Martinsville Circuit Court judge Kennon C. Whittle told prosecutors and defense lawyers that all the defendants "will be tried as though both parties were members of the same race. I will not have it otherwise." There was a good reason for that. Whittle may have known that up to that point, all 45 men executed for rape in Virginia since the introduction of the electric chair in 1908 were blacks convicted of attacking white women. Not one of the 808 white men convicted of rape in that period had been executed. Whittle knew he could easily find himself presiding down the same slippery slope.

Whittle also agreed to a defense request to hold individual trials except for Taylor and James Hairston, who agreed to be tried jointly. During jury selections, Judge Whittle's admonition faded when the prosecution vetoed all potential black jurors, mostly because they opposed capital punishment, leaving white male juries to hear all six cases. It was a portentous omen of the final phase of southern racial justice about to occur.

Ruby Floyd testified in all six so-called assembly-line trials, sometimes for as long as forty minutes. Juries heard evidence that included medical verification of Floyd's physical injuries and testimony from local residents she had appealed to for help after the rape. Defense lawyers argued that Floyd's failure to forcibly repel the men constituted consent and that their clients' confessions were coerced by the local police.

SEVEN MEN, SEVEN DEATH PENALTIES

While all seven defendants admitted their presence at the attack, only Frank Hairston freely admitted to raping Floyd. On the stand, each of the defendants at least partially rejected his earlier confession. Some claimed that the police had written the confessions, and when they signed them, they did not notice that their own words had been changed.

While there was a noticeable absence of the prosecutorial race-baiting such as seen in the 1931 Scottsboro trial and other similar prosecutions across the South, Virginia law at the time authorized capital punishment for not just rape but also attempted rape and for aiding and abetting. Thus, all the juries convicted the young men of rape, and on May 3, 1949, they recommended the death penalty for all seven of them.

Conservative southern Virginia newspaper editorials were unanimous in their praise for the fairness of the arrest and trials. "No infringement of their rights occurred," wrote the *Danville Register* on June 6, 1950. "The seven were tried in an atmosphere free from excitement and were represented by the ablest counsel available."

After the convictions, the men were represented by Richmond civil rights lawyers Martin A. Martin, Oliver Hill and others. In requesting some execution statistics from the penitentiary, Martin received a response from Superintendent W.F. Smyth Jr. that they had combed through 51,780 inmate records dating back to January 1, 1908, and replied, "No white person has ever been electrocuted in Virginia for the crime of rape; or attempted rape."

Governor Battle was indifferent to the startling electrocution statistic in the clemency petition, writing, "No fair minded person can read the evidence in these cases without being convinced, beyond the shadow of a doubt, of the guilt of all the defendants." Appeals were also rejected by the Virginia Supreme Court, and the U.S. Supreme Court declined to hear the case. Coming at the earliest beginnings of the civil rights movement, the Martinsville case was a stark reminder of the excessive punishments still reserved for blacks who violated entrenched southern racial codes.

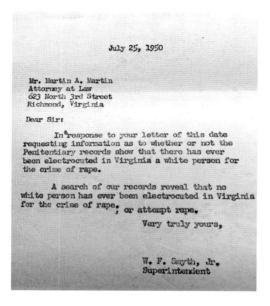

July 25, 1950

Mr. Martin A. Martin
Attorney at Law
623 North 3rd Street
Richmond, Virginia

Dear Sir:

In response to your letter of this date requesting information as to whether or not the Penitentiary records show that there has ever been electrocuted in Virginia a white person for the crime of rape.

A search of our records reveal that no white person has ever been electrocuted in Virginia for the crime of rape.; or attempt rape.

Very truly yours,

W. F. Smyth, Jr.
Superintendent

A letter from penitentiary superintendent W.F. Smyth to attorney Martin A. Martin. *Library of Virginia.*

Martin confronted this violation head on: "The prime reason [these men] were sentenced to the electric chair was because all of them are colored and the prosecutrix was a white woman and the juries were composed of all white men."

Richmond was deluged by thousands of telegrams to stop the executions, including one from Russia signed by numerous Russian writers and artists, including film director Grigori Alexandrov, singer Ivan Kozlovski and composers Dimitri Shostakovich and Sergei Prokofiev, expressing "deepest indignation at this act of infamy and brutality inspired by race hatred." Many letters—especially from northern states—compared the Martinsville defendants to the "Scottsboro boys" and warned Governor Battle that he was doing a grave disservice to Virginia and southern racial justice by allowing the executions to move forward. Charged terms such as "legal lynching" and "Jim Crow justice" abounded.

There was good reason for the dissidence toward the sentencing. First Baptist Church pastor W.L. Ransome reminded the governor that in January 1947, two white Richmond policemen—Carl Burleson and Leonard Davis—were convicted of raping a thirty-two-year-old black woman, Nannie Strayhorn, in the rear of their patrol car on a dead-end street and were sentenced to seven years in the penitentiary.

Also, the October 16, 1948 *Norfolk Journal and Guide* reported that a white farmer in Amherst County, Corbett Witt, raped a pregnant nineteen-year-

An appeal from artists and writers in Russia to stop the executions of the Martinsville Seven. Most notable is Sergei Prokofiev (*bottom right*). *Library of Virginia.*

George Hailey. *Library of Virginia.*

old black woman. He was found guilty and fined $350. Even more egregious was the rape of Bertha Rose, a "feeble-minded colored woman," by a white man, Murrel Dudley, near Glasgow, Virginia, on August 29, 1948. According to the *Norfolk Journal*, Dudley was found guilty and fined $20.

On February 2, 1951, at 8:04 a.m., seventy-five people silently prayed at Richmond's capitol building while George Hailey, a white Halifax County man convicted of raping and murdering a twelve-year-old girl—who had nothing to do with the Martinsville cases—was executed first in this grisly sequence, proving that even in execution, the white man still goes first. Unlike the Martinsville defendants, who went calmly, Hailey fought the guards all the way from his cell and had to be restrained while he was strapped in the chair.

Joe Hampton, in stark contrast to Hailey, was very composed. His last words were "Everything's all right. We'll see you on the other side." Declared dead by 8:12 a.m., he was followed by Howard Hairston, who needed a second charge to kill him at 8:22 a.m. Booker Milner was dead by 8:29 a.m., and finally, Frank Hairston was dead by 9:05 a.m. "Gentlemen," Hairston said to the witnesses after he was strapped in, "I want all of you to meet me in Heaven."

Five dead in sixty-one minutes.

In Washington, D.C., several people from as far away as New York City held a "death watch" in front of the White House. A spokesman said President Harry Truman was "very familiar with the [Martinsville] case" but he was "not seeing anyone about it."

In between the executions, Governor Battle received many more letters and telegrams, including a particularly angry one from the National Negro Congress that stated, in part, "You white sons of bitches will suffer for crucifying these innocent boys.…Soon the glorious Negro race will revolt and rule in your place and you will be strung up from the Courthouse flagpole and your carkass [*sic*] thrown to the dogs. YOU MUST DIE!!" It was signed, "Booker Carver Washington III, Grand and Imperial Regent."

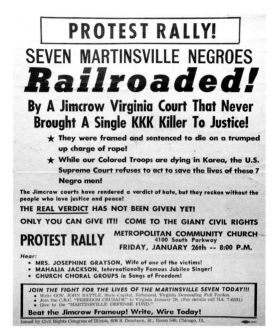

A flyer for a rally in Chicago to stop the executions of the Martinsville Seven. *Library of Virginia.*

On February 5, John Taylor went to the chair at 7:35 a.m. and was pronounced dead six minutes later. He was followed by James Hairston, who, like his brother, needed a second charge, and then Francis Grayson. All three were dead by 8:15 a.m.

Behind the penitentiary walls, life goes on, and unlike the Powhatan case, the executions of eight men in three days seemed to have little to no effect on the day-to-day operations.

Nine years later, on March 1, 1960, a bill introduced in the General Assembly to abolish the death penalty was soundly defeated.

CHAPTER 13
GREAT ESCAPES AND NOT-SO-GREAT ATTEMPTS

JAMES WILSON: THE FIRST ESCAPE

In late August 1800, only four months after the penitentiary opened, James Wilson, alias Jeremiah Whitson, discovered his cell window bars unsecured and disappeared into the Henrico countryside. A report by acting inspector John Buchanan, dated September 1, stated in classic understatement, "We beg leave to suggest the propriety of having the grates and windows of the prisoners apartments better secured." It is unknown if Wilson was recaptured.

In 1802, a group of five got out through another unsecured window grate but were immediately recaptured inside an enclosure built after Wilson's escape. In 1803, three men escaped by somehow getting to the roof, and in 1806, a group of eight "ingenious and dangerous desperados" tunneled their way to freedom.

LIZZIE DODSON: RECIDIVIST ESCAPEE

Lizzie Dodson was a sixteen-year-old black teenager in 1897 when she was convicted of burglary in Fairfax County and sentenced to five years in the penitentiary. On March 24, 1900, after serving half her term, maintaining a good prison record and obtaining post-release employment, she was granted a conditional pardon by Governor James Tyler.

Dodson went to work at Robertson's grocery store in Richmond, but on June 5, she was arrested and convicted of grand larceny. This time, she was sentenced to three years in the penitentiary, plus the remaining time from her first conviction and the obligatory five additional years for a second conviction. She was the first prisoner to violate a conditional pardon and be returned to the facility.

Dodson was not a model prisoner the second time around. The *Richmond Times* reported that her conduct was

Lizzie Dodson. *Library of Virginia.*

"very unseemly, and it was necessary, on several occasions, to whip her."

At 5:30 a.m. on Christmas Eve 1900, while the other prisoners were preparing for breakfast, Lizzie and another convict, a Norfolk woman named Lou Gallagher, initiated an escape they had been planning for months. In the foggy, black morning, no guard could see them as they slid a bench from the shoe department to the twelve-foot west wall. Dodson shed most of her clothing, climbed on the bench and then scaled over the wall, dropping to freedom on the other side. Gallagher, however, lost her nerve and remained behind.

A few minutes after 6:00 a.m., a guard discovered Dodson was not in her cell. During questioning, Gallagher admitted that Dodson had escaped and intended to jump a freight train to points unknown.

In April 1901, Dodson was spotted in Fairfax County by Deputy Charles Pierpont. Determined not to go back, Dodson went berserk, fighting Pierpont like "a veritable amazon" before pulling a pistol from under her dress and shooting him in the groin. It was later revealed that Dodson had gotten pregnant while free and did not want her baby to go to jail with her.

Despite being shot, Pierpont managed to arrest Dodson. She was later convicted of malicious shooting; however, since this was her third conviction, by law she was sentenced to life. On September 2, while still in Fairfax Jail,

Dodson gave birth to a son, Junius Raymond Dodson, who accompanied her back to the penitentiary on November 1.

A few years after her son left the penitentiary, Dodson attempted another escape on April 7, 1908. She used a stolen chunk of metal to somehow dig through her wall into the next cell, which had been left unlocked while being whitewashed. She stole a set of keys from a sleeping guard, ducked from the building and scaled the same west wall. This time, however, she broke her ankle when she dropped to the other side and, unable to flee, was quickly recaptured.

On April 24, 1918, Dodson petitioned Governor Westmoreland Davis for another conditional pardon under the stewardship of local store owner John T. Willard, this time promising to behave herself. It was granted on May 25, and the notorious Lizzie Dodson walked out of the penitentiary and vanished from history.

Walter Turpin: Too Talented for His Own Good

By age thirty-one, Lynchburg native Walter Turpin had spent seventeen years behind bars. His troubles started in 1890 at age thirteen, when he was arrested for stealing cigarettes and spent seven years in a reformatory. Three years after his release, he was arrested and sent to the penitentiary for breaking into a Southern Railway storehouse on Richmond's Dock Street. While he was discharged in October 1901, the very next year he was sentenced to five years for breaking into a Lynchburg hardware store. An additional five years were added for his second offense.

Turpin decided he had to make a change. On October 25, 1902, he finished his work in the shoe manufacturing shop at about 4:00 p.m. and returned to his cell. A few hours later, when the prisoners were counted and locked in their cells, Turpin was discovered missing. He had exchanged his prison stripes for civilian clothes he had stolen from J. Carper, a shoe shop guard. He also took a ladder from the building and climbed over the wall to freedom. A passing Oregon Hill resident actually saw him leap from the wall down onto Belvidere Street, but dressed in a brown suit, overcoat and bowler hat, he quickly blended into a crowd and disappeared. A reward of $100 was offered for his capture.

Two days later, Turpin wrote a letter to Carper (which Carper gave to the *Times-Dispatch* newspaper for publication) promising to pay him for

Walter Turpin. *Library of Virginia.*

his pants "as soon as I get on my feet." He added that he was going to Liverpool, England—a plan many believed was a ruse. They were correct; Turpin was captured in Georgetown, Delaware, in February 1903 and returned to the penitentiary.

Not one to sit on his hands, on July 3, 1904, Turpin and his cellmate, W.G. Donahue, gathered two crude saws, a homemade rope, a fake plywood pistol covered with tinfoil and a convict suit dyed black with shoe polish. They first gouged an eighteen-inch-diameter hole through the wall between their windowless cell and the adjoining cell, which was occupied by Joseph Seybold and another inmate named Hamlin, who refused to join them. As Turpin began to saw through the cell window bars, Hamlin began yelling for guards, despite the others threatening to cut his throat if he did not shut up.

The guards stopped the escape attempt. Turpin received an additional three years for attempting to escape and for cutting out of his cell.

In February 1905, Turpin turned his energies from escaping to counterfeiting. Ingeniously adapting shoe shop equipment into coin molds, he made quarters, dimes and nickels from tin and lead from tomato cans, shoe buckles and scrap metal. The counterfeits' size and thickness were exact, but the coins reportedly felt "greasy" and were the wrong weight. The operation was terminated when a convict who had received one of the fake coins reported it to a guard.

In May 1908, the Ex-Prisoners' Aid Society of Virginia requested a pardon for Turpin, which was granted by Governor Swanson in December.

One month later, Turpin's friend Thomas Seybold was arrested for buying a half pint of whiskey with counterfeit quarters at Seventeenth and Broad Streets in Richmond. A street informant told detectives that he had seen another man with Seybold earlier, and at the Methodist Mission House they found Walter Turpin, with his counterfeiting equipment under his bed. Turpin was convicted and sentenced to five years at the federal penitentiary in Atlanta.

Released in 1913, Turpin returned to Virginia, and in October 1914, he was convicted of housebreaking in Charlottesville under the alias John Johnson. Weeks after "Johnson's" arrival at the Virginia Penitentiary, it was discovered he and Turpin were the same person. Turpin was pardoned by Governor Davis in 1918.

WILLIAM STIARS: THIRTEEN DAYS IN A SEWER

For pure grit and pitbull tenacity, no penitentiary escape matches the ordeal of William Stiars. In fact, it was the disappearance of Stiars in 1906 that led to the penitentiary adopting the Bertillon system of "Anthropometric Measurements" and of photographing inmates for identification purposes.

A Lynchburg native, Stiars was convicted in February 1905 of breaking into Vaden's Store in Manchester. Considered dangerous and an escape risk since he told the officials that they would have a hard time keeping him in prison, he was put to work in the Davis Shoe manufacturing office, mostly so he would have no access to tools. For months, he used his meager earnings to purchase snacks and canned goods.

On June 15, 1906, the noon dinner bell rang and the roll was called. Stiars did not answer.

The alarm was sounded, and the penitentiary was searched top to bottom. Nothing was left unturned: packing boxes were opened and searched and blanket, shoe and coat stacks were prodded. Outgoing barrels and boxes of manufactured goods were opened and examined. It was assumed that if Stiars did not get out in a shoe box or a barrel then he must have been hiding, as there were no signs of an escape. Guards were stationed along the penitentiary walls to watch for indications of an attempt.

After several days, the guards were withdrawn, as it was not believed that a convict could remain in hiding that long.

But Stiars was indeed hiding. He had pried away a panel inside an office closet and then stealthily crawled behind a waste pipe under the office into a narrow opening, where he slithered into a corner against an outside wall. This is where Stiars lived and worked for thirteen straight days—under shoe factory no. 2, lying down in a wet, murky twenty-two-inch-tall crawl space, surrounded by rats, cockroaches, the excruciating stench of two raw sewage pipes and the unbearable heat of a steam boiler directly overhead. He subsisted on the canned food he had bought and stashed there as he worked slowly and deliberately with a chisel used to open shoe crates, cutting a hole in the twenty-four-inch brick exterior wall.

Around June 28, Stiars finally broke through the wall. Carrying a roll of webbing and piece of steel made into a grappling hook, he walked under the arch to the western wall—the same wall Walter Turpin had scaled—and, after a couple of attempts, threw his hook onto the rail surrounding an empty guard house. He then used webbing to slide down the other side and disappeared into the Richmond night.

Later that night, Superintendent Morgan offered a $100 reward for Stiars's recapture. "How he lived in that awful hole for 13 days, I cannot understand," he told the June 29, 1906 *Times-Dispatch*. A guard named Penn and another inmate went down into the described "cesspool," finding a homemade "code" book, a tattered copy of the *Times-Dispatch* and Charles Dickens's *Our Mutual Friend*. Also strewn about were both empty and full cans of beef, salmon, potted tongue, sardines, crackers and even cigarette butts, a knife, a blackjack and a chisel. The men were forced out after five minutes, however, retching from the blistering humidity and suffocating stench Stiars had endured for almost two weeks.

After ten months of freedom, Stiars was arrested in April 1907 on a burglary charge in Mansfield, Ohio. Before he could be extradited to Virginia, however, he escaped and was never heard from again.

Ed Baker: One-Legged Escapee

Ed Baker, a "one leg Italian," was a cook at the state road crew camp near Williamsburg. On Sunday, January 20, 1907, a guard sent him for wood to start the day's cook fire. When Baker did not return by 6:15 a.m., the alarm was sounded and search parties fanned out. Despite having a wooden leg and a scant eight-minute head start, Baker eluded guards and local volunteers for nearly nine hours before being caught around 3:00 p.m. by a guard named Morris over twenty miles from the camp. Baker received thirty-nine lashes and had to wear a ball and chain on his one good leg to prevent future escapes.

Hamilton, Atkins, Burton and Hanley: Delicate White Songbirds

On January 11, 1915, four white prisoners overpowered a guard, a night watchman and a prison shop foreman and bound their hands and feet. After changing clothes, they slid down a rope from a fourth-story window and then scaled the thirty-foot wall, making a clean getaway.

They were:

- #11264, H.L. Hamilton: twenty-four years old, from Danville. He was convicted twice for forgery, with seven years left to serve.
- #8115, Siler Adkins: twenty-seven years old, from Lee County. Serving eighteen years for second-degree murder, with ten years left to serve.
- #7462, Al Burton: thirty-one years old, from Russell County. Serving twenty-five years for two counts of second-degree murder, with seventeen years left to serve.
- #10993, E.B. Hanley: twenty-eight years old, from Norfolk County. Serving eight years for robbery, with five years left to serve.

All four of these men were employed as cutters with Star Clothing and Manufacturing, a St. Louis company contracted by the penitentiary. The men ranked in prison society as "men of better class" and frequently sang as a quartet in the penitentiary choir.

At 6:15 p.m., one of the men stepped behind guard J.T. Bullock to retrieve a bolt of cloth. Then, as two others stepped in front of Bullock, the man behind him pinned his arms to his sides. He was bound securely with baling ropes and gagged with a handkerchief.

Shortly after, the night watchman, George Cardona, and the shop foreman, Mr. Kircher, both wandered into the fourth-floor cutting room. Upon entry, they were accosted by one of the men with Bullock's pistol. They, too, were bound and gagged beside Bullock. The prisoners assured the men they would do no harm as long as no resistance was offered. "They kept their word to the letter," reported the *Times-Dispatch*.

When all three were securely tied, Hamilton—the "boy forger from Danville"—made pillows from loose cloth and placed them under the men's heads.

The four convicts switched their black-and-white striped prison uniforms for overalls before they rifled through the pockets of the three men and took their money. Hamilton leaned over Bullock and asked him to turn his head to the side, which he did, expecting a punch or, worse, a gunshot. Hamilton instead kissed Bullock on the cheek. "Bye-bye, old sport," Hamilton reportedly said. "And good luck."

The inmates then stitched together a long rope made from the cloth bale bindings and then, one by one, swung out the window and climbed fifty-eight feet down to the ground. Once on the ground they swung another rope weighted with a brick on one end over the outside wall, climbed the rope and then dropped to freedom on the other side.

After the night watchman failed to appear from his rounds, a trusty named William Bailey found the three men tied and gagged. Superintendent J.P. Wood sounded a general alarm. The penitentiary was searched and the train yards were put under heavy surveillance, but no trail of the escapees was discovered.

Al Burton was known for his fine handwriting and left behind in the cutting room a beautifully written note:

> *Richmond, VA. January 11, 1915.*
> *To whom it may concern:*
> *We, the undersigners, agree individually to make our escape from the Virginia State Prison, if possible. We further pledge ourselves to harm no one. Why we go to such extremes, is, briefly, that is the only way we can get justice. Three of us at least have made applications for executive clemency, and found none. The fourth is, as anyone can see, serving an*

unjust additional term of five years. It is true we have utmost confidence in
Major Wood, yet we are assured he cannot change the laws and customs of
Virginia. Lastly, we agree to take nothing from either guard or foreman. If
so, such must be returned by mail.
(Signatures) "R.A. Burton"
"Harry Hamilton"
"Siler Adkins"
"E.B. Handy"

Believing the four escapees were headed to Newport News to escape the country on one of the many livestock ships leaving for the European war zone, Superintendent Wood notified the Newport News police. That was not the case: Burton and Adkins were recaptured the next day, January 12, and Hanley and Hamilton were both recaptured on January 14. Despite the escape attempt, all four were pardoned by 1920.

ERNEST HARPER: CLEAN GETAWAY

Ernest Harper and his cellmate, Frank McGee, planned and executed on November 8, 1924, one of the most extraordinary and physically challenging breakouts in the history of the penitentiary.

Harper was convicted of the first-degree murder of Norfolk woman Alice Moore and sentenced to twenty years. McGee was serving a fifteen-year sentence for housebreaking.

Upon Harper's arrival in May 1923, he and McGee began planning their seemingly impossible escape. For weeks, the two men made chisels, picks, a crude sledgehammer and drills using only scrap iron from the penitentiary's blacksmith shop. Then, since musical instruments and singing were allowed

Ernest Harper. *Library of Virginia.*

in cells between 5:00 and 7:00 p.m., the two worked only during those two hours every day, chopping, hammering and drilling through an eighteen-inch concrete and steel floor and a thick steel reinforcing plate, using the music for cover and their mattresses to muffle their noise.

It took the men months to chip and claw their way through the tough cement floor. Incredibly, they managed to keep their heavy tools hidden in their cells and were able to somehow carry out the broken concrete in their toilet buckets. In a move right out of a Warner Brothers cartoon, they simply spread a rug over the hole, being careful not to step on it.

On November 8, 1924, they eventually broke through to a little-used basement shower room below them. They lowered themselves down and then out into the yard. They first scaled a fifteen-foot iron fence and then used rope to scramble over the twenty-foot brick outer wall facing Belvidere Street, where they separated and vanished.

McGee remained free for almost three years before he was caught in May 1927. Ernest Harper, on the other hand, was never found.

Bob Addison: Thirty Years on the Lam

Tazewell County native Bob Addison holds the distinction of being the longest known escapee in penitentiary history, living as a free man from 1936 until his recapture in 1966.

Convicted and sentenced in December 1935 for six years on a malicious wounding charge in Russell County only five days after getting married, Addison escaped a Fauquier County road crew on May 16, 1936, by using a fake shackle on his leg irons. He made his way back to Russell County; picked up his wife, Edna, and they moved to Kentucky, where he changed his name to Elbert Roy Clark.

For thirty years, the Clarks raised six children in Kentucky and West Virginia, never telling them their dad was a fugitive. Around July 1966, however, someone recognized Clark as Addison, and he was arrested by the FBI on December 27 of that year. Addison voluntarily returned to the penitentiary on January 3, 1967. A deluge of letters recommended clemency for the prisoner, including one from the governor of West Virginia, and Governor Mills Godwin pardoned him on January 27, 1967.

Who Shot Powhatan B. Bass?

Eight dangerous inmates all serving long sentences saw an opening on June 18, 1936, when a convoy of trucks was getting ready to leave the penitentiary. Jumping one of the trucks and seizing two guards and a trusty as hostages, the eight men attempted to ram the truck through the penitentiary's west gate.

Unfortunately for them, a guard named Smith immediately suspected something was wrong. He shouted "Stop!" and fired a warning shot, but when the truck did not stop, it was quickly met with a hail of machine gun fire.

Guards surrounded the bullet-riddled truck and in the back found guard Powhatan B. Bass dead of a bullet wound to the head. Another guard, Robert Reams, and the trusty, Oscar Fields, were wounded. Five convicts were also wounded in the attempt, which was over literally in seconds.

Commonwealth Attorney Haddon, citing a Texas precedent, claimed he would seek the electric chair for the eight convicts, but on September 17, one of the inmates, Ralph Stonebreaker, who was serving sixty-four years for highway robbery, was acquitted of murdering Bass. That set the stage for the remaining seven to also be acquitted of murder due to the prosecution being unable to determine who actually shot Bass.

Franklin Meekins: Blasted His Way Out

By 1970, the penitentiary had gone a remarkable fourteen years without a single escape. Then, Franklin O. Meekins, a twenty-six-year-old sentenced in 1967 to thirty-five years for robbing the First and Merchants National Bank in Petersburg, blasted his way out with a homemade bomb.

Meekins was the son of a faculty member of Virginia State University in Petersburg and was himself a former pre-law student at Wayne State in Detroit. On October 2, 1970, he sawed through a window bar with a hacksaw and wiggled out of his cell into a small first-floor hallway facing Spring Street.

Minutes later, an explosion rocked the building. Guards rushed through thick smoke to discover a hole blown through a barred window. Meekins had built a bomb out of a section of steel pipe filled with match heads and some other combustible material and then used a cloth rag for a fuse. The explosion was so intense that pipe fragments shattered nearby glass windows and chunks pierced an overhead drain pipe.

Meekins made his way to Washington, D.C., where he turned up shot to death in August 1977.

Melvin Wilson: Dude Looks Like a Lady

Penitentiary corrections officer William Estep was watching a group of visitors leave the chapel after a gospel sing at 10:45 p.m. on August 9, 1976, when he noticed an odd, out-of-place woman mingling in the crowd. Despite a modest dress, jewelry and "padding in the appropriate places," Estep said the visitor "just didn't look that much like a woman." He politely asked her to step aside.

She wasn't a female visitor at all; it was (male) convict Melvin Wilson, who was serving two life terms for murder and robbery. He had somehow gotten hold of a dress, wig, makeup and jewelry; stuffed the dress with mattress fill; and attempted to walk out by blending into a crowd of visitors.

He was charged with attempted escape and placed in isolation.

Vincent Rawlings: "A Hood Ornament on Belvidere"

One of the more audacious and visually spectacular penitentiary escape attempts occurred on December 22, 1979, when convicted murderer Vincent Rawlings attempted to fly a homemade hang glider over the wall facing Belvidere Street.

Rawlings was serving life plus fifty-nine years for abducting, raping and murdering a Portsmouth woman when he hatched the idea of building a makeshift glider out of rope, balsa wood and bedsheets.

With a fourth-floor recreation area in the main building being renovated into a classroom, Rawlings stashed the pieces of his glider there. Three days before Christmas, he fastened them all together and carried them to the top of the four-story structure. It had to look daunting; the wall was only twelve feet away, but he was twenty-five feet higher.

Rawlings—with no helmet, safety equipment or straps—grasped his homemade, V-shaped glider, took off running and leaped from the building, intending to majestically soar over the wall. Instead, he dropped like a rock, crashing hard into the top of the wall and becoming entangled in the razor wire. A guard who witnessed the flight reported a "white flash, and it seemed to be just zooming down…like a plane crashing."

The twenty-one-year-old Rawlings was taken to the Medical College of Virginia Hospital with a broken pelvis, several other fractures and numerous razor-wire cuts.

Penitentiary assistant director Robert Landon commented that had Rawlings cleared the wall, "he would have been a hood ornament on Belvidere."

CHAPTER 14
CULTURE INSIDE THE PEN
SPORTS, ART, MUSIC, THEATER AND LITERATURE

"ALL OUR GAMES ARE HOME GAMES"

The first Biograph Theatre softball team in 1976 was called the Swordfish, after a joke in a Marx Brothers movie. They were a very good team and lost only two of seventeen games that year—one of which was inside the walls of the penitentiary.

The penitentiary recreation director frequented J.W. Rayle, a bar located at Pine and Cary Streets in Oregon Hill. There he ran into Biograph manager F.T. Rea and asked if the Swordfish would consider playing the prison's softball team on a Saturday afternoon. Rea said sure.

A couple weeks later, the Swordfish entered the penitentiary. They were searched, and each got a stamp on their hands that could only be seen under blacklight as they passed through the gates. "Someone asked what would happen if the ink got wiped off, inadvertently, during the game," said Rea. "He was told that was not a good idea."

The umpire for the game was Dennis "Dr. Death" Johnson, a high-profile Richmond Fan District character and former professional wrestler. The fence in left field was a 30-foot-high brick wall only about 230 feet from home plate that ran along Belvidere Street. Because of its imposing height, a lot of hard-hit balls caromed off it. What would have been a routine fly ball on most fields was a home run there. "It was a red brick version of Boston's Green Monster," said Rea.

The prison team, known as the Raiders, launched ball after ball over that towering brick wall, and about one hundred prisoners seated in stands loudly cheered each one.

During a conversation with a couple of his teammates behind the backstop, Rea referred to the home team as "the prisoners." Their opponents' coach immediately stepped toward him.

"Call us the Raiders," he advised sternly, as he pointed to an awkward-looking mural on the prison wall that said "Home of the Raiders." According to Rea, it looked like a jailhouse tattoo, blown up large. "It was obvious," Rea explained, "I had made a faux pas."

"While we are on this ballfield, we're not the prisoners," he said seriously. "We're the Raiders."

"Raiders," Rea said. "Right."

"And all our games," he deadpanned, "are home games."

They all laughed, grateful the tension had been broken. The Raiders coach patted Rea on the back and thanked him for playing them.

In a tight, high-scoring affair, the Raiders prevailed. "Afterward, I was glad the Swordfish had met the Raiders," Rea explained. "And I was glad to leave them, too."

Penitentiary Music

Yes, I'm goin' to Richmond
And I'm leavin' for paradise
Gonna see that woman
That sure don't rag my life.
—*"Goin' to Richmond," by Jimmie Strothers,*
State Farm, Virginia, 1936

The earliest mention of music inside the penitentiary is found in the May 25, 1890 *Richmond Dispatch*, which mentions a "flower mission" to local prisons by the Woman's Christian Temperance Union (WCTU) and several local church ladies. Inserted among the prayers and scripture texts were "hymns by the Penitentiary Choir." Another similar mission was held the next year, with visits by the WCTU again to Richmond's jails and almshouses, with "exercises interspersed with singing by the young ladies of the party and the penitentiary choir."

John Lomax's *Field Recordings*, with Jimmie Strothers and Joe Lee on the cover. *Document records/Library of Congress.*

The choir apparently was still together in 1915, as four prisoners who briefly escaped on January 11 of that year "possessed excellent voices," according to the *Richmond Dispatch*, and frequently performed in the choir as a quartet.

By 1930, inmates were allowed singing and musical instruments in their cells for two hours per day, between 5:00 and 7:00 p.m. The rule was rigid; the punishment ledger frequently lists prisoners receiving up to fifteen lashes with the whip for "singing after hours."

Music was legitimized in Virginia's prison system in 1936, when inmate Jimmie Strothers was called by Superintendent Rice Youell to play at the

Goochland State Farm for musicologist John Lomax and Harold Spivacke, head of the Music Division of the Library of Congress.

Lomax's goal of recording in American prisons was in the hopes of "discovering an isolated musical culture 'untouched' by the modern world," where musicians "thrown on their own resources for entertainment, they still sing—especially the long-term prisoners who have been confined for years and who have not yet been influenced by jazz and the radio—the distinctive old-time Negro melodies." A true music pioneer, Lomax discovered singers like Lead Belly, Clear Rock and Iron Head, Captain Nye, Kelly Pace and others. He uncovered "Home on the Range," "Git Along Little Dogies," "Goin' Walk Around in Jordan" and "Boll Weevil."

Strothers, who lost his sight years earlier in a mining accident, was incarcerated on April 2, 1934, for shooting his wife at their home in Culpeper. Although he claimed he only intended to scare her, he was found guilty of second-degree murder and sentenced to twenty years.

Steeped in the spirituals of the ex-slaves as a child in the Tidewater area of Virginia, this former "medicine show" and street performer was a consummate "songster," as comfortable with dance tunes as with religious hymns, popular and blues numbers. His song "Goin' to Richmond" (supposedly about his admission to the penitentiary) displays his comfort with the relatively new blues genre and its instrument of choice, the guitar.

At the State Farm, Strothers recorded twelve songs for Lomax and Spivacke on banjo and guitar. On one number, "Do Lord, Remember Me," he recorded with fellow inmate Joe Lee.

Strothers and Lee were not the only inmates recorded in these legendary sessions. A listing prepared by Library of Virginia music scholar Dr. Gregg Kimball shows that twenty-six musicians recorded at Richmond, Goochland and Culpeper (although not all of them were prisoners). One group of eight penitentiary inmates recalled the days on the West Virginia railroads in a song titled "Can't You Line 'Em?" Roanoke native James Henry "Crip" Diggs, serving twelve years for a third housebreaking conviction, recorded "Freight Train Blues" for Lomax. In 1955, during another arrest in Roanoke, Diggs sang "Hearts of Stone" to the investigating officers. Upon his acquittal one week later, he rejoined the detectives and appropriately performed "Let Me Go, Lover."

"The Ballad of Claude Allen"

In addition, songs have been written not just by but about notorious penitentiary inmates. At least two ballads were recorded about the Allen clan of Hillsville after the courthouse massacre, including "The Ballad of Claude Allen." The original composer is unknown, but in 1914, Clarence Ashley taught it to Hobart Smith, who made a recording of it right around 1940.

Claude Allen and his father,
Have met their fatal doom at last,
Their friends are glad their trouble's ended,
And hope their souls is now at rest.

Claude Allen was that tall and handsome,
He still had hope until the end,
That he in some way or other,
Escape his death from the Richmond Pen.

The Gov'nor being so hard-hearted,
Not caring what his friends might say,
He finally took his sweet life from him,
In the cold, cold ground his body lay.
[...]

"The Ballad of Henry Clay Beattie"

On March 22, 1927, Grayson County native Kelly Harrell recorded for the Victor Talking Machine Company "The Ballad of Henry Clay Beattie," about the infamous Richmond wife killer who was executed on November 24, 1911. Harrell's lyrics were original, but he borrowed the music of Welling and McGhee from their hymn "Knocking at the Door."

Friday as the sun was lifting,
After the sun shone clear;
Down in a cell set a prisoner,
Trembling with mercy and fear.

In came his grey headed father,
Says, "Henry this day you must die,
If [you] don't confess that you killed her,
You'll go to your doom with a lie."

In came his brother and sister,
To bid him their last farewell;
"If [you] don't confess that you killed her,
You'll spend eternity in hell."

"Yes, I confess that I killed her,
I've taken her sweet life away;
But oh, how greedy and brutish,
I was for taking her sweet life."

'Twas late on Thursday evening,
After the sun went down;
Henry Clay Beattie was saying
Farewell to his friend native town.

Then Friday, as the sun was rising,
Just before the sun shone clear;
Henry Clay Beattie was dying,
Down in a 'lectric chair.

Almost all the songs recorded by Strothers, Lee and these other inmates are today available at the Library of Congress website. "The troubling fact remains," said Kimball, "that if Jimmie Strothers had not murdered his wife, old-time and blues music aficionados would not be extolling his musical gifts today."

In September 1939, Jimmie Strothers received a conditional pardon and disappeared.

Penitentiary Literature and Creative Writing

Death Row Poetry

On June 3, 1910, a forty-five-year-old penitentiary inmate named Henry Smith (not to be confused with Henry Smith from Portsmouth, who was executed on October 13, 1908) died in the electric chair for the murder of Chicago artist Walter F. Schultz.

Records and accounts prove that Smith's execution is one of the more appalling examples of law enforcement misconduct in Virginia's early criminal justice history. Smith was arrested in Alexandria on a false charge (watch stealing) and was held hostage by a desperate local police department for four days in a cell with no food or water while coerced into a confession that implicated three other most likely innocent men: James Dorsey, Richard "Dick" Pines and Calvin "Sonny" Johnson.

While lingering on death row through numerous stays, Smith wrote an untitled poem. Dated January 14, 1910, it is possibly the earliest surviving example of primitive death row poetry in penitentiary history:

> *People of this city, will you listen to what is true?*
> *And I will tell you with all my heart,*
> *What the chief made me do.*
>
> *He locked me close in a cell,*
> *Where I was bound and compelled to do just like he says,*
> *But if I did but only refuse I should go through a terrible spell.*
>
> *I wrung my hands together,*
> *And wondered what I must do.*
> *He then gave me a little Bible,*
> *And told me to read,*
> *For the lynchers may be coming after you.*
>
> *Then the tears were streaming down my cheeks,*
> *As I did holler and cry,*
> *"Chief, let me see my wife and child once more.*
> *Be fair, for I die, for no more liberty shall I see.*
> *Chief, please take out your gun and kill me."*
>
> *But God is still looking and sees all over the land.*
> *I wish he would point down his finger and show who murdered that man.*

Beacons in the Darkness

Eleven years after the second Henry Smith's execution, in the midst of the 1921 reforms, an inmate-produced literary magazine called *The Beacon* was launched.

The monthly *Beacon* is a surprisingly articulate, well-written and well-produced publication. In consecutive 1939 issues, an inmate named G.D. Roberts wrote a feature titled "Our Literary Heritage," in which he explored the function of great literature down through history and what makes it enduring. "Much literature is preserved for its sheer beauty," Roberts writes, "but to be beautiful it necessarily has morally uplifting and inspiring qualities which are imparted to the reader, even though his only purpose in reading is pastime."

Roberts goes on in subsequent editions to write of the Roman occupation of Britain after AD 43, when Latin was blended into the Old English language. He notes

The Beacon, December 1938. *Library of Virginia.*

Caedmon's *Paraphrase of Scriptures*, its similarities to *Beowulf* and works of Bede (673–735) as being hugely influential in the development of modern literature.

On a lighter note, inmate W.P. Gempp's column "Ramblings and Mutterings" frequently displays an almost whimsical look at penitentiary life, with inside jokes and good-natured put-downs. "Some men regard themselves a penitentiary asset," he wrote in the December 1939 edition. "Well they are merely exaggerating by two letters." "A number of men here are trying to carve a future for themselves, but some are chiseling theirs."

Other issues include a sports column, an update on classes offered both at the penitentiary and at the State Farm and even a crossword puzzle.

While it is unknown exactly how long *The Beacon* was published, the last issues on file at the Library of Virginia are from 1939.

FYSK ("*Facts You Should Know*") was a magazine of news and commentary produced by and for inmates from 1973 until August 1977. Its purpose was to create "a better public awareness of the prison system and to serve as an agent for change, providing alternative concepts to our criminal justice system." Under editor Ron Greenfield, *FYSK* won fifteen prison journalism awards of excellence.

Freelance writer Ben Cleary taught a weekly volunteer creative writing class at the penitentiary from the early 1980s until constant troubles shut down classes shortly before the facility closed. Cleary says that unlike prisoner

Left: FYSK magazine, August 1977. *VCU James Branch Cabell Library Special Collections and Archives.*

Right: A collection of poetry by inmate Hasib Muqsit, 1976. *VCU James Branch Cabell Library Special Collections and Archives.*

writers such as Evans Hopkins, whose work appeared in the *New Yorker* and the *Washington Post*, "most of the men in the class were less interested in creative writing but were instead trying to involve themselves in something positive and intellectually stimulating to help pass the time and counter the negativity of their surroundings."

Cleary says that one of the most interesting arrangements of the class involved bringing in guest speakers. The guests gave short presentations on their areas of expertise, and then the lively discussion became a learning experience for both the guests and the inmates. Tim Kaine, 2016 vice presidential candidate, was a guest, as were Gordon Davies, head of the Virginia Council of Higher Education; Lorna Wyckoff, *Style Weekly* publisher; and Garrett Epps, author and law professor. Cleary says that he is still in touch with several members of the class today.

Penitentiary Theater, Film and Broadcasting

"Inside the Virginia State Penitentiary there exists no outlet for emotions because to show emotion is to show weakness," stated a grant proposal dated July 1, 1976, to the Virginia Commission of the Arts and Humanities to create the Spring Street Theatre. "We want to let the inmate use the theatre to express the emotions that are pent up inside him and give him a chance to communicate with a world he has been locked away from."

Theater was not an entirely new concept. VCU theater professor Kenneth Campbell introduced the penitentiary inmates to theater in 1971, producing a version of *One Flew Over the Cuckoo's Nest.* Jim Drewry, who attended a performance, reported that per regulations, they stamped his hand upon entry with invisible ink. When he left, he held his hand under a blacklight, revealing the word "Free."

Sara Shifflette related how some VCU students went to the penitentiary to produce Lenny Bruce's *Are There any N****** Here Tonight?* After a few tense moments, one inmate started laughing, after which the entire audience started laughing. Afterward, she reported they had a "great" Q&A.

Encounters

Inmate Ron Greenfield started the Spring Street Theatre as a four-part concept, including education, workshop, theater and communication. According to the proposal, education was intended to teach inmates acting, directing, speech and playwriting. Workshop's purpose was the staging of experimental productions inside the chapel that had been converted into a theater space for honing writing and acting. Theater was the actual staging of four productions per year.

Communication was their most ambitious component. Greenfield and his partner, Henry Clere, actually started recording and producing a radio program called *Encounters* that was taped inside the penitentiary and aired every Saturday morning from 8:30 to 9:00 a.m. on Richmond-based WGOE radio.

Encounters was recorded on secondhand equipment in whichever penitentiary office had an available desk, giving the broadcast a rough, spontaneous quality. Interviews were sandwiched between opening and closing commentaries by Clere and Greenfield. During the 1976 Christmas program, while inmates and their families were interviewed, a loudspeaker suddenly went out on the air, ordering inmates back to their cells—but not before the families gathered and sang "Silent Night" in the dankness of their surroundings.

Guests on *Encounters* included Catholic bishop Walter Sullivan, ACLU attorneys, editors of the Richmond newspapers and even Warden Robert Zahradnick. Clere and Greenfield both told *Times-Dispatch* columnist Carole Kass that their interviews were intended to "educate the public to the realities, problems and complexities to the Virginia penal system"; thus, their questions centered on issues pertinent to not just other inmates but the public at large, including rehabilitation and the death penalty, which was on hiatus at the time.

Clere was familiar with the death penalty. Convicted of murder in Chesapeake in 1969, he was sentenced to the electric chair but had his sentence commuted in 1972 when the Supreme Court temporarily abolished capital punishment. With a new lease on life, he became a model prisoner and went on to win "prison writer of the year" by the American Penal Press for 1976 and win an additional six national awards in prison journalism, including photography.

Reaction to *Encounters* was mostly favorable. WGOE producer Patrick O'Neill said that while they did no promotion for the show, it proved to be a good public affairs service, despite the poor time slot.

Time to Learn

The 1977 strike and near-riot proved devastating to literature, theater and broadcasting inside the penitentiary. Henry Clere, advertising editor Willie Williams and theater producer Ron Greenfield were all transferred out when officials deemed their presence "detrimental to the welfare of the prison." Clere and Williams were sent to maximum-security building M at the State Farm, while Greenfield went to Mecklenburg Correctional "in order to let emotions at the [penitentiary] to die down."

Carole Kass did not just report of cultural activities inside the penitentiary; around 1980, she started a film screenwriting program there. Then, in the mid-1980s, inmate Evans Hopkins created a script called *Time to Learn*, about a new inmate struggling with the system and his own illiteracy. The film moved into production, with funding attained from the Virginia Department of Correctional Education.

Jones pleaded guilty, as he was told, but before sentencing, he told the court of the sexual abuse he had endured at the State Farm. Visibly irritated, the judge stated that he could not believe that the authorities would ever allow such things to happen, and besides, he was not going to get involved in jail management. Jones received a ten-year sentence despite his plea.

On Jones's first day at the penitentiary, a group of seven men cornered him and threatened to sexually assault him, but an inmate known as Donnie XX stopped the attack. He warned Jones that in view of his young age and attractiveness to the more vicious homosexuals, he could either accept a boy-girl reputation and submit to the assaults or risk permanent injury by fighting back. Donnie XX befriended Jones, however, and stimulated in him an interest in the Muslim faith.

After Jones's conversion, he requested certain publications related to his culture and faith, such as the *Richmond Afro-American* newspaper. After repeated requests, he was padlocked with no administrative hearing in his cell for a month and not allowed basic privileges, such as toiletries or cigarettes. "Padlock" was a punitive segregation where a padlock was placed on the offending convict's cell so it could not be opened electronically like the others. Sometimes the padlock stayed on for weeks, depending on the infraction.

In the summer of 1959, Jones wrote to the American Civil Liberties Union (ACLU) seeking arbitration on the constitutionality of his treatment. The next day, he was transferred with no explanation to maximum-security C block.

Thirty days later, Jones received a reply from a volunteer ACLU attorney requesting more information on his case. Jones, then sixteen, read the letter to a more educated prisoner in the next cell in order to compose the best reply. Prison officials heard about the exchange and the next day transferred Jones to solitary confinement for "agitating."

Jones remained in solitary for ninety-eight days, with ninety on bread and water. He was given no reading or writing materials. He lost thirty pounds, aggravating a stomach ailment. His health problems got worse when his mattress and blankets were taken away as punishment for whispering to another prisoner held temporarily in the same cell. Despite the health dangers of his bread and water diet, sleeping on concrete and the tear gas shot into his unventilated cell, Jones was not examined by a doctor until after his release from solitary.

Jones spent most of the next two years in C on a reduced diet of two daily meals. He was allowed no visitors and had limited writing privileges, all because of a second and then third charge of "agitating."

No one ever told Jones which rules he had allegedly violated. While he remained in C, he was not considered for parole. Superintendent C.C. Peyton stated later in testimony that he had never spoken to Jones and that the disciplinary actions taken against him were based on one-page reports filed by guards.

On January 1, 1969, at age twenty-five and after serving ten years for a first-offense felony, Leroy Jones was finally released from the Virginia State Penitentiary, a victim of the crime of punishment.

[This section is paraphrased from "The Unconstitutionality of Prison Life" by Philip J. Hirschkop and Michael A. Millemann, *Virginia Law Review* 55, no. 5 (June 1969).]

THE 1950s: SETTING THE STAGE

At the Virginia Penitentiary, C Building was a prison within a prison, the worst building with the most dangerous inmates. Dirty, loud, isolated from the rest of the prison compound and surrounded by a concrete wall, this fortress was built in 1955 and divided into two sections, with one designated segregation and the other solitary confinement—or more euphemistically called "meditation."

To minimize escapes and riots, C could only be entered by first passing through a single locked gate in the surrounding concrete wall. There was only one key, and it was held in the guard tower overlooking the compound. When entry into C was sought by anyone, including the superintendent, the key was lowered on a string, the gate unlocked and then again locked after the person entered. Then, the string was pulled up and the key returned to the tower guard. No one, including the superintendent, held an extra key to C.

Prisoners confined in segregation were not permitted to work and earn money in any of the shops or on the grounds. They were allowed only two meals a day and were denied television, radio and movie privileges. They did not have access to the facility library and were not permitted to attend classes. They were allowed to shower only once a week, as opposed to the daily showering allowed other convicts.

Convicts in solitary confinement in C suffered additional deprivations. They had no writing or visiting privileges, except in an emergency. Their diet consisted of water and two servings of four slices of bread for two days, then two regular C Building meals on the third day. Those inmates could have a Bible but no personal items. Bedding consisted of a mattress and one or two blankets, and the only clothing provided was one pair of pants, one shirt and one pair of socks.

The meditation cells measured about six feet by ten feet and contained only a sink and commode during the day, with a mattress brought in at night. A convict could be denied his mattress for up to three days as punishment, forcing him to sleep on the steel frame or bare cement floor. If a convict continued to be disorderly in solitary, he could be chained to the bars, tear-gassed, have his clothes taken away or, in more severe cases, be transferred to B basement, where additional deprivations could be incurred. These punishments were not covered by regulation but left to the discretion of the unit superintendent or, more often, the guards.

C Goes to Court

Prison administrative hierarchy proved that a specific rule or order deteriorated in content and specificity as it traveled from chief officer to subordinates down the line. Higher prison officials maintained a confident but often theoretical awareness of the application of rules and procedures in various situations. Lower officers implementing those rules, however, were far less confident of the regulations governing not only the prisoners' conduct but their own and frequently interpreted those rules as they saw fit. This anomaly came forward in several court cases throughout the next two decades that forever changed prisoner treatment.

In the 1966 case *Landman v. Peyton*, penitentiary officials admitted to not only a prevailing negligence in the supervision of C Building but also the inherent abuse and arbitrariness by guards in the treatment of the inmates confined there.

Robert Jewell Landman Sr., sentenced to eight years for robbery in 1963, was the author of over twenty lawsuits for himself while assisting in almost two thousand others. He petitioned the District Court on March 11, 1965, to order his release from C, where he had been periodically confined since November 1963, and to place him back in general population. He alleged that his confinements stemmed solely from his "habitual writ-writing." An amended petition, which went nowhere, sought full release from the penitentiary on the grounds that his confinement in C Building constituted cruel and unusual punishment.

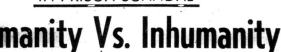

Olympic Boycott
Still Alive
(See Sports Page)

Richmond Afro-American

AND THE RICHMOND PLANET

Did Race Figure
In Gonder Trade?
(See Sports Page)

5th Year, No. 44   Copyright 1968 by THE AFRO-AMERICAN Co., Inc all material previously printed in the current National Edition   RICHMOND, VA., AUGUST 10, 1968   24 PAGES ★★★   20 CENTS

IN PRISON SCANDAL

Humanity Vs. Inhumanity

PHILIP HIRSCHKOP

GOV. MILLS GODWIN

"Humanity Vs. Inhumanity." Richmond Afro-American, *August 10, 1968*.

Superintendent Peyton testified that he did not make periodic inspections of C Building, and that while he "was supposed" to have made surprise visits, he could not recall a single one. Notably, the penitentiary disciplinary committee, the commission charged with investigating disciplinary measures taken against inmates by guards, had no jurisdiction in C. Thus, the treatment (and fate) of inmates confined in either segregation or meditation was left generally to the unsupervised discretion of C guards.

Landman's problems started after writing a letter to the *Richmond News Leader* without submitting it first to penitentiary censors, which earned him twenty days in solitary. This was followed with correspondence to the governor, which landed him in punitive segregation in C for 150 days. In C, he endured a series of transfers to and from solitary confinement; in at least one instance, he was put in solitary for fifty-eight days and never given any reason why. In fact, he was again placed in solitary after the March hearing.

Landman testified that guards in C withheld food, struck inmates with clubs and used tear gas indiscriminately as punishment. His testimony was in turn buttressed by several other inmates.

Superintendent Peyton testified that guards had a blanket authorization to use tear gas against "recalcitrant" inmates and to prevent escapes and riots. A written report on its use was required only after a gas shell was fired; however, no record was kept of the number of shells issued, and no verifications were made to determine if reports were accurately filed covering each time gas was used. While it was admitted that tear gas was used inside the penitentiary approximately twelve to fifteen times in a typical year, Peyton insisted that this was done in the "legitimate exercise of disciplinary authority."

While Landman lost this case, it did prove there was poor and subjective enforcement of regulations in C, and it opened the door for similar lawsuits throughout the '60s, most all alleging mistreatment by guards and a lack of hearings for arbitrary punishments.

Desegregation Maybe

The year 1968 was a transformative one for the penitentiary and Virginia's prisoners. On February 2, two inmates, Leroy Mason and Thomas Wansley, filed a class-action lawsuit (*Mason v. Peyton*) in U.S. District Court against the entire Virginia prison system, alleging unlawful racial segregation and "general unconstitutional conditions of confinement." The suit asked that a three-judge federal court consider complaints that the 1950 prison segregation law violated the Civil Rights Act of 1964 and five amendments to the U.S. Constitution.

Thomas Wansley was one black inmate very familiar with mistreatment. On December 6, 1962, a story in the Carter Glass–owned *Lynchburg Daily Advance* newspaper reported that two women had been raped and two more attempted by a local black man and that Lynchburg was gripped in fear of another attack. On December 17, seventeen-year-old Wansley was arrested, given a court-appointed lawyer who called no witnesses and in only a few weeks was tried under Criminal Court judge Raymond Cundiff and convicted of two capital crimes. He was sentenced by an all-white jury to two executions in the electric chair in addition to twenty years for a robbery.

The sensationalism surrounding Wansley's arrest and convictions was whispered among civil rights workers to be the result of the Glass-led white ruling class's bullying of Lynchburg's black community and was payback for a sit-in that had occurred earlier that year. Refusing to back down, Lynchburg's local chapter of the Southern Christian Leadership Conference (SCLC) contacted Dr. Martin Luther King Jr. and civil rights attorneys William Kunstler, Arthur Kinoy and Philip Hirschkop for support. While on death row in the penitentiary, Wansley began studying law while Kinoy and Hirschkop worked to overturn his convictions. They appealed, and the second jury in 1967 commuted his two death sentences to life in prison.

Undeterred, and with the hysterical Lynchburg media proclaiming that Kunstler was a communist in an attempt to discredit him, the New York attorney appealed again, and finally in 1973, federal District Court judge

Robert Merhige Jr. reversed Wansley's convictions on grounds that his trial was unfair and that vile, prejudicial newspaper accounts had biased the jury. Wansley's life was saved, providing him the opportunity to provide assistance to other prisoners later in the decade.

While he was denied full clemency by Governor Linwood Holton in 1974, he was finally cleared of all charges and released in 1984.

STRIKE

On July 16, 1968, Wansley, Landman and a few others suddenly sat down in the penitentiary yard and refused to do any more work. Soon they were joined by dozens of other prisoners, protesting their fifteen- to twenty-cents-per-day wages. Their contention was that since the penitentiary was grossing about $3 million annually, they could afford a raise to one dollar per day so they could at least afford basic toiletries at the penitentiary canteen.

Inmates and even some prison employees argued that the penitentiary had become more consumed with production and profits than rehabilitation. Many spent their entire terms doing tedious assembly-line tasks such as threading a needle in the tailor shop or polishing a table top rather than learning a trade as their rehabilitation.

Virtually the entire penitentiary population refused to work, and officials reacted strongly to the stoppage. All visits, mail and communications were immediately halted. Inmates were confined in 110-degree cells, with the hallway windows closed for weeks until inmates managed to break some of them by throwing coffee cups to let in air. Anyone caught breaking windows or who dared criticize the harsh conditions was tear gassed in locked cells.

Leroy Mason was named a spokesman by the striking inmates and agreed only if the stoppage remained totally nonviolent. The next day, on July 19, four guards went to Mason's cell, handcuffed him and, with no hearing or explanation, took him to the isolation cell block (called a "nut cell") in the penitentiary hospital, where he remained in solitary confinement "for his own safety," even though he had never been threatened (except possibly by guards). Another spokesman, Roger Pegram, was treated in the same manner.

Mason spent the entire month alone, spending his time killing cockroaches and piling them in a corner. In a letter that reached attorney Hirschkop, Mason wrote, "This cell is roach-infested, no beds, I am not permitted a light at night, and no toilet articles."

Arthur J. Probst Jr.

When asked about the roach problem during testimony, Superintendent Peyton waved it off, stating that "there are roaches in the White House kitchen. I have them in my home. But I can't deny that there is a cockroach here and there."

On August 20, Mason was released from isolation but was transferred to C Building segregation and was held there for eight months. In addition, he lost ninety days' good conduct time with no explanation why. Hundreds of cockroaches lay in a pile in the corner.

While the strike was declared over after three days, the stoppage continued and the grievances expanded in the coming weeks to cover charges of prisoners' continued denial to counsel; the recurrent, indiscriminate use of tear gas; unsanitary living conditions; denial of health facilities; widespread unchecked homosexual assaults; instigation of the strike by guards; and racism in the penitentiary's administration. It is critical to note that these issues were raised not just by convicts but also by former prison employees, the NAACP, the ACLU and the Virginia Council on Human Relations.

There was widespread reason to believe that during and after the strike, convicts were enduring even more brutal mistreatment. One released prisoner named James May told the *Richmond Afro-American* that he saw stunned prisoners in handcuffs brought back to C with blood on their shirts.

May also said that prisoners in C kept in touch with one another by dipping the water out of their commodes and talking through the pipes. It was a huge risk; punishment for "talking through the commodes" included getting shot with tear gas and having their mattress taken away.

Virginia Department of Corrections director W.K. Cunningham told Barry Barkan at the *Afro-American* that he was "inclined to doubt" any prisoner's account of what was happening behind the wall during the lockdown because they "had their own axes to grind."

"As far as any systematic beatings," he added, "I'd know about them sooner or later."

"DACHAU ON SPRING STREET"

During the stoppage, civil rights workers and Quakers holding a vigil in support of the inmates heard the unmistakable bang of gas grenades going off inside the cell blocks. Herbert Sykes and Theodore Slaughter, who were both released just after the strike started, confirmed gas was shot on prisoners inside their cells. "They shoot us right in the face," Sykes told Barkan. When confronted, Director Cunningham acknowledged that tear gas had indeed been used several times on convicts after the strike commenced.

"The tear gassing of prisoners locked in their cells is an oppressive act intolerable to a generation that has seen the horrors of Nazi extermination camps," said Frank Adams, executive secretary of the Virginia Council on Human Relations. "This commonwealth can ill-afford a Dachau on Spring Street."

The picketers in support of the striking prisoners were soon joined by several area activists who feared a state police–led massacre. "We held a picket line out there for twenty-eight days, night and day. We had as many as forty or fifty during the day and three or four all night, there at the main entrance on Spring Street," former civil rights activist Bruce Smith said in a 2017 interview. He went on at his website brucejsmithblog to describe the mix of protestors:

> *Ruth and Wally Bless brought out their friends from the Richmond Council on Human Relations as well as members of the Unitarian Church.... Marie and Phyllis brought out members of the Women's International League for Peace and Freedom (WILPF) and other members of the Quaker meeting in Richmond. Rev. Curtis Holt brought out residents of the housing project in Church Hill, Richmond's east end, in which he was a resident advocate and leader. Also from Church Hill, was William Crump, owner of a reupholstering shop and Black Nationalist since the 1940s. All were community activists dedicated to preventing an attack on the prisoners. Of course, we were also happy that the picket line attracted some high-schoolers and students from* [Richmond Professional Institute].

Sykes also told Barkan that the guards egged on the convicts when they became aware of the plans to strike. The prisoners then coupled their demand for higher wages with a demand for higher wages for the guards, with the thought that better wages would attract better guards.

The strike also united the black and white convicts most likely better than the pending desegregation law, in a somewhat backhanded way—the white inmates stereotypically believed all black inmates already knew how to strike, so they were willing to give up traditionally "white only" areas in favor of uniting for the strike. "We don't have time to hate each other as long as we have to put up with all the abuses that all of us suffer over there," Sykes claimed.

In fact, an unnamed penitentiary employee told the *Afro-American* that the prison was still operating under the old 1950 segregation statute. He also claimed the best jobs were always assigned to white convicts.

THE SLOW–BURNING FIRE OF RESENTMENT

By August, the work stoppage and the war of words between Philip Hirschkop and Governor Mills Godwin had intensified. Godwin dismissed allegations of brutality inside the penitentiary, stating, "I don't know of anyone connected with the administration of the penal system who wants to inflict cruel and inhumane punishment on anyone." While acknowledging that convicts had been locked in cells for two straight weeks, Godwin said, "I don't think any injustice has been done to anyone over there."

The disagreement among Hirschkop (privately nicknamed "Horseshit" by a Richmond commonwealth's attorney), Adams and the Godwin administration boiled down to the definition of "inhumane treatment." Prison authorities did not dispute Hirschkop's claims but maintained that solitary, 110-degree cells, roach infestation, tear gas used in an enclosed area, reduced food rations and a lack of due process was not, in their opinion, "cruel and unusual." "The prison authorities must maintain discipline," said Godwin, "and they must do so over a group of men who are in the prison in the first place because they could not discipline themselves."

On August 8, inmate Alexis Madden killed himself with a homemade shiv in his cell. An enraged Hirschkop maintained that Madden was "murdered by prison authorities" because they knew he was mentally ill yet kept him locked in a sweltering cell with several other inmates. Madden's cellmates told Hirschkop that they witnessed him pleading with the guards for help but that the guards "just laughed" at his requests. In addition, two inmates asked penitentiary physician Dr. David Pollack to see Madden, but he never did. Cunningham acknowledged that Madden spoke to the penitentiary chaplain shortly before he slashed his own throat but gave no indication to anyone he was about to do that.

Hirschkop was finally allowed inside the penitentiary on August 10 and came out shaken by what he saw. Cells were hot, filthy, roach- and rat-infested and overcrowded with convicts, many with no mattresses and wearing the same dirty clothes for almost two weeks. Many bore tear gas burns and bruises. He reported that "ringleaders" in solitary were losing weight at an alarming rate because of the heat and their mandated bread and water diet.

Still, he expressed hope that a solution could be worked out.

"*Qui Custodiet Custodem?*"

In mid-August 1968, the State Board of Welfare and Institutions made a surprise visit to the penitentiary at the request of Governor Godwin. After emerging, the board's vice chairwoman, Mrs. Jackson Fray, indicated her "satisfaction" with the prison administration's handling of the situation inside and, in a preliminary report to Godwin, gave the facility a clean bill of health.

No sooner had the report been issued than cries of "whitewash" rose up from prisoner advocates. Frank Adams, noting the fact that journalists were barred from the tour, told the *Afro-American* that the Romans had a saying that fit the current dilemma inside the penitentiary: "*Qui custodiet custodem?*" or, "Who will watch the watchmen?"

"Naturally," he claimed, "they will not tell the press they saw men bearing the scars of mistreatment."

The call for reform was soon picked up politically. Norfolk senator Henry Howell said he would make the Virginia prison system a major point in his campaign for governor. Fairfax senator Omer Hirst stated that an evaluation of the state penal system was in order and that he would ask Manassas delegate Stanley Owens to call a public hearing.

On August 17, Hirschkop was told by Superintendent Peyton that he would not comply with any prison desegregation order, claiming that he "would never put a black prisoner in a cell with a white prisoner." Hirschkop argued that the matter went beyond simple accommodations, maintaining that Jim Crow pervaded all aspects of penitentiary life. He contended that all working areas were segregated, as were the barbershop, shower stalls, Saturday night movies and Sunday morning worship services. Worse, the attorney claimed the black prisoners were purposefully denied access to newspapers like the *Afro-American* and other periodicals dealing with black culture.

That same week, Judge Merhige issued a multi-point injunction prohibiting certain practices by prison guards after allegations of mistreatment were again brought forward by Hirschkop. The injunction prohibited guards from barring inmates from meeting with attorneys or denying them prompt access to the courts; they could not use instruments that could cause pain against inmates; there could be no "unrestrained" use of tear gas; inmates could not be placed in solitary for extended periods that could harm their physical or mental health; and they must allow toilet articles and other necessities of health for inmates.

While this order drew applause from both sides, the next day, Robert Landman was placed in solitary after he was badly beaten by another prisoner while "guards looked the other way." He remained there for forty days, allegedly for conferring with another prisoner but in his opinion as punishment for attracting unwanted attention to the prison system from the courts. His attempts to contact his lawyer were fruitless. Then, from March 15 to July 1969, he was placed on padlock.

(By November 1969, Landman had served 266 total days in solitary, many of those on bread and water, and 743 total days on padlock, with not even a rudimentary hearing to defend allegations made against him.)

The prison desegregation case *Mason v. Peyton* commenced in December 1968 under U.S. District Judge Merhige to "enjoin segregation between white and negro inmates in penal institutions in Virginia." Inmate after inmate took the stand and told of brutal mistreatments. Calvin Arey said he was placed in solitary confinement for attempting to mail an "illegal letter." Roger Pegram testified he was shot with insecticide in his cell by a guard and then placed in solitary. Fifteen-year-old Bobby Lee Taylor, a prisoner at the State Farm in Goochland, testified that he was tear gassed by a guard when he asked for medical aid for a sick fellow prisoner. Roy Hood claimed he was isolated from other prisoners by being placed on padlock as punishment for conferring with his attorney.

After separating claims of general prisoner mistreatment from the segregation claims, on August 13, 1969, the court ruled that inmates must have reasonable access to attorneys; that physical violence toward inmates be restrained; that the use of tear gas be limited; and that inmates be provided mattresses and toilet articles as required. Then, on October 16, 1969, the court entered an order calling for full desegregation of the Virginia prison system, including all field units and farms, within ninety days.

A LANDMARK COURT CASE

For a prisoner, going to court was never a slam-dunk, as judges sometimes unexpectedly upheld seemingly indiscriminate decisions of penitentiary superintendents. For example, Harold Lee Jones, who was serving twenty years for a 1952 armed robbery, killed a penitentiary guard in 1963. He was tried in Richmond's Circuit Court on January 16, 1967, and acquitted by reason of self-defense. Despite the acquittal, Superintendent Peyton personally escorted Jones to C block and padlocked him in a single cell.

Three months later, Jones took Peyton to court over his solitary confinement, but the court took a "hands-off" policy in deference to Peyton's twenty-eight years' prison experience. A stunned Jones remained padlocked in his single cell almost continuously for six years.

Facing this uphill battle, the American Civil Liberties Union filed the mother of all prison class-action suits in April 1969 on behalf of those five inmates who contended their constitutional rights were continually violated. The United States District Court under Judge Merhige convened in what would become a landmark case regarding incarceration methods and prisoner treatment. *Landman et al v. Royster et al* pitted Virginia prison administrators, the Department of Welfare and Institutions, the director of the Division of Corrections, the superintendent of the state penitentiary and the superintendent of the State Farm against convicts stripped of constitutional guaranties "of so grave a nature as to violate the most common notions of due process and humane treatment by certain of the defendants, their agents, servants and employees."

The five plaintiffs in this case—Robert Landman, Leroy Mason, Thomas Wansley, Roy Hood and Calvin Arey—sought $750,000 in damages. Defendants were W. Cunningham, director of the Division of Corrections, and Otis Brown, director of the Department of Welfare and Institutions, a state agency. The other two plaintiffs, former superintendent C.C. Peyton and a guard, M.L. Royster, were both deceased by the court date but still named in the suit.

A parade of forty-six inmates illustrated arbitrary and almost indescribable treatments under guards who appeared to operate with little guidance and virtually no impunity. Calvin Arey was charged with possessing a pair of scissors and being an escape risk when he was placed in solitary confinement on December 6, 1965. He remained there for more than four and a half years until July 1970, when he was finally released into general population. Caught allegedly discussing with Landman an order of the court, both were transferred to solitary confinement for forty-two days, during which time neither of them was permitted to file legal pleadings or send letters to attorneys.

The court also found that on August 13, 1968, as radio news reported the District Court's injunction against corporal punishment, Arey yelled to inmates in C that tear gas and the taking of mattresses had been prohibited. As punishment, Superintendent Peyton committed Arey to solitary with no hearing. He was on a bread and water diet for two days out of three, in a cell that contained only a sink and a commode, with a mattress and blanket provided at night.

When Arey was released from isolation on September 23, 1968, he found on his mattress a letter he had tried to send to an attorney the previous August 14. Three days after his release from solitary, he wrote another letter describing penitentiary conditions to Senator Henry Howell, only to also have it returned to him without having been mailed. Assistant Superintendent Oliver later told the court, "I don't think it is the prisoner's place to be describing to the State Senator his description of how we operate the penitentiary." Later on, Arey was again placed in solitary for thirty days on bread and water for reading to inmates a letter that he had finally received from Senator Howell. No notice or hearing of any kind was held for him regarding these punishments, and he lost an entire year of "good time" as a result.

SCREAM UNTIL YOU DIE

Conditions at the State Farms were scrutinized during this trial, with many disturbing allegations uncovered. Nathan Breeden testified he was incarcerated in Goochland's C5 high-security section at his own request because of his fears of other convicts in general population. While there, Breeden witnessed in the next cell the death of a mentally disturbed inmate named William Lassiter, whose psychiatric records Breeden had acquired from another inmate in a fruitless attempt to get him help.

Breeden claimed Lassiter screamed day and night seeking help and plugged the commode with his shirt, flooding his cell. The next day, Lassiter and a guard apparently fought over a food tray and struck each other at least once. Breeden, meanwhile, attempted to alert the prison nurse of the records he had secured, and on August 27, he finally gave a lieutenant a copy of a doctor's letter diagnosing Lassiter as a chronic schizophrenic.

Remaining ignored, Lassiter screamed for help until he died on August 31 of unknown causes. Four inmates in nearby cells corroborated Breeden's account. Superintendent Oliver testified that he knew that Lassiter was under psychiatric care but stressed that he had been placed in solitary confinement at his own request. He also said he never received reports of him screaming.

The testimony went on and on. Edward Belvin testified that in April 1970, he was in the prison hospital for treatment of a nervous disorder. After loudly insisting on getting a shot he thought he needed, he was taken to solitary confinement without a hearing, and the guards handcuffed him, chained his body to the cell bars and, in a final humiliation, duct-taped him by his neck to the bars. Belvin remained in that position for fourteen hours until a sympathetic guard finally cut him down. He was then kept nude in the bare solitary cell for seventeen straight days, his clothing taken because he refused to hand over a food tray.

Barry Johnson, who was under a death sentence, told of numerous harassments due to his alleged "poor attitude" and "nasty comments" to guards. After he had written a letter of complaint to the governor, he was taken to C solitary for the third time. There he was punched by a captain with a tear gas gun and then, at that captain's orders, chained by his waist and arms to the cell bars in such a way that he could not recline. He remained there for five days and was forced to urinate and defecate where he sat.

Robert Landman was eventually released from the penitentiary on August 28, 1970, after serving his full term. He had technically been eligible for parole for six years prior to his release but was continually turned down. The court stated it was satisfied that "Landman's exercise of his right to file petitions with the courts, and his assisting other prisoners in so doing, were the primary reasons for the punishments put upon him."

Landman went straight to Washington, D.C., where he supposedly had a job with an attorney's office.

FINDINGS IN THE SHADOW OF ATTICA

On September 17, 1971, while the Richmond prison case neared closure, a riot followed by a multi-day strike by inmates protesting inhuman treatment at Attica State Prison in New York resulted in 1,700 state troopers, national guardsmen, sheriff's deputies and prison guards storming the facility on orders of Governor Nelson Rockefeller with rifles containing unjacketed dum-dum bullets. In the fifteen-minute slaughter, 33 prisoners and 10 hostages died, and 85 were injured.

But the true horror of Attica was the dehumanizing aftermath. Hundreds of prisoners were stripped naked and made to walk, stagger and crawl across a muddy yard covered in debris, shell casings and broken glass and then forced through a gauntlet of corrections officers who viciously beat them and showered them with racial epithets. Medical care was denied many of them for weeks. Individual prisoners were later tortured for days to reveal leadership names, including being forced to play Russian roulette and drink officers' urine.

Attorney William Kunstler likened Attica to the My Lai massacre in Vietnam. "They may have been convicts," he told the Associated Press, "but they were infinitely more decent than the man who was elected governor of the state."

The *Richmond Afro-American* was quick to point out the inevitable comparisons between the Virginia Penitentiary and Attica, stating that only 6 percent of the guards at the Virginia Pen were black versus 60 percent of the prisoners. Guard supervisor Lieutenant E.K. Walker was equally quick to respond that most every complaint the prisoners had at Attica they had already addressed in Richmond, including the hiring of black guards; therefore, in his opinion, a similar riot was unlikely.

"UNCONSTITUTIONALLY EXCESSIVE"

By November 1, 1971, the Virginia court had found proof of several general classes of constitutional deprivation in the Virginia prison system. Discipline was imposed for the wrong reasons—not that the infractions were genuinely punishable but that inappropriate punishments were utilized without due process. The court then ruled that all good time lost by inmates as a result of court hearings be restored. Prisoners confined in padlocked or solitary cells would immediately be released and receive retrials. The court also ruled that inmates in C Building would be given hearings within thirty days or they were to be released into general population.

Injunctive relief was likewise granted regarding those practices determined to be cruel and unusual or in violation of other constitutional rights. This ruling eliminated the practice of punishment with bread and water, which the court decried as "an unnecessary infliction of pain" and a penalty "designed to break a man's spirit not just by denial of physical comforts but of necessities.…The bread and water diet is inconsistent with current minimum standards of respect for human dignity."

Restraining and controlling misbehavior by placing an inmate in chains or handcuffs inside his cell was declared "unconstitutionally excessive." The court noted that the restraints frequently prohibited the men from eating or proper toileting. "Further details are not necessary in order to reveal that it constituted physical torture."

In addition, the court ruled against such practices as "handcuffing to cell doors or posts, shackling so as to enforce cramped position or to cut off circulation...deprivation of sufficient light, ventilation, food or exercise... forcing a prisoner to remain awake until he is mentally exhausted, etc.... Corporal punishment of this variety is outmoded and inhuman. The Constitution forbids it, and this Court shall enforce that ban."

The court ruled that the practices of stripping inmates of their clothing while in unheated solitary cells with open windows in the winter was corporal punishment, "never to be used under any circumstances."

Finally, the court addressed tear gas. It found that the problem of dealing with convicts who persisted in disturbing entire cell blocks and inciting others was a real one; however, the use of gas to disable a convict who posed no immediate physical threat constituted a form of corporal punishment. "Undoubtedly it is effective," the court said, "but it is painful, and its abuse is difficult to forestall."

The court barred any official who reported a violation from ruling on the punishment, stressing that utilization of charges based solely on written reports were unfair. "Prisoners are not as a class highly educated men, nor is assistance readily available," the court said. "If they are forced to present their evidence in writing, moreover, they will be in many cases unable to anticipate the evidence adduced against them." Also, if an inmate was unable to represent himself in a disciplinary hearing, he could present his case through a lay adviser or a volunteer inmate.

Ruling that the State of Virginia could not be held liable for the actions of the man who oversaw the day-to-day management of the prisons, the court found Director Cunningham personally liable for damages against Robert Landman in the amount of $15,303.20. "The traumatic neurosis suffered by Landman results not from individualized instances of tortious behavior, but from the continued frustration of six years of arbitrary, illegal and unjust treatment...treatment calculated to dehumanize the man."

Mason was awarded $3,605.00 from Cunningham for lost wages and pain and suffering. Finally, the court awarded a judgement against Cunningham of $2,357.25 to Thomas Wansley.

The decisions obviously had an impact on Governor Linwood Holton. "All of us know we have a prison that is obsolete and overcrowded," he said at a press conference on December 21, 1971, before declaring that the penitentiary would be closed in 1978—two years earlier than his original target date of 1980.

Virginia was far from alone in dealing with prison reform, and Eastern and Western Virginia District courts especially led the nation in the volume of prisoner litigation. A nationwide series of prison revolts, strikes and riots in the mid-'60s into the '70s were all inspired by the social turmoil of the decade, and in all fairness, the prison rights movement is as relevant as other sociopolitical crusades of those decades, such as the civil rights, gay rights, anti-draft and women's liberation movements, among others.

Inside Richmond and in many American prisons, individual rebellion morphed into collective action. Black and white prisoners united against what they saw as an inherently brutal and prejudiced system that robbed them of personal liberties and stole their self-respect. They saw huge gains.

Ruffin v. Commonwealth was finally dead.

CHAPTER 16
ODD, STRANGE AND CURIOUS

FIVE YEARS' HARD LABOR FOR INTERRACIAL MARRIAGE

A mixed-race Augusta County couple, Andrew Kinney (a black man) and Mahala Miller (a white woman), began living together in 1867 in defiance of Virginia law against interracial marriage. In 1874, they got married in Washington, D.C., where interracial marriages were legal, and then returned to near the town of Churchville, where they raised five boys. They were charged with miscegenation in 1878 and fined $500, which they paid. The 1880 census showed them still living together.

Incensed by their audacity, the General Assembly hurriedly modified the statute to severely punish not just miscegenation but also going out of state to circumvent Virginia law.

In October 1878, Edmund Kinney (no apparent relation to Andrew), a black man, married Mary S. Hall, a white woman, also in Washington, D.C. After returning to their home in Hanover County, they were convicted of violating the 1878 statute. Both were sentenced to five years at hard labor in the penitentiary.

When petitioned, U.S. district judge Robert W. Hughes rejected all constitutional intervention. Kinney, he declared, was "a citizen of Virginia amenable to her laws," and though married in the District of Columbia, he cannot "bring the marriage privileges of a citizen of the District of Columbia any more than he could those of a citizen of Utah, into Virginia, in violation of her laws."

Penitentiary records show the couple were separated to serve their full five-year sentences. Both were released in 1884.

TOO PRETTY FOR PRISON

"The heavy iron gates of the Virginia Penitentiary closed August 11, 1892 on perhaps the prettiest prisoner who has ever been confined in the institution," gushed the *Washington Post* on the penitentiary admittance of twenty-five-year-old Octavia Hodges. The Rocky Mount woman was sentenced to six years for killing a sewing machine salesman named R.J. Cunningham. "[Hodges] is tall, well-formed, has black hair and eyes, and is quite pretty."

Hodges's mother ran a house of ill repute, and Hodges claimed at her Franklin County trial that Cunningham entered the house intoxicated and, during a card game, had some words with her about a sewing machine. Her own mind "inflamed with liquor," Hodges ordered the salesman to leave several times, and when he refused to do so, she took a pistol from a cupboard and shot him through the chest, severing his aorta.

Clemency was discussed for Hodges almost immediately, due to her exceptional looks and quiet, prim demeanor. Citing that she had been raised under "immoral influences" and that "she was only charged with killing a sewing machine agent," Hodges was pardoned and released on December 24, 1896.

"FIFTEEN YEARS IN HELL"

Eight hundred people arrived at the Richmond Academy of Music on the bitter cold nights of January 11 and 17, 1911, to hear Charles Morganfield, a recently released train robber, deliver lectures castigating Virginia's penitentiary and convict labor system. His hour-long speech was titled "Fifteen Years in Hell."

Morganfield and his accomplice, Charles Searcy, robbed a passenger train Wild West style near Aquia Creek just north of Fredericksburg on the Richmond-Washington line in 1894. After the robbery, Morganfield dynamited the mail and express cars, disconnected the engine and tender, tossed out the engineer and sent the engine at full speed up the track, where it very nearly collided with another loaded passenger train. He and Searcy made off with about $50,000 in the daring robbery, with all but $7,000 eventually recovered.

Ten days later, Searcy was caught. He confessed, implicated Morganfield and received a ten-year sentence. Morganfield was arrested in Cincinnati, brought back and sentenced to eighteen years. Searcy's actions enraged Morganfield, and he repeatedly said that he would kill his former partner on sight once released.

When Searcy was released on May 3, 1902, after serving eight years, his behavior as an inmate had been so good that he was offered a clerkship in the very railroad he had robbed. Instead, he asked for transportation to Stafford County, where many believed he had hidden the remainder of the stolen money, and then disappeared south. He was so terrified of Morganfield that he periodically sent out announcements that he was dead.

Morganfield was released on January 5, 1911, and instead of hunting down and killing his former accomplice, he decided to expose the "inner workings" of Virginia's penal system. "Train Robber Charles Morganfield," stated newspaper display ads for his speeches, "in his exposure of the penitentiary. A gripping discourse on 15 years in hell."

He gave several talks from January through March, and reviews were overwhelmingly negative. "He rambled to such an extent that a connected account of his charges is almost impossible," wrote a *Times-Dispatch* critic on January 17. Morganfield denounced the Thacker Shoe Company, stating that inmates were kept working there past their parole dates. He said he had been punished for unexplained false charges. He spoke of corporal punishments, especially the crucifixion and the barrel.

By March, the novelty had worn off, and his crowds had dwindled to a scarce few. "If Morganfield had the pen of a D'Annunzio or a Bernstein, he might hope to gain wealth and fame in his vivid denunciation of the Richmond prison," stated the March 21, 1911 *Roanoke Evening News*, "but being a rude and crude fellow…having only the tools of an unformed, uncultured man, rough in manners and rough in ideas, he is doomed to failure."

SQUIRREL CHARLIE

Charles Davis was a former circus trapeze performer charged with breaking into Cordes & Mosby's store in Richmond in 1900. While on patrol that night, a watchman named Hunter first spotted a fire starting inside the building and then saw Davis and ordered him to halt. Startled by the watchman's shout, Davis exited the burning building through a first-floor window. As fire crews and other police officers showed up and formed a cordon around the building, Hunter watched in stunned surprise as Davis deftly scrambled up the outside of the three-story building.

Just as Davis reached the roof, Hunter took a shot at him, missing but forcing Davis to give himself up. After Davis was brought down and the fire was extinguished, a pistol that he had thrown away was found inside the building. "Squirrel Charlie," as he became known, was sentenced to four years in the penitentiary for housebreaking.

THE NURSEMAID'S VISION

On July 18, 1911, Henry Clay Beattie, the spoiled and irresponsible son of a wealthy Richmond businessman, arrived at home in his car with his lifeless wife, Louise Wellford Owen Beattie, bleeding profusely from what appeared to be a gunshot wound to her head. Beattie claimed that they had been accosted along Midlothian Turnpike near a railroad crossing by a tall man with a long beard who had stepped out into the road and forced the car to a stop, then fired a shotgun through the window, striking Mrs. Beattie in the face and killing her.

Beattie's marriage to Miss Owen, a native of Dover, Delaware, pleased his father, whom he depended on for support, but the marriage was not a happy one. Yet in March 1911, they had a child, named Henry Clay Beattie III. The pregnancy was difficult, and Louise had to remain in bed before and after the birth, cared for by her black nursemaid, Maizie Green. It was Miss Green who had a horrifying premonition of Louise Beattie's death a month before it happened.

After the murder, followed by an investigation and questioning, the police concluded that Henry Beattie himself had pulled the trigger on his wife inside the car and then threw the shotgun out onto the tracks.

The case dominated the front page of the *Richmond Times-Dispatch* newspaper for days and aroused much interest in Richmond's society circles. At Beattie's trial, the sixteen-year-old Miss Beulah Binford, who had a torrid off-and-on affair with Beattie since 1907, took the stand and directly contradicted much of Beattie's testimony. She described in detail her relations with the accused before and since his marriage and their trips to hotels and "questionable resorts," even as recently as midnight the day before the crime. Obviously, Beattie killed his wife to carry on his affair with Miss Binford.

Beattie's cousin Paul Beattie then signed an affidavit that weeks before the murder, he had purchased the shotgun used to kill Louise Beattie at a pawnshop.

Henry Clay Beattie was found guilty of murdering his wife and on November 24, 1911, was electrocuted in the penitentiary electric chair.

But one night about four weeks before this tragedy even started, the nursemaid Maizie Green was sleeping in the same room with Mrs. Beattie and the newborn baby. She had a nightmare, awakening Mrs. Beattie with a shriek.

"What is the matter, Maizie?" Mrs. Beattie reportedly asked, startled from her slumber.

"Miss Louise," she explained, "I saw a man creep into this room, pass around my couch and point a gun in your face and pulled the trigger. Just as the gun exploded, it tore into your face, and you were killed."

THE ALLENS OF HILLSVILLE

On March 28, 1913, Floyd and Claude Allen, the notorious father-and-son ringleaders of the Hillsville, Virginia massacre that wiped out of existence all law enforcement and the Circuit Court of Carroll County, were put to death in the electric chair for first-degree murder.

Long regarded as desperadoes in and around the Hillsville area, the Allens were far from being just rough and uneducated mountaineers. Claude Allen had even completed two years of business college in Raleigh, North Carolina.

Over one hundred years later, the story is still controversial. In January 1912, Floyd Allen beat up two deputies who were arresting his nephews Sidna and Wesley Edwards for disturbing a Primitive Baptist Church meeting and reputedly parading them through the streets. On March 13, Floyd was tried in Carroll County Circuit Court for "illegal rescue of prisoners." While Judge Massie had been advised to go to the courthouse armed, he reportedly stated that he would not demean the office of judge by wearing a pistol on the bench.

The next morning, Floyd and numerous family members were permitted in court loaded down with guns and ammunition that had been openly shipped in beforehand. Reports suggested that the officers knew the men were armed but were afraid to disarm them.

Floyd (*left*) and Claude Allen while on death row. *Library of Virginia.*

After the trial, the jury rendered a verdict of guilty, with a recommended punishment of one year's confinement in the state penitentiary. Floyd Allen stood and told Judge Massie, "If you sentence me on that verdict, I will kill you."

Unintimidated, Judge Massie proceeded to sentence him the jury's recommendation. Sheriff Webb left his stand to take charge of the prisoner when Floyd Allen—who claimed he would die and go to hell before spending one minute in prison—allegedly announced, "Gentlemen, I ain't a-goin." He produced a pistol and fired toward Judge Massie. Almost immediately, Sheriff Webb drew his own gun and shot Allen, wounding him. But then other members of the Allen family produced revolvers, and the courtroom erupted in shooting, terror and panic. Members of the Allen clan shot down court officers, members of the jury and even spectators.

The Allens left the courthouse and began firing at jurors fleeing down the street. Clerk Dexter Goad, despite his wounds, wounded Sidna and Floyd Allen outside the building.

When it was over, Judge Massie (with his dying breath claiming he was shot by Sidna Allen), Sheriff Webb and Commonwealth's Attorney William Foster were dead. A juror named Fowler died two days later. Dexter Goad was badly wounded, shot through the neck and in both legs. Also wounded were Ridney Allen, brother of Floyd; two jurors; and three court spectators.

After the courthouse carnage, Floyd was too badly wounded to travel, so his son Victor remained with him inside the Elliott Hotel. They were taken into custody the next morning, and on his way to the jailer's quarters, Floyd attempted suicide by cutting his own throat.

Carroll County was left without any court system or law enforcement. Local residents quickly telegraphed the news to Governor Mann, who in turn wired W.G. Baldwin of the Baldwin-Felts Detective Agency in Roanoke to "take such men as you think may be necessary and proceed at once to Hillsville and arrest murderers and all connected with the crime. Spare no expense."

Sidna Edwards surrendered, and Claude Allen was caught by detectives two weeks later. Friel Allen was delivered through the intervention of his father. Six months later, Sidna Allen and Wesley Edwards were captured in Des Moines, Iowa.

From April through December 1912, members of the Allen family were tried for murder in the Wythe County Circuit Court. Floyd Allen was convicted of first-degree murder on May 16, even though it is unclear who he shot. Claude was first convicted of second-degree murder for killing Judge Massie and first-degree murder for killing Sheriff Webb. He and Floyd were both sentenced to die in the electric chair.

The remaining family members, including Sidna Allen, Sidna Edwards, Friel Allen and Wesley Edwards, were all sentenced to penitentiary terms ranging from fifteen to thirty-five years for various charges, mostly second-degree murder.

Since in the confusion of the courtroom fusillade it was impossible to ascertain exactly who shot whom, petitions to commute Claude and Floyd gathered almost seventy-five thousand signatures, from Sunday school classes, Washington and Lee University, the University of Virginia law school and retail businesses. Mountaineers donated the costs of presenting appeals to Governor Mann.

Unmoved, the governor released a statement on March 6 denying commutation of the death sentences. The U.S. Supreme Court refused to hear the case.

In a final statement on March 27, 1913, Floyd Allen stated that "a great injustice has been done" and that he was in fact the victim of a political plot to kill him. "I believe that the attempt on my life was made for no other cause except for my active work in the Democrat[ic] party and the bitter feeling that had gotten up between Dexter Goad and others."

After execution, the bodies of the two men were sent by train back to Hillsville, and on March 30, over five thousand people from surrounding

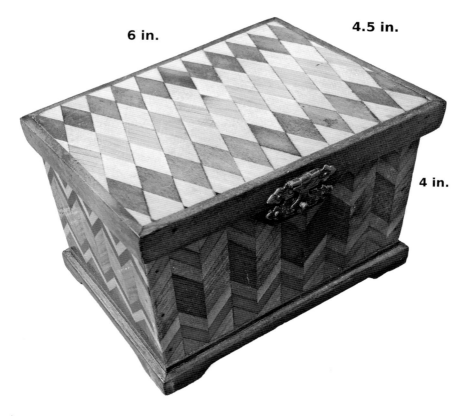

An expert woodworker, Wesley Edwards made this box as a gift to penitentiary guard William D. Rock in the 1920s. *Richard Moss.*

counties attended their open-casket funerals. Then they were buried side by side.

On April 29, 1926, Sidna Allen and Wesley Edwards were both pardoned by Governor Harry Byrd and walked out of the penitentiary after serving almost fourteen years. Wesley ran a restaurant and beer joint on Route 1 north of Richmond prior to his death in 1939. After living in North Carolina until 1940, Sidna moved back to Carroll in poor health to live his final days with his daughter. He died there in 1941.

Mob Law in Patrick County

On September 12, 1898, in Patrick County near the town of Stuart, a mob of fifteen to twenty furious men, many of them drunk, wrestled Lee Puckett from a deputy at the home of Justice of the Peace C.T. McMillan during a preliminary hearing. They dragged Puckett outside into a field and "shot him to pieces" with numerous weapons. The act was done in broad daylight, and the perpetrators made no attempts to conceal themselves.

Described as a "half-witted fellow" who had spent time in Central State Hospital, Puckett had been accused of "making a criminal assault" on a "respectable and accomplished young lady" named Phoebe Gates, who fought back "so manfully that [Puckett] failed to accomplish his purpose."

It was another horrifying southern lynching; however, in this case, Puckett was white.

It is unknown if the Puckett case was the first white lynching in Virginia, but it was the first lynching where the ringleaders were caught, convicted and sentenced—undoubtedly solely because the victim was a white man.

Soon after the lynching, Commonwealth's Attorney J.M. Hooker vowed in a letter to Governor J. Hoge Tyler to bring Puckett's killers to justice, although the attitude of the county residents was that Puckett "needed killing" because no woman felt safe walking alone with him prowling the countryside. "Puckett was a dangerous man," stated a headline in the March 31, 1899 *Richmond Times* of the prevailing attitude toward Puckett. "The evidence showed he was a menace to the safety of the women in his community."

Five men were apprehended and tried in Patrick County court for the first-degree murder of Puckett: Madison Montgomery, Robert Montgomery, L.D. McMillan (son of the justice of the peace) and W.D. Branch. The fifth, C.T. Thompson, was a minister who claimed to have said that "he had served God so long and now he had laid his Bible by with murder in his heart and that nothing but the blood of Lee Puckett would justify it."

The black-owned *Richmond Planet* newspaper praised the quick action of law enforcement, declaring, "The lynching of Lee Pickett [*sic*] (white) near Stuart. Va....was murder, and the lynchers of this man are murderers." White or black, the *Planet* declared, "Lynch law must go!"

Despite overwhelming evidence of the men's participation, the jury was unable to reach a verdict of first-degree murder, and a mistrial was declared. At a retrial in July, all five men were convicted of a lesser charge of manslaughter and sent to the penitentiary. Thompson and Madison and

Robert Montgomery all received five years, although they were all pardoned by 1902. McMillan received twenty-three years, and Branch, after a third trial, received ten years.

"I Shall Die by My Hands"

Portsmouth's Capital Theater was the scene of a terrifying public robbery on May 11, 1943, at 10:00 p.m. during a showing of *Casablanca*. In full view of almost one thousand people, Joseph "Cocky Joe" Robinson and his girlfriend, Margaret Fowler Barnes, approached theater manager Marc Terrell, who was walking through the theater with about $700 in box office cash. Robinson pulled a gun, shot Terrell in the stomach and then fired several shots in the air, creating pandemonium. Terrell died several days later.

Robinson and Barnes fled to New York, where they were eventually arrested for several robberies. They were extradited to Virginia and stood trial for murder, armed robbery and assault. Barnes was convicted on all counts and sentenced to three life terms in the penitentiary. Robinson was convicted on April 9, 1951, to death for first-degree murder, thirty years to life for robbery and ten years for malicious assault. After several appeals, he was sentenced to die on May 4, 1954.

At 5:12 a.m. on the day of execution, Robinson asked Officer in Charge L. Gangwer how much time he had left. When informed he had approximately two hours before he was to die, Robinson told another guard that he was going to sleep.

But he did not sleep. Robinson broke off a wooden spoon in his cell lock, and at 5:30 a.m., Officer Bradley found him hanging by the neck from a bedsheet tied to a ceiling pipe. When Bradley and two others finally got the door open, Robinson was dead. For good measure, he had also slit his wrist with a Gillette razor blade smuggled inside the sole of his shoe.

Robinson had left three notes in his cell. One said, "i shall Die By my hands i cannot think of any Reason why i Should let the State have Me put to Death. Die i must as it has Been said. i will Die By my hands it cannot, it will not Be Said I Joseph Robinson were kill by the State By Joseph Robinson, May 3, 1954, P.S. you cant live forever."

In another, Robinson apologized to Officer Bradley for killing himself while he was on duty, saying, among other things, "i didn't wont to Do this

"Cocky Joe" Robinson. *Library of Virginia.*

The piece of wooden spoon and razor blade used by Joe Robinson to jam his cell door and take his own life on the day of his execution. *Library of Virginia.*

on your time. you is a Fined man.…Mr. [Bradley] i Just cant let these Rats Kill Me.…Be Good Mr. [Bradley.] May God be with you always."

Death row inmate John Kensinger told investigators that Robinson wanted to kill himself because he did not want Captain Weatherspoon, a particularly sarcastic guard on duty from 4:00 p.m. to 11:30 p.m., to see him die.

PORTRAIT OF A SERIAL KILLER

A Blacksburg native and the youngest of nine children, Henry Lee Lucas, while growing up in the 1940s, endured unspeakable abuse by his alcoholic mother, Viola Waugh. Viola would beat young Henry and force him and even her disabled husband, Anderson, to watch her prostitute herself in their dirt-floor, two-room cabin. Henry lost an eye at age eight because Viola refused him medical care. Anderson—nicknamed "No Legs" because he lost both in a railroad accident—later chose to lie down in the snow and freeze to death rather than spend one more day with the vicious woman. By age ten, Henry was an alcoholic, sexually abused regularly by a stepbrother and had developed a sick fascination with bestiality and rape.

Henry Lucas left home in the early 1950s and was living with another stepbrother, Harry Waugh, near Lyndhurst, Virginia, when, on May 13, 1954, the seventeen-year-old was stopped on a traffic violation in Waynesboro by Officer R.L. Stover. A check of his car revealed money, a coat and keys, all believed to be stolen.

While Lucas claimed that the car was his brother's, he was charged with breaking and entering and car theft. According to the June 28, 1954 penitentiary admittance ledger, the "Augusta County youth" was found guilty of statutory burglary in Juvenile Relations Court and sentenced to two years as prisoner #65971. Two unsuccessful escape attempts from a road crew in 1957 extended his sentence, and he was finally released in September 1959.

After his release, Lucas went to his older sister's home in Tecumseh, Michigan, and the following year, his mother showed up, demanding he return to Blacksburg. Refusing, they got into a fight, and he stabbed her to death. He received twenty to forty years in a Michigan prison but was released in 1971 because of overcrowding.

After a failed marriage and serving another four years in Michigan for attempted kidnapping, Lucas met a sadistic drifter named Ottis Toole and his mentally disabled niece Freida Powell in Florida, and they traveled for

Henry Lee Lucas, age seventeen, 1954. *Library of Virginia.*

years doing odd jobs across thirty-eight states. In 1982, Lucas killed and dismembered Freida and then killed a former employer named Kate Rich in Ringgold, Texas.

After being arrested on an illegal weapons charge in Texas, Lucas began confessing to hundreds of murders, some so outlandish they were dismissed as hoaxes by the media. Still, he was flown from state to state to meet with detectives and police, who used his dubious and coached confessions to prematurely close the books on hundreds of inactive cases.

Lucas confessed and then withdrew to killing a Lynchburg girl in 1951 named Laura Burnsley and burying her body near Harrisonburg. He was eventually convicted of eleven murders and sentenced to death for killing a woman known only as "orange socks," as that was all she was wearing when found.

Becoming a born-again Christian, Lucas's death sentence was commuted by Governor George Bush in 1998. He died of heart failure in prison on March 12, 2001.

In a shocking postscript, Ottis Toole was posthumously determined in 2008 to be the killer of six-year-old Adam Walsh, son of *America's Most Wanted* host John Walsh, in 1981.

Henry's life inspired the 1986 John McNaughton movie *Henry: Portrait of a Serial Killer.*

THE COLD CREAM BANDIT

On February 24, 1972, Rex Wardell Albright Jr. stood in Staunton Circuit Court and quietly answered "guilty" to two counts of statutory burglary, larceny and possessing burglary tools after an October 30, 1971 break-in. He was then sentenced to twenty years' hard labor in the penitentiary, with fifteen suspended.

This was not the first time; Albright had a bizarre fetish that landed him in prison twice.

Albright's first crime spree began in 1958 when he began burglarizing houses "for kicks" in West Virginia and then Pennsylvania before he found Augusta County "by chance" and began robbing homes in Harrisonburg, Waynesboro and Staunton. At the time, he frequently used a propane torch to gain entry, earning him the nickname the "blowtorch burglar."

Albright was arrested in Uniontown, Pennsylvania, on August 15, 1964. He pleaded guilty to twenty-four Uniontown burglaries and served five years in prison there.

Claiming that he always hoped people would be home when he broke in, and admitting that the magnetic thrill of getting caught was "a sexual desire," he said prior to going to jail that he "hoped to get some medical help."

After his release from prison, Albright not only resumed his old habits but also began indulging the bizarre pattern of smearing some of his sleeping female victims with Vaseline or some similar drugstore lotion, usually with the husband lying nearby. This led to him this time being dubbed the "cold cream bandit."

He returned to Augusta County, stealing cash and trinkets and smearing women with Vaseline. Several of his victims woke screaming during his break-ins, and he frequently had to escape barking dogs and furious, cursing husbands.

Albright's luck ran out in Staunton on October 30, 1971. Just after 2:00 a.m., he was found sleeping in his car after an Augusta Street break-in. He was arrested again, and authorities determined he had been involved in two hundred robberies in three states, although it is unknown exactly how many victims he smeared with ointment.

Commonwealth's Attorney T.C. Elder said Albright had "quirks of personality" rather than a mental illness and proposed the sentence that was accepted by Judge William Moffett. Then, on March 13, Albright became Virginia Penitentiary prisoner #98477. After serving only two and a half years, he was discharged on December 20, 1974, and placed on supervised probation for fifteen years.

Rex Albright Jr. died on February 24, 2000, in Elkins.

CHAPTER 17
NEVER STOMP THE KITTEN

1978-1992

If the prisoner is locked up primarily for the purpose of revenge,
then perhaps this retribution should be acknowledged openly.
That way, if you ever meet an ex-con with a thirst for vengeance,
at least you will know that the feeling is mutual.
—penitentiary inmate Evans Hopkins, "Pariahs Seek Reforms," ThroTTle
magazine, July 1983

"...YOU KNOW SOMETHING IS WRONG"

Governor Linwood Holton's confident prediction of closing the
penitentiary in 1978 was ultimately a pipe dream. With many new prisons
held up in construction and budget issues, and with an inmate receiving
and holding facility planned for Louisa County shot down by a consulting
firm, the Virginia State Penitentiary—now a creaking, decaying urban
fortress, obsolete, out of place and completely surrounded by the city of
Richmond and a frustrated Virginia Commonwealth University—lurched
into its final decade.

Prisoners emboldened by the early 1970s court decisions and perhaps
sensing the penitentiary was in its death throes continued to strike and riot
sporadically throughout the decade into the 1980s in an effort to win more
concessions and perhaps hasten the facility's demise. Just after the court-
ordered changes in early January 1973, guards had to use tear gas to flush

out twenty-nine barricaded inmates in a disturbance over living conditions in the first of several insurgences to rock the facility.

"The penitentiary was already antiquated in the 1970s," said Alan Katz, a retired attorney formerly with the attorney general's office, in a 2017 interview. "The mindset among the guards at the time was 'we can do anything we want, because they're just inmates.'"

From May through June 1973, the penitentiary was the scene of six consecutive Friday night inmate fights, resulting in six prisoners stabbed, one fatally. One inmate was fatally set on fire in his cell by another inmate who splashed him with a chemical from the paint shop. One particularly brutal fight in a receiving cell on May 29 resulted in one inmate beaten and forced to commit oral sodomy on twelve other prisoners. Those attacks finally led to a total lockdown and a weapons search. Over one hundred weapons were confiscated, including a twenty-five-inch machete with a sharpened eighteen-inch blade.

"We know we're in trouble when we find something like this machete," Assistant Superintendent Edward Murray told *Washington Post* reporter Paul Edwards. "When a prisoner has time to make something like this and not be observed, then you know something is wrong."

Something was wrong, indeed. Almost a decade of strikes and court challenges, coupled with gang rapes and discoveries of stashes of homemade weapons, had a cumulative discomfiting effect. A state crime commission report piled on the bad news, concluding that life for the nine hundred inmates at the penitentiary had been "reduced to a struggle for survival that is devoid of any of the moral or ethical standards usually associated with western civilization." These all led to calls to not only close the woefully outdated facility but also dismiss and legally prosecute all the top state prison officials for their continued mishandling of the state's penal system.

To rub salt in the wounds, a withering 157-page grand jury report on prison conditions and methods issued two weeks into the Mills Godwin administration in late January 1974 resulted in six penal system officials being indicted. Otis Brown, secretary of human affairs; William Lukhard, director of the Department of Welfare and Institutions; James Howard, director of corrections; Dennis Gallagher, administrative assistant; Robert Mason, assistant superintendent of security; and Frank Dunn, former chief security officer, faced charges including "a discouraging deficiency in leadership of those responsible for corrections," a "stubborn refusal by too many entrenched management people to accept the necessity for change" and "antiquated, inadequate and often inhumane housing facilities and obsolete or inadequate industrial and vocational equipment and insufficient effort to maintain what was available."

All charges were eventually dismissed.

Black Codes Redux

Meanwhile, the state and federal wars on drugs kept sending more and more mostly young black men into the prison systems and particularly into the penitentiary in a contemporary implementation of the notorious post–Civil War black codes. All the court rulings that in the 1970s changed prisoner treatment mattered little within certain Virginia counties' notorious "cruel and unusual" drug sentences.

The unspoken saying at the time was "don't be convicted in Pittsylvania," as it was home of the harshest juries in the state. Quadriplegic Robert Moore Jr. learned this hard lesson in September 1977 when he was sentenced to twenty-one years in the penitentiary for selling one-third of an ounce of marijuana and five sleeping pills for $25. Conversely, one week later, David and Thomas McNamara, sons of a Norfolk Circuit Court judge, were given suspended sentences by a lenient Norfolk jury for selling $20,000 worth of marijuana and cocaine to an undercover policeman. Moore and the McNamaras were white, proving the existence of not just racial but also class disparities in local sentencing.

There were some bright spots in this decade, however. In 1975, civil rights worker and VCU professor Dr. Edward H. Peeples designed a Family Life Program to "preserve family ties of prisoners and their families and to prepare prisoners for reintegration into society." Peeples wrote in a letter to Warden James Mitchell that in visits to the penitentiary, he was "not only distressed about the deplorable physical facilities, the inhuman social conditions, and the paucity of effective rehabilitation programs, but I was very uneasy about the apparent lack of self-awareness and commitment among inmates themselves to take responsibility for reshaping their own lives."

Mitchell, however, along with some of the guards, did not always appreciate the program, and Peeples related in a 2017 interview that conditions eventually grew hostile. The program ended around 1985, when other groups began coming in with resources of their own. "I gave them faith," Peeples said of his seminal program, adding that he learned if he showed solidarity within the group and with the inmates, it gave them assurance that he was on their side.

STABBINGS, SHAKEDOWNS AND A HUGE LEGAL AWARD

The inmate population has already reached a breaking point, caused by the insensitivity and arrogance of a bigoted Warden. It was like a raging fire waiting for a strong wind that would set an entire forest on fire, and that's exactly what happened.
—*press release written by Latif Rashe'd, resident Emam and convict #94958, about the 1977 strike*

On August 1, 1977, three hundred inmates gave prison administration a list of thirty-two demands and then staged a strike beginning at 8:00 p.m. The prisoners wandered uneventfully around the yard until around 4:00 a.m., when some broke into storage areas and armed themselves with pipes, garden tools and broken furniture. Negotiations on the demands, which included the immediate removal of Superintendent Robert Zahradnick, broke down, and sixty heavily armed state police and guards massed quickly inside the gate. It looked extremely ugly.

But a confrontation was avoided when a sudden thunderstorm pounded the area. Guards gave inmates five minutes to clear the yard, and by 5:00 a.m., all inmates were peacefully back in their cells.

After the disturbance, a cell-by-cell sweep turned up almost one hundred homemade weapons, highlighting the adversarial relationships not just from inmates toward guards but toward other inmates as well.

The next major riot occurred on January 9, 1983, when up to 150 inmates attacked 3 guards, looted the commissary, set fire to the barbershop and smashed multiple windows in an attempt to let out the tear gas fired at them. After the guards were beaten, 50 inmates refused to return to B Building, and another 75 milled around the recreation field, wielding chair and table legs, before attempting to break into the guard station.

Reinforcements from Powhatan and Deep Meadow Correctional arrived, and when confronted, the inmates returned to their cells at 10:00 p.m., five hours after the riot commenced. The inmates were protesting recent rule changes that, among other things, stopped them from padlocking their own cells to protect their belongings and restricted time out of their cells in the evenings following a New Year's Day stabbing that was fatal to inmate Edward Jones. Another shakedown after that stabbing turned up thirteen homemade knives.

In 1979, the largest out-of-court legal decision against an inmate in American history was settled when Henry Tucker was awarded $518,000 in

Aftermath of the 1983 riot. *Library of Virginia.*

damages for negligence, medical malpractice and violations of his civil rights. Sentenced to forty years in 1964 for intent to rape, he became emotionally disturbed after being denied parole in 1976 and was administered a powerful anti-psychotic drug by untrained, unsupervised inmates. He lapsed into a coma, developed a joint disease that drew his legs up into his chest and then lay untreated in a bed for six months, his body covered in maggot-infested bedsores. Eventually, his hip joints were entirely removed so his legs could be straightened, but his legs and arms remained paralyzed. "It was like something out of the inquisition," ACLU attorney Stephen Bricker said of his client's treatment inside the penitentiary.

"Justice that Is Criminal"

At the time, a major lawsuit, initiated by the National Prison Project of the American Civil Liberties Union on behalf of the inmates, was being adjudicated in federal court. The suit charged administrators with fostering "an aura of violence" and refusing to improve living conditions.

The National Prison Project (NPP) evolved out of independent work done in Virginia and New York, with attorney Phil Hirschkop handling dramatically increasing complaints from prisoners in Virginia prisons. As word of his work spread, he found himself inundated with about one hundred letters a week.

Meanwhile, in Buffalo, New York, law professor Herman Schwartz began handling prisoner rights complaints at the New York State Penitentiary at Attica several years before the notorious 1971 riot. In 1972, both of these efforts coalesced into the foundation-funded NPP.

"I am reminded of the sentiments of several persons who called in to a segment of CBS' 'Nightwatch' that aired following a takeover by prisoners at Sing-Sing in New York," inmate Evans Hopkins wrote in the July 1983 issue of *ThroTTle* magazine. "Many expressed the view that criminals should be made to 'pay their debts to society' in harsh environments....In thinking about these 'debts' that ensue from criminal activity, it seems that moral justice should demand humane limits to the remuneration exacted from a lawbreaker. Does not society owe at least this to the pariahs it produces? Instead of justice for criminals we have justice that is criminal."

The crime of punishment.

"What strikes me hardest about the discourse on prisons is that race is seldom mentioned, even though the prison population in this country is largely made up of black and Hispanic people," Hopkins wrote. "By ignoring this fact it is much easier to avoid facing up to the racism that permeates our social structure, to obscure the widely felt sentiment that penitentiaries are needed to keep black hands from reaching for white pockets, or white throats."

After the January 9 riot, twenty-one inmates were transferred out of the penitentiary to Mecklenburg County maximum-security facility. Eighteen more were sent in subsequent weeks as ringleaders were identified.

SHUT IT DOWN

About 50 lifers were transferred to Staunton [Correctional] *from the penitentiary just before it closed. They were old guys—one had been in since 1942—and they were in for heinous crimes. In Staunton, they befriended this mother cat who had three kittens, feeding her and watching out for her. Then one day someone through a window saw another inmate stomp one of the kittens to death. The lifers put up a reward of fifty cartons of cigarettes for that prisoner's name. They were going to kill him. The heat got so bad that prisoner had to be transferred to Mecklenburg, and even there he had to serve out his term in segregation for fear of his life for killing that kitten. Never stomp the kitten.*
—retired corrections analyst Danny Link, 2017 interview

After years of false starts, the penitentiary was scheduled to close on July 1, 1990; however, construction delays at two new correctional facilities in Greensville and Buchanan Counties kept it open until December of that year. A Building—the oldest remaining structure in the complex—was the first cell block to be vacated, with the inmates going to B in April. It was about time: an inspection by the ACLU for the National Prison Project, Judge Merhige and representatives of the attorney general's office revealed the buildings were filthy and roach-infested; the heat was unbearable; there was standing water everywhere; and the toilets frequently stopped up. After this tour, the ACLU declared the penitentiary "the most shameful prison in America."

("That wasn't a rat," Judge Merhige said when someone pointed out a scurrying rodent on the tour, "that was a mouse.")

The last condemned convict to die in the electric chair in Virginia's crumbling penitentiary was a lanky, southern-talking drifter named Buddy Lee Justus, who was executed on December 13, 1990, for the 1978 rape and murder of twenty-one-year-old nurse Ida Mae Moses. He was also found guilty of murdering Rosemary Jackson in Georgia and Stephanie Hawkins in Tampa, Florida.

The very next day, on December 14, 1990, the penitentiary closed. The final four inmates—Bobbie Rogers, Paul Stotts, Albert Vanderstuyf and Dean Ratliff—left in a van to Greensville Correctional, telling reporters they were glad to be leaving. On the other hand, some of those lifers who had earlier been moved to Staunton told Danny Link that they were sorry to leave the old pen.

Left to right: Author and former inmate Evans Hopkins, former corrections officer Jerry Givens and Dale Brumfield at the dedication of the penitentiary historical marker at 500 Spring Street in Richmond, February 24, 2017. *Hunter Brumfield*.

At the closing ceremonies, Warden Raymond Muncy asked for the penitentiary's official prisoner count. Major Early T. Turner stepped forward, opened a ledger and announced in a loud, clear voice that the prisoner count was officially zero. Many in the crowd laughed. Warden Muncy stared straight ahead. It was the first time the prisoner count was zero since the evacuation of Richmond in 1865. Muncy stated, "Accordingly, in my capacity as warden, I now declare the Virginia State Penitentiary closed."

But not really. By Virginia law, the electric chair had to be always on standby, so technically the penitentiary remained open until the new death chamber in Greensville could be completed. In early February 1991, condemned murderer Joseph Giarratano was brought to the penitentiary for execution. On February 19, his sentence was commuted to six life sentences, and he was transferred to Deerfield Correctional.

From Merryman to Giarratano. The circle was complete.

On February 26, the electric chair was boxed up and moved to its new home at Greensville. Starting in August, Thomas Jefferson's "Gaol and Penitentiary-House" was physically erased by Wrecking Corp. of America of St. Louis, Missouri, for the property owner, Ethyl Corporation. Ethyl had purchased the sixteen acres in 1987 for $5 million. The demolition took almost one year.

Until 2017, there was no plaque, sign or marker indicating the penitentiary's existence until this author applied for one with the Virginia Department of Historic Resources (DHR), a division of the Virginia Historical Society. The marker was unveiled on February 24, 2017, at the intersection of Belvidere and Spring Streets.

The only thing saved from the penitentiary complex were three cupolas off the roof of the main building. Today, those cupolas are located behind the Tredegar Museum.

The property is the home of Afton Chemical.

CHAPTER 18
FACT CHECK

SEPARATING FACT FROM RUMOR AT THE VIRGINIA PENITENTIARY

Oregon Hill streetlights dimmed briefly during electrocutions.
False. The penitentiary had its own power plants: one coal, one oil and one gas-fired. The electric chair was on its own dedicated 2,500-volt circuit, and activation did not affect any other electrical functionality either inside the facility or outside the walls.

Doug Dobey.

There were at least two prisoners unaccounted for when the penitentiary shut down in 1990.

False. In 1990, the older inmates transplanted to the Staunton Correctional facility bragged to a corrections analyst that at least two of their brethren who angered someone may have exited the institution through the incinerator or in pieces in multiple trash bags.

In January 2015, however, the absconsion unit director for the Virginia Department of Corrections wrote in an e-mail, "I reviewed records I have, and spoke to several old timers and I can't find any evidence that would support your claim that prisoners vanished inside the penitentiary." Retired attorney Alan Katz, who spent almost forty-one years in prisoner litigation, reported also, "I have never heard that."

The oldest man to die in Virginia's electric chair was eighty-three. The youngest was sixteen.

Half-true. Joe Lee, charged with the murder of Frank Grymes near Rappahannock Academy in Caroline County, was executed on April 21, 1916, claiming to be eighty-three years old. The court, however, had reason to believe he was more realistically sixty-eight. Regardless, he is still the oldest prisoner executed in Virginia's electric chair to date. His execution coincidentally followed the youngest prisoner to date to be electrocuted, Percy Ellis, who was verified as sixteen years of age. Ellis was the youngest to be executed in Virginia since a slave named Clem was hanged for murder at age twelve on November 5, 1787.

The George Washington equestrian statue at the state capitol is facing the General Assembly but deliberately pointing to the penitentiary as a warning to legislators.

True, but purely coincidental. The rumor apparently was started by a disgruntled post–Civil War Confederate senator who maintained that General Washington was pointing to the penitentiary as a warning for legislators to walk the straight and narrow. It was merely a fluke of placement that made that impression.

"Pointing to the penitentiary": the George Washington statue at the Virginia State Capitol. *Author's collection.*

The penitentiary prisoner who placed the capstone on the Confederate Monument in Hollywood Cemetery was awarded his freedom for doing so.

Most likely false. The construction of the ninety-foot memorial to the Confederate dead was plagued with accidents (but only minor injuries), as the stone blocks composing the monument were stacked with no cement bonding. The placing of the top capstone proved to be especially daunting until a convicted horse thief named Thomas Stanley, who was working on the monument as a public works project, agreed to climb the structure and place it there.

Stanley's prison record, however, does not state he was "released" for his brave accomplishment but "transferred," a catch-all term that meant he could have been released but more likely meant he was leased or put to labor on one of the railroads in West Virginia.

When the penitentiary was demolished, skeletons were found in the walls.

False. This rumor may have started from the fact that...

Almost three hundred skeletons were found buried on the penitentiary property during demolition.

True. The General Assembly allowed the penitentiary to create its own cemetery in 1877, presumably to handle the large influx of dead and dying inmates returning from the West Virginia railroad tunnels. Then, on March 11, 1992, an excavator for Wrecking Corp. of America accidentally unearthed pine boxes containing forty-six skeletons near the north end of the penitentiary property, from six to eight feet below ground level. Eventually, many more boxes were uncovered, ranging in size from an orange crate to a piano box, with each containing as many as eight skulls and bones. Demolition was briefly halted, and the area became an archaeological dig, under the direction of Kathy Biedleman.

The remains were shipped to the Smithsonian Institute in 1992 as part of Biedleman's doctoral research, but only preliminary studies have been done

Penitentiary demolition, March 1992. *Library of Virginia.*

Arthur J. Probst Jr.

since her death in 2013, and evidence still needs to be matched with prison records. The remains are confirmed to be from the nineteenth century, and the majority are males, but there are females and children also. Most are also of blacks, but there are whites present also.

According to Kari Bruwelheide, a skeletal biologist at the Smithsonian Institute's Division of Physical Anthropology, the commingled remains could have been single graves combined to create more space for additional graves or the burials of multiple individuals dying in single events. There is also the possibility that an original cemetery may have been disturbed by prison expansions and those graves removed and redeposited.

Scott Reynolds Nelson states in his book *Steel Drivin' Man* that the evidence of abnormal bone formations and lesions on several individuals are indicative of silicosis from working in the West Virginia railroad tunnels. But according to Bruwelheide, certain conditions within the prison, such as tuberculosis and pneumonia, could also have resulted in these pathologies.

Perhaps one day we will have closure.

BIBLIOGRAPHY

Abernathy v. Royster. U.S. Court of Appeals for the Fourth Circuit April 1, 1968. (Justia, Dist. file). 393 F.2d 775.

Alexander, Michelle. "The New Jim Crow. Mass Incarceration in the Age of Colorblindness." *Kritikon Litterarum* 40, nos. 3–4 (2013).

Alexandria Gazette. "Attempted to Escape." July 7, 1904.

———. "Smith Sentenced." January 14, 1910.

———. "A State Farm." November 5, 1893.

Annual Report(s) of the Board of Directors of the Virginia Penitentiary with Accompanying Documents. Fiscal Year(s) Ending September 30, 1900–1910.

Associated Press. "Booby-Trap' Slayer Dies in Va. Chair." *Washington Post*, January 4, 1947.

———. "Flogging Ban Is Deplored by Va. Penal Head." *Washington Post*, September 19, 1946.

———. "Official Discounts Fugitive's Charge of Va. Brutality." *Washington Post*, January 23, 1946.

———. "Prisoner Tries Hang-Gliding Escape." *Courier-Post* (Camden, NJ), December 23, 1979.

———. "Prisons in Va. Ban Flogging Ahead of Law." *Washington Post*, March 13, 1946.

———. "Shackling of Ill Prisoners, Other Abuses Charged in Va." *Washington Post*, November 21, 1945.

———. "Social Gain Seen Offsetting 'Loss' in Flogging Ban." *Washington Post*, September 20, 1946.

———. "State Prison Aides Cleared of Brutality." *Richmond News Leader*, December 17, 1945.

———. "Virginia Wife Raped; 6 Held, 7th Sought." *Washington Post,* January 10, 1949.

Barkan, Barry. "Attica Conditions at Va. State." *Richmond Afro-American*, September 25, 1971.

———. "Charges Fly: Prison Scandal Grows." *Richmond Afro-American*, August 3, 1968.

———. "Godwin, Prison Officials Accused of 'Whitewash.'" *Richmond Afro-American*, August 24, 1968.

———. "Humanity vs. Inhumanity. Big Protest Set for the Weekend." *Richmond Afro-American*, August 10, 1968.

———. "Inmate Work Stoppage Still in Effect at Prison." *Richmond Afro-American*, August 17, 1968.

Barrow, Bernard, MD. "Vasectomy for the Defective Negro with His Consent." Lecture transcript, Southside Virginia Medical Association, Petersburg, June 28, 1910.

Beaumont, Gustave De, Alexis De Tocqueville and Francis Lieber. *On the Penitentiary System in the United States: and Its Application in France; with an Appendix on Penal Colonies, and Also, Statistical Notes.* London: Philadelphia, 1833.

Becker, Balthazar. "Blackmon, Douglas A. Slavery by Another Name. The Re-Enslavement of Black Americans from the Civil War to World War II." *Kritikon Litterarum* 40, nos. 3–4 (2013).

The Bee (Danville, VA). "Convicted Bank Robber Escapes State Prison." October 1, 1970.

Bredemeier, Kenneth. "6 Prison Officials Indicted in Virginia." *Washington Post,* January 26, 1974.

———. "Virginia Rape Case Figure Wansley Freed After 10 Years, Isn't Bitter." *Washington Post,* January 18, 1973.

———. "Virginia State Penitentiary to Close in '78, Holton Says." *Washington Post*, December 21, 1972.

Brooklyn Daily Eagle. "Negro Youth Executed." October 30, 1908.

Bruce, Allan R. "Attica: Another 'My Lai.'" *Richmond Afro-American*, September 18, 1971.

Brumfield, Dale M. "An Executioner's Song." *Richmond Magazine*, April 2016.

———. "Stopping Sanism." Guest editorial. *Richmond Times-Dispatch*, September 4, 2016.

Cable, George W. *The Silent South.* Reprint; New York: Wentworth Press, 2016.

Cahalan, Margaret. "Trends in Incarceration in the United States Since 1880." *Crime and Delinquency* 25, no. 1 (1980). (JSTOR).

Carrington, Charles, MD. "Asexualization of Hereditary Criminals." *Journal of the American Institute of Criminal Law and Criminology* 1 (March 10, 1910): 124–25.

———. "Hereditary Criminals: The One Sure Cure." Lecture transcript, Tri-State Medical Association, Richmond, Virginia, February 15, 1910.

———. "The History of Electrocution in the State of Virginia." Lecture transcript, forty-first annual session of the Medical Society of Virginia, Norfolk, October 25–28, 1910.

———. "Mistreatment at the Penitentiary." Guest commentary. *Richmond Times-Dispatch*, October 3, 1912.

———. "Sterilization of Habitual Criminals." *Journal of Prison Discipline*, January 1909, 48–51.

———. "Sterilization of Habitual Criminals." *Virginia Medical Semi-Monthly*, April 9, 1909, 421–22.

———. "Vasectomy, from the Eugenical Standpoint, with Report of Cases." *Transactions of the Forty-Third Annual Session of the Medical Society of Virginia*, 1913, 150–52.

Carwile, Howard. Letter to the Editor. *Richmond Times-Dispatch*, July 28, 1946.

———. Transcript of radio address on WRNL radio, February 2, 1946.

———. Transcript of radio address on WRNL radio, February 24, 1946.

Childs, Dennis. *Slaves of the State: Black Incarceration from the Chain Gang to the Penitentiary*. Minneapolis: University of Minnesota Press, 2015.

Christian, W. Asbury. *Richmond, Her Past and Present*. Richmond: L.H. Jenkins, 1912.

Clinch Valley News. "Punishment in the Penitentiary." April 18, 1919.

A Collection of the Several Acts of the Assembly Concerning the Penitentiary. Richmond, VA: Samuel Pleasants, 1807.

Commonwealth of Virginia. *Acts and Joint Resolutions Passed by the General Assembly of the State of Virginia…* Richmond, VA: J.H. O'Bannon, Supt. of Public Print, 1874–76, 1904–6.

———. *Annual Report(s) to the Board of Directors*. Richmond: Virginia Penitentiary, 1900–15, 1918–24.

———. *Calendar of State Papers*. September 1798, 1799–1804.

———. *Governor's Message and Annual Reports of the Agents of Public Institutions*. Richmond, VA: William F. Ritchie, 1851.

———. *Governor's Message and Reports of the Public Officers of the State, of the Boards of Directors, and of the Visitors, Superintendents, and Other Agents of Public*

Institutions or Interests of Virginia. Richmond, VA: William F. Ritchie, public printer, 1850, 1855–60.

———. Grant Application, Spring Street Theatre, Inc. Virginia Commission of the Arts and Humanities. Richmond, VA, 1976.

———. *Journal of the House of Delegates,* 1797–1805, 1808–41, 1846–59, 1861, 1863, 1866–67.

———. "Report of the Virginia Penitentiary." *Annual Reports of Officers, Boards, and Institutions of the Commonwealth of Virginia.* Richmond, VA, 1800–30, 1892, 1893–97.

———. *Report(s) of the Virginia Penitentiary.* 1902–12, 1921, 1924–26.

———. "Senate Action on Bills." *Journal of the Senate of Virginia,* January 1796–1800.

———. "Senate Action on House Resolutions." *Journal of the Senate of Virginia,* 1798–1801, 1803–21, 1823, 1828–43.

———. "Surgeon's Report." *Journal of the House of Delegates,* 1821–44, 1847–59, 1870–73, 1875–76, 1881–83, 1886–88, 1900.

Crisis magazine. "Christian Virginia vs. Virginia Christian." September 1912, 237–39.

Culbertson, Charles. "In 1895, Man Almost Got Life in Prison for Bacon Theft." *Staunton News Leader,* March 10, 2017.

Danville Register. "Escape Foiled." August 10, 1976.

———. "Martinsville Trial." June 6, 1950.

———. "Virginia Prison Inmates Tell of Abuse by Guards." December 13, 1968.

Davis v. Commonwealth. 186 VA 937. Hustings Court, Richmond, VA, November 24, 1947.

Deans, Mal. "Youth Says Chains Cut into Legs." *Richmond Times-Dispatch,* November 20, 1945.

Dix, Dorothea Lynde. *Remarks on Prisons and Prison Discipline in the United States.* Philadelphia: J. Kite, 1845.

Dugdale, Richard. *The Jukes: A Study in Crime, Pauperism, Disease and Heredity.* New York: Knickerbocker Press, 1895.

Dun, Michael. "War of 1812: Privateers and Letters of Marque." www.1812privateers.org. Includes list of British prisoners captured by the United States during the War of 1812.

Earley, Mark L. "A Pink Cadillac, an IQ of 63, and a Fourteen-Year-Old from South Carolina: Why I Can No Longer Support the Death Penalty." *University of Richmond Law Review* 49 (2015): 811–23.

Edwards, Paul G. "Hunt Yields 100 Weapons at Va. Prison." *Washington Post,* June 3, 1973.

Engerman, Stanley L., and Peter Kolchin. "American Slavery, 1619–1877." *Journal of American History* 81, no. 2 (1994): 643.

Espy, M. Watt, and John Ortiz Smykla. *Executions in the United States, 1608–2002: The Espy File.* 4th ed. Ann Arbor, MI: Inter-university Consortium for Political and Social Research, 2004.

Free Lance (Fredericksburg, VA). "Morganfield Assails 'Pen.'" January 17, 1911.

Friedman, Lawrence J., and Pete Daniel. "The Shadow of Slavery: Peonage in the South, 1901–1969." *American Historical Review* 78, no. 1 (1973): 179.

Gaines, William, Jr. "The 'Penitentiary House.'" *Virginia Cavalcade* (Summer 1956).

Goddard, Henry Herbert. *The Kallikak Family: A Study in the Heredity of Feeble-Mindedness.* New York: Macmillan Company, 1913.

Goode, William O., and Edmund Ruffin. *Internal Improvements and Banks.* 1st ed. Richmond: Commonwealth of Virginia, 1852.

Grant, Mary Agnes. "History of the State Penitentiary of Virginia." Master's thesis, College of William and Mary, Williamsburg, VA, 1936.

Green, Frank. "Witnessing Executions." *University of Richmond Law Review* (2015).

Griffin, Larry J., and W. Fitzhugh Brundage. "Lynching in the New South: Georgia and Virginia, 1880–1930." *Contemporary Sociology* 23, no. 6 (1994): 814.

Grinnan, Dr. A.G. "The Burning of Eve in Virginia." *Virginia Historical Magazine,* June 1896. www.archive.org.

Hampton Monitor. "Murder of Mrs. Belote." March 21, 1912.

———. "Virginia Christian, Murderess, Pays Penalty of Awful Crime." August 22, 1912.

———. "Virginia Christian Must Die." June 13, 1912.

Harris, LaShawn. "The 'Commonwealth of Virginia vs. Virginia Christian': Southern Black Women, Crime & Punishment in Progressive Era Virginia." *Journal of Social History* 47, no. 4 (2014): 922–42.

Hemstock, G. Kevin. *Injustice on the Eastern Shore.* Charleston, SC: The History Press, 2015.

Hirschkop, Philip J., and Michael A. Millemann. "The Unconstitutionality of Prison Life." *Virginia Law Review* 55, no. 5 (June 1969): 795–839.

Holmberg, Mark. "Meet Chris Baker—Richmond's Grave Robber." WTVR-6. November 17, 2010. WTVR.com.

Hopkins, Evans D. *Life After Life: A Story of Rage and Redemption.* New York: Simon & Schuster, 2005.

————. "Pariahs Seek Reform." *ThroTTle*, July 1983.

Howe, Henry. *Historical Collections of Virginia*. Charleston, SC, 1852.

Hunter, Joel D. "Sterilization of Criminals (Report of Committee H of the Institute)." *Journal of the American Institute of Criminal Law and Criminology* 5, no. 4 (1914).

Inmates of the State Penitentiary. *The Beacon* magazine. Consecutive issues, December 1938–January 1940.

The Intelligencer (Wheeling, WV). "Interesting from Richmond." April 9, 1865.

Jet. "Va. Prisoner Beats Electric Chair, Hangs Self." 1954.

Joyner, Nancy D. "The Death Penalty in Virginia: Its History and Prospects." *University of Virginia Institute of Government Newsletter* 50 (1974): 37–40

Kahan, Paul. *Eastern State Penitentiary*. Charleston, SC: The History Press, 2008.

Kass, Carole. "Prison Inmates' Voices Fly Over Walls by Radio." *Richmond Times-Dispatch*, April 4, 1976.

Keeler, Clarissa Olds. *The Crime of Crimes, Or, The Convict System Unmasked*. Washington, D.C.: Pentecostal Era Co., 1907.

Keve, Paul W. *The History of Corrections in Virginia*. Charlottesville: University Press of Virginia, 1986.

Kimball, Gregg D. "Jimmie Strother, Virginia Songster." *64 Magazine*, January 2002.

Kollatz, Harry, Jr. "Life in the Time of Cholera." *Richmond Magazine*, August 8, 2015. www.Richmag.com.

Landman v. Brown. U.S. District Court, E.D. Virginia, Richmond Division, November 7, 1972. 350 F.Supp. 303. casetext.com/case/landman-v-brown.

Landman v. Peyton. U.S. Court of Appeals, Fourth Circuit, November 28, 1966. 370 F.2d 135. www.courtlistener.com/opinion/274090/robert-jewell-landman-sr-v-c-c-peyton-superintendent-of-the-virginia.

Landman v. Royster. U.S. District Court for the Eastern District of Virginia, October 30, 1971. 333 F. Supp. 62. www.leagle.com/decision/19731656354FSupp1302_11457/LANDMAN%20v.%20ROYSTER.

Latimer, James. "Charge that Medical Attention Was Refused Dying Prisoner at State Farm Meets Denial." *Richmond Times-Dispatch*, November 21, 1945.

Letter from Benjamin Latrobe. *The Papers of Thomas Jefferson Digital Edition*, ed. James P. McClure and J. Jefferson Looney. Charlottesville: University of Virginia Press, Rotunda, 2008–17.

Lewter F. Hobbs to Governor William Mann, July 16, 1912, Secretary of the Commonwealth, Executive Papers, June 24–July 18, 1912, Archives & Manuscript Division, Library of Virginia.

Lichtenstein, Alex, and Matthew J. Mancini. "One Dies, Get Another: Convict Leasing in the American South, 1866–1928." *American Journal of Legal History* 43, no. 1 (1999): 87.

Lima News. "Negro Girl Put to Death in Chair for Murdering Woman." August 16, 1912.

Lindholm, Jeff. "Briley Execution Brings Out the Worst." *ThroTTle* magazine, November 1984.

Lombardo, Paul A. *Three Generations, No Imbeciles.* 1st ed. Baltimore, MD: Johns Hopkins University Press, 2010.

Lovely, Collis. "Report on Southern Prisons." *The Shoe Makers Journal*, July, August, September, October 1905.

Lumumba, Altrice. "Inmates Refute Prison Report in White Press." Letter to the Editor, *Richmond Afro-American*, August 18, 1968.

Lynchburg Daily Advance. "Police Continue All-Out Search for Negro Rapist." December 7, 1962.

Manarin, Louis. "The Richmond Evacuation." *Philadelphia Weekly Times*, August 27, 1881.

Mason v. Peyton. U.S. District Court for the Eastern District of Virginia, February 19, 1974. www.clearinghouse.net/detailDocument.php?id=4939.

Mathews Journal. "Dr. Carrington Would Sterilize All Felons." January 27, 1910.

———. "Sterilization of Criminals." February 3, 1910.

May, Robert. *A Voice from Richmond, and Other Addresses to Children and Youth.* Philadelphia: American Sunday-School Union, 1857.

McClure, James P., and J. Jefferson Looney. *The Papers of Thomas Jefferson Digital Edition.* Charlottesville: University of Virginia Press, Rotunda, 2008–2017.

Menninger, Karl. *The Crime of Punishment.* New York: Viking Press, 1968.

Meyers, David, and Elise Meyers Walker. *Inside the Ohio Penitentiary.* Charleston, SC: The History Press, 2013.

Murphy, Caryle. "Quadriplegic Gets 21-Year Sentence." *Washington Post*, September 14, 1977.

Nelson, Scott Reynolds. *Steel Drivin' Man: John Henry—The Untold Story of an American Legend.* New York: Oxford University Press, 2006.

Newport News Daily Press. "Alleged Counterfeiters Taken into Custody." January 16, 1909.

————. "Die on Different Days." April 16, 1909.

————. "Electric Chair May Get Eight Negroes." March 13, 1909.

————. "Electrocution in Penitentiary Friday." October 31, 1908.

————. "Gov. Mann Grants Respite to Negress." June 14, 1912.

————. "Murder Confessed by Negress, Slayer of Mrs. Ida Belote." April 11, 1912.

————. "Murder of Mrs. Belote Is Deplored by Negroes." March 20, 1912.

————. "No More Hangings in the Old Dominion." March 6, 1908.

————. "Petition for Appeal in the Christian Case." May 12, 1912.

————. "Virginia Christian Goes to Chair Today." August 16, 1912.

————. "Virginia Christian Must Die August 2." July 19, 1912.

New York Times. "A Horror Case in Prison Medicine Costs $518,000." January 7, 1979.

Norfolk Journal and Guide. "Two Police Convicted in Richmond Rape Case." January 25, 1947.

————. "White Man Charged with Rape on Feebleminded Woman Gets Fine of $20." October 16, 1948.

"Notes on Plan of a Prison." Thomas Jefferson to Governor James Wood, March 31, 1797. www.Rotunda.upress.virginia.edu.

O.L. "Reformatory Needed for Youthful Colored Criminals." *The Reformer,* January 16, 1897.

Oshinsky, David M. "Convict Labor in the Post–Civil War South Involuntary Servitude after the Thirteenth Amendment." *The Promises of Liberty,* 2010.

Penitentiary Employee News, December 1990.

Pescud, Edward. "Penitentiary Store." *Petersburg Republican,* August 11, 1820.

Pittsburgh Post-Gazette. "Mrs. Beattie's Nurse Tells of Awful Dream." July 28, 1911.

Ploski, Harry, and James Williams. *The Negro Almanac: A Reference Work on the Afro-American.* 4th ed. New York: Wiley, 1983. JSTOR.

Powell, T.C. *The American Siberia, or Fourteen Years' Experience in a Convict Labor Camp.* Chicago: Conkey, 1891.

Prison Reform League. *Crime and Criminals.* Los Angeles: Prison Reform League Publishing, 1910.

Public Opinion. "Capital Punishment—Execution by Electricity—The Kemmler Case." April 12, 1890, 432–35.

Pyle, G.F. "The Diffusion of Cholera in the United States in the Nineteenth Century." *Geographical Analysis* 1, no. 1 (2010): 59–75.

Rappahannock Record. "Escapee Acquitted in Guard's Death." September 17, 1936.

————. "A Parole System." April 4, 1935.

————. "To Enlarge State Prison." May 5, 1938.

Rayner, B.L. *The Life of Thomas Jefferson.* Boston: Lilly, Wait, Colman & Holden, 1834.

Richmond Afro-American. "Judge Merhige Bars Cruel Treatment in State Prisons." November 6, 1971.

————. "Last of Doomed 7 Says 'Meet Me in Heaven.'" February 10, 1951.

————. "Prison Boss Quoted as Saying 'Never.'" August 17, 1968.

Richmond Dispatch. (Acts of the General Assembly). October 21, 1900.

————. "The Board and Its Duty." September 30, 1911.

————. "Convict Labor Bill." February 11, 1900.

————. "Davis Company Contract." February 3, 1900.

————. "Dead to the World: Twelve Hundred Inhabitants of the Virginia Penitentiary." December 14, 1902.

————. "A Disgrace." September 15, 1897.

————. "The Handsome Franklin County Convict." August 12, 1892.

————. "An Inside View of the Virginia Penitentiary." November 30, 1868.

————. "Lynchers Convicted." August 10, 1902.

————. "The Need of a State Farm." December 4, 1892.

————. "Negro Convict Fatally Shot by Pen Guard." November 7, 1924.

————. "Negro Executed." May 31, 1869.

————. "Prison Day Exercises." May 25, 1890.

————. "A Prison's Profits." November 10, 1897.

————. "The Treatment of Convicts." December 15, 1895.

Richmond Inquirer. "Fire at the Penitentiary." May 16, 1804.

Richmond News Leader. "Carwile Plans New Demand on Governor for Personal Investigation of State Farm." November 9, 1945.

————. "Chair Claims First Woman Victim Today." August 16, 1912.

————. "Think Electrocution of Girl Would Be a Disgrace." July 25, 1912.

Richmond Planet. "The Reign of Lawlessness." September 24, 1898.

————. "She Is Free." January 2, 1897.

————. "White Man Lynched." September 17, 1898.

Richmond Times. "Assassin at the Wedding." January 9, 1892.

————. "Awful Conditions in State Prison." March 27, 1901.

————. "Denied Admission, Doctor Indignant." April 3, 1919.

————. "Dr. Harrison Passes Away." September 12, 1900.

————. "An Eyewitness Describes Death in the Electric Chair." January 12, 1902.

————. "Female Convict Makes Escape." December 25, 1900.

————. "Leaped to Freedom." October 26, 1902.

————. "No Verdict in Lynching Case." March 31, 1899.

————. "The Patrick Lynching." September 16, 1898.

————. "Searcy Is Free." May 3, 1892.

————. "Sickening Condition of the Penitentiary." December 15, 1901.

Richmond Times-Dispatch. "Carrington May Not Answer Board." December 26, 1911

————. "Carwile Is Ejected from Hearing on Phillips Bill." February 14, 1946.

————. "Christian Girl Must Die To-Day." August 16, 1912

————. "Crowd Eluded by the Sheriff." February 26, 1909.

————. "Doctors Working for Race Purity." October 28, 1913.

————. "Dr. Carrington Resting Well after Operation." October 5, 1919.

————. Editorial. "Virginia Should Get in Step." November 21, 1945.

————. "Four Long-Term Men Escape from State Prison." January 12, 1915.

————. "House Defeats Sterilization Bill." February 18, 1910.

————. "How It Feels to Die in the Electric Chair." March 5, 1916.

————. "Killers Bullets Fatal to Officer." October 4, 1934.

————. "Nation Shocked by Crime at Hillsville." March 29, 1913.

————. "Negro Girl Pays Death Penalty." August 17, 1912.

————. "Newspaper Would Save Girl's Life." August 14, 1912.

————. "Ought We Revive the Barbarous Whipping Post?" August 17, 1913.

————. "Respite Granted Young Murderess." June 14, 1912.

————. "Seybold Takes Blame on His Own Shoulders." January 16, 1909.

————. "Stairs's [*sic*] Escape Is Sensational." June 29, 1906.

————. "A State Farm for Women." November 10, 1931.

————. "State Makes Switch to Electric Chair." Editorial, April 12, 1908.

Rise, Eric W. *The Martinsville Seven: Race, Rape and Capital Punishment in Virginia.* Charlottesville: University Press of Virginia, 1995.

————. "Race, Rape, and Radicalism: The Case of the Martinsville Seven, 1949–1951." *Journal of Southern History* 58, no. 3 (August 1992): 461–90.

Rizzo, Dennis C., and Dave Kimball. *The Burlington County Prison.* Charleston, SC: The History Press, 2011.

Roanoke Evening News. "Finney's Sentence Has Been Commuted." October 10, 1908.

————. "Five to Die." October 6, 1908.

————. "Sensationalism." March 21, 1911.

Roanoke Times. "Convict Labor." January 22, 1896.

Russell, John Henderson. "The Free Negro in Virginia, 1619–1865." PhD diss., Johns Hopkins University, Baltimore, MD, 1913.

Salem Times Register. "Shot Dead by a Woman." May 23, 1890.

Salt Lake Herald. "Young Woman Attacked by Burly Negro in Richmond, Va." January 11, 1909.

Scott, Ned, Jr. "An Eye for an Eye: The Strange Death of Frank Coppola." *ThroTTle* magazine, October 1982.

Second Annual Report of the Board of Managers of the Prison Discipline Society. 1st ed. Boston: published by Perkins & Marvin, 1827.

Shires, Carl. "Electric Chair, after 232 Executions, Loses 'Elegance.'" *Richmond News Leader*, March 8, 1961.

Silverman, Richard. "B. Henry Latrobe's Penitentiary House, Richmond, Virginia." Graduate thesis, School of Architecture, University of Virginia, Charlottesville, 1991.

Slaughter, Phillip. *Virginia History of African Colonization.* Richmond, 1855. Web.

Smith, Bruce J. "Transformation from Republican to Radical Activist in the 1960s." brucejsmithblog.wordpress.com, 2017.

Smithfield Times. "Guard Killed in Escape Attempt." July 2, 1936.

Southside [VA] Sentinel. "Pardoned Negro Seeks Return to Prison." June 13, 1940.

———. "Two Prisoners Killed in Penitentiary." September 22, 1949.

Staunton Spectator. "Carrington Barred from Pen by Warden." December 8, 1911.

———. "Mob Law in Patrick." September 22, 1898.

The Sun (New York). "Kemmler's Death Chair." April 29, 1890.

Tazewell Republican. "Hiram Steele Arrested." March 11, 1897.

Teeters, Negley K. *The Cradle of the Penitentiary: The Walnut Street Jail, 1773–1835.* Philadelphia: Pennsylvania Prison Society, 1955

———. "The State of Prisons in the United States, 1870–1970." *Federal Probation*, December 1969.

Times-Herald. "The Case of Virginia Christian." July 20, 1912.

Trotti, Michael A. "The Scaffold's Revival: Race and Public Execution in the South." *Journal of Social History* 45, no. 1 (2011): 195–224.

Tyler, Lyon Gardiner. *Men of Mark in Virginia Ideals of American Life; a Collection of Biographies of the Leading Men in the State.* Washington, D.C.: Men of Mark Pub. Co., 1907.

United States, Commissioner of Labor. *Convict Labor.* Washington, D.C.: U.S. Government Printing Office, 1886.

U.S. Congress. *United States Historical Corrections Statistics, 1850–1984.* By Margaret Werner Cahalan and Lee Anne Parsons. Cong. Rept. NCJ-102529. Rockville, MD: Westat, Inc., 1986.

Vaughan, Charles. *Grant Me to Live: The Execution of Virginia Christian.* Pittsburgh, PA: Dorrance Publishing, 2010.

Vincent, Jay E. "Martinsville Seven." *Washington Post,* February 6, 1951.

Wallenstein, Peter. "Slavery Under the Thirteenth Amendment: Race and the Law of Crime and Punishment in the Post–Civil War South." *Louisiana Law Review* 77, no. 1 (September 2016).

Washington Post. "Convict Wants to Return." September 15, 1897.

———. "Inmate Uses Bomb in Virginia Escape." October 2, 1970.

———. "Outfit and Bogus Coins Made by Convicts in Virginia Penitentiary." February 21, 1905.

———. "Penitentiary Disorder in Va. Quelled." January 21, 1973.

———. "A Pretty Prisoner in the Pen." August 12, 1892.

———. "Probers Urge Virginia Form Parole Bureau." April 30, 1935.

———. "Riot Troops, Rain End Prison Strife." August 2, 1977.

———. "Virginia Will Speed Plans for Execution." January 19, 1935.

Wheeler, Linda. "On the Track of Railroad Folk Hero John Henry." *Washington Post,* December 26, 1998.

Wilson, Theodore Brantner. *The Black Codes of the South.* Tuscaloosa: University of Alabama Press, 1965.

The World (New York). "Extra Brutal: Kemmler Dies a Terrible Death in the Electric Chair." August 6, 1890.

Collections

Library of Virginia. Governor Claude Swanson executive papers, 1906–10.

———. Governor James Wood executive papers, 1796–99.

———. Governor John S. Battle executive papers, 1950–54.

———. Governor Mills Godwin executive papers, 1966–70 and 1974–78.

———. Governor William Hodges Mann executive papers, 1910–14.

———. Guide to the Records of the Virginia State Penitentiary.

———. Microfilm collection, Virginia State Penitentiary admissions and discharges, 1865–1984.

Virginia Commonwealth University, James Branch Cabell Library Special Collections and Archives (2006). "A Guide to the Edward H. Peeples Jr. Papers." 1915, 1920s–2005.

Video and Music

MonumentAve. *Time to Learn* (Spring Street Penitentiary). YouTube. February 20, 2017.

Sterowski, Brian. "Virginia State Penitentiary 1991—Prison Tour." YouTube. October 20, 2015.

Strothers, Jimmie. "Goin' to Richmond." YouTube. State Farm, VA: Document Records, 1936.

Strothers, Jimmie, and Joe Lee. "Do Lord Remember Me." YouTube. State Farm, VA: Document Records, 1936.

werewolfmanjackal. "Execution by Electric Chair Explained at Virginia State Prison." YouTube. March 6, 2011.

Web and Digital Collections

Ancestry.com.

California digital newspapers collection. cdnc.ucr.edu.

Death penalty information center. deathpenaltyusa.org/usa1/state/virginia.

Facebook. facebook.com.

Find a Grave Cemetery records. findagrave.com.

Hathitrust digital library. hathitrust.org.

Internet Archive digital library. www.archive.org.

Library of Congress. loc.gov.

Library of Congress digitized newspapers. chroniclingamerica.loc.gov.

Library of Virginia online digitized newspapers. virginiachronicle.com.

Murderpedia, encyclopedia of murderers. www.murderpedia.org.

Newspapers.com, digitized newspapers. www.newspapers.com.

Virginia Center for digital history. www.vcdh.virginia.edu.

Virginia Heritage Guides to Manuscript and Archival Collections in Virginia. vaheritage.org.

"Archive of American Folk Songs." The American Folk Life Center. Library of Congress, Washington, D.C., 1936.

Christman, Roger, and the Library of Virginia. "Notes from the Archives at the Library of Virginia." www.virginiamemory.com/blogs/out_of_the_box. Entries November 14, 2016; March 4, 2015; September 8, 2014; September 23, 2013; March 14, 2012; March 7, 2012; December 19, 2011; November 21, 2011; October 10, 2011; October 13, 2011; December 8, 2010; September 14, 2010.

INDEX

A

absconsion unit director 240
A Building 137, 141, 157, 236
ACLU 192, 197, 204, 236
Adams Electric Company 121, 160
Adams, Frank 204, 207
Addison, Bob 178
Afton Chemical 238
Alabama 69, 72, 152
Albright, Rex Wardell 228
Allen, Claude 186, 219, 221
Allen, Floyd 219, 220, 221
Allen, Friel 221
Allen, Sidna 220, 221, 222
American Civil Liberties Union.
    See ACLU
American Colonization Society 41
American Prison Association 102
Andersonville Prison 71
Arey, Calvin 208, 209, 210
armory 25, 31, 38
arson 86, 137

Attica State Prison 211, 212, 235
Auburn 20, 27, 29, 40, 45, 120, 145

B

Baker, Ed 175
Baldwin-Felts Detective Agency
    221
ball and chain 56
ball and spike 56
Barbour, James 34
Barkan, Barry 204, 205
Barrow, Dr. Bernard 109
Bass, Colin 64
Bass, Powhatan B. 179
Battle, John S. 163
Bayliss, Captain William 54
B Building 158, 199, 233, 236
Beacon, The 188, 189
Beattie, Henry Clay 186, 187,
    218, 219
Belote, Ida 128, 129, 130, 131,
    132, 133

Belvidere 18, 98, 139, 171, 178, 180, 181, 182, 238

Belvin, Edward 211

Bentham, Jeremy 20

Bertillon system 69, 173

Bible 17, 20, 45, 188, 199

Biedleman, Kathy 242

Binford, Beulah 218

black codes 69, 72, 77, 79, 80, 232

blacksmiths 47, 78

blowtorch burglar 228

Blue, Charles 63

Board of Public Welfare 95

Botts, Benjamin 34

Bowles, Dr. E.W. 104

bread and water 40, 57, 60, 197, 206, 208, 210, 212

Briley, Linwood 138

Bristol Coal and Iron Railroad 82

British prisoners of war 35

Broocks, Dr. J.N. 45, 46, 50

Brown, Henry "Box" 54

Brown, Otis 209, 231

Bruce, Lenny 191

Bruwelheide, Kari 243

Buck v. Bell 108

Burr, Aaron 29, 33, 34

Bush, George 227

Byrd, Harry 222

Byrd, Richard 111

Byrd, William, III 18

C

Cabell, William 32

Cain, Herbert 19

Callis, Thomas 22, 23, 24, 25

Campbell, Kenneth 191

Cape Mesurado 41

capital punishment 119, 120, 122, 138, 163, 164, 192

Capital Theater 224

Caple, Herbert 134

carnivals of death 118

carpenters 22, 47, 48, 52

Carrington, Dr. Charles 57, 79, 102, 103, 104, 105, 106, 108, 109, 110, 111, 112, 113, 114, 115, 116, 124

Carroll County 219, 221

Carwile, Howard 150, 151, 152, 153, 154, 155, 156, 157

Castle Thunder 71

C Building 197, 198, 199, 200, 201, 203, 204, 209, 211, 212

Central State Hospital 105, 108, 110, 112, 123, 223

Cherry Hill 45

Chesapeake and Ohio Railroad 74

cholera 43, 44, 46

Christian, Virginia 128, 129, 130, 131, 132, 133

Church Hill 18, 205

Civil War 62, 72, 77, 90, 117, 232, 240

Clanton, Earl, Jr. 193

Clarke, John 25, 29

Cleary, Ben 189, 190

Clem 240

Clere, Henry 191, 192

Clover Hill coal mines 68

C&O. *See* Chesapeake and Ohio Railroad

Cockerell, Samuel Pepys 19

cold cream bandit 228

Connally, Jeff 87

consumption 76, 100

contraband 31

convict lease system 53, 72, 81

coopers 48, 78

Coppola, Frank 137

corporal punishment 16, 32, 34, 36, 41, 49, 56, 57, 58, 145, 155, 156, 209, 213

Cottrell, Walker 148, 149

Covington and Healey Springs Turnpike 68

Covington and Ohio Railroad 53, 72

Cowley, Robert 22

crime of punishment 198, 235

Crisis, The 133

Cumberland County 25, 26

Cunningham, W.K. 204, 209

D

Dale, Thomas 17

Darden, Colgate 152

Davis & Company 81

Davis, Jefferson 71

Davis, Westmoreland 144, 171

de Beaumont, Gustave 46

Declaration of Independence 42

Deep Meadow Correctional 233

DeJarnette, Dr. Joseph 111, 115

dementia vasectomy 106

de Tocqueville, Alex 46

Dickens, Charles 17, 47, 174

Diggs, James Henry "Crip" 185

"Divine, Moral and Martial Laws" 17

Dobie, Samuel 19

Dodson, Lizzie 92, 169, 171

Douglas, Abraham 25, 32

Dugdale, Richard 109

dungeon 39, 44, 60, 104

E

Edwards, Sidna 219, 221

Edwards, Wesley 219, 221, 222

electric chair 119, 120, 121, 122, 125, 127, 128, 131, 135, 136, 137, 142, 160, 163, 179, 187, 192, 193, 201, 219, 221, 236, 237, 238, 239, 240

Eliza, the 19

Ellis, Percy 240

Emancipation Proclamation 72

Encounters 191, 192

Ethyl Corporation 238

eugenics 102, 106

Evans, Wilbert Lee 141

Ex-Prisoners' Aid Society of Virginia 173

F

Ferrets 71

Fiber Craft Chair Company 147

Finney, William 122, 123

fire 29, 34, 37, 38, 40, 47, 52, 62, 64, 65, 67, 80, 85, 94, 96, 137, 217, 218

firemen 48

Fletcher, John 55

flogging 41, 59, 151, 154, 155, 156, 157, 158

Florida 60, 69, 72, 97, 152, 226, 236

Floyd, John 44

Floyd, Ruby Stroud 161

Fourteenth Amendment 70

Franklin, Benjamin 16

free blacks 36, 41, 49, 50, 53, 63, 69

Freedmen's Bureau 69

Furman v. Georgia 137
FYSK 189

G

Gabriel 27, 28
Gabriel's Rebellion 27, 28
gag 40, 59
Gallagher, Dennis 231
Gallaher, Johnny "Johnny G" 138
gallows 94, 118, 121
Garland, Carroll 136
General Assembly 16, 18, 28, 29,
    34, 40, 42, 45, 47, 55, 62, 67,
    70, 74, 77, 80, 82, 85, 90, 93,
    95, 98, 99, 104, 111, 117,
    119, 137, 144, 146, 147, 155,
    168, 215, 240, 242
Georgia 60, 69, 71, 72, 81, 97, 128,
    152, 236
Giarratano, Joseph 122, 237
Gilbert, Benjamin 127
Giles, William 22, 41
Givens, Jerry 137, 138
Glass, Carter 201
Goad, Dexter 220, 221
Godwin, Mills 137, 178, 206, 231
Gordonsville 72
grand larceny 34, 36, 68, 70, 79,
    88, 148, 162, 170
Grayson County 36, 186
Greenfield, Ron 191, 192
Green, Maizie 218, 219
Greensville 236, 237, 238
Green, Winston 125, 126
Gusler, Amon 135, 136

H

Hairston, Frank 162, 164, 167
harness makers 47
Harper, Ernest 177, 178
Harrison, Dr. Benjamin 102
Harvie, John 19, 22
Haupt, Herman 88
Hawes-Cooper Bill 147
Henry, John 69, 70, 71, 74, 75, 76
Henry, Patrick 15
Henry: Portrait of a Serial Killer 228
Hill, Oliver 164
Hillsville 186, 219, 221
Hirschkop, Philip J. 198, 201, 202,
    206, 207, 235
Hirst, Omer 207
Hodges, Octavia 216
Hollywood Cemetery 116, 241
Holmes, J.B. 65
Holmes, Oliver Wendell 108
Holton, Linwood 202, 213, 230
Hood, Roy 208, 209
Hopkins, Evans 190, 192, 230, 235
horse stealing 34, 36
hospital 39, 40, 42, 46, 50, 52, 64,
    76, 77, 83, 85, 91, 96, 104,
    106, 112, 144, 145, 146, 152,
    158, 202, 211
housebreaking 69, 70, 79, 87, 94,
    110, 148, 173, 177, 185, 218
House of Delegates 25, 33, 39, 42,
    45, 63, 74, 79
Howell, Henry 207
Hoysradt, Lieutenant Lyman 65
"Humming-Bird" 61
Hunt, Gilbert 38, 41
Hustings Court 87

I

Industrial Farm for Women 148
iron mask 57, 115, 145

J

Jackson, Thomas "Stonewall" 62
James River 18, 31, 32, 44, 46, 47,
    53, 138, 148
James River and Kanawha Canal 68
James River Company 53, 80
Jefferson, Thomas 15, 16, 17, 18,
    19, 27, 29, 42, 77, 95, 146,
    154, 238
Jim Crow 119, 165, 207
Johnson, Dennis "Dr. Death" 182
Jones, Leroy 196, 198
Jukes family 109
Justus, Buddy Lee 236
juveniles 86, 95
J.W. Rayle 182

K

Kaine, Tim 190
Kass, Carole 192
Katz, Alan 231
Keeler, Clarissa Olds 97
keeper 25, 29, 32, 33, 34
Kemmler, William 120
Kemper, James 88
Keziah 54
Kimball, Gregg 185, 187
King County Prison 93
King, Dr. Martin Luther, Jr. 201
Kinoy, Arthur 201
Kloch, John 141
Kunstler, William 201

L

labor in confinement 16, 29, 30, 39
Landman et al v. Royster et al 209
Landman, Robert J. 199, 200, 201,
    202, 208, 209, 211, 213
Landman v. Peyton 199
Larus Brothers Tobacco 80
Lassiter, William 210
Latrobe, Benjamin H. 19, 20, 22,
    23, 24, 25, 31, 38, 146
Lee, Joe 185
Legenza, Walter 134, 135
Lewis Tunnel 76
Libby Prison 63
Liberia. *See* Cape Mesurado
Link, Danny 236
Lomax, John 185
Louisa County 230
Louisiana 69, 81, 97, 152
Lovely, Collis 57, 84
Lucas, Henry Lee 226
Lukhard, William 231
Lynchburg 93, 115, 171, 173,
    201, 227
Lynds, Elam 27
Lynn, Bushrod Washington 98

M

Madison, James 17
Mais, Robert 134, 135
malaria 76
Mann, Dr. Herbert 113
Mann, Horace 113
manslaughter 36, 62, 86, 87, 223
Marshall, John 34
Marshall, Justice Thurgood 137
martial law 71

Martin, Martin A. 164
Martinsville Seven 159, 161, 162
Mason, Gooch and Hoge 72
Mason, Leroy 201, 202, 209
Mason, Shanahan & Hoge 81
Mason v. Peyton 201, 208
Maud, Ebenezer 19
McDowell, James 50
McGuire, Dr. Hunter 102
Mecklenburg Correctional 141, 192, 193, 235
Medical College of Virginia 121, 145, 146, 181
Medical Society of Virginia 113, 145
Meekins, Franklin 138, 179, 180
Merhige, Judge Robert, Jr. 202, 207, 208, 209, 236
Merryman, Thomas 25
Mims, Martin 22, 23, 25, 32
miscegenation 215
Mississippi 33, 69, 152
Mitchell, James 232
Moisant, John 101
Monroe, James 27
Monticello 18, 42
Morgan, Charles 46, 53
Morganfield, Charles 114, 216, 217
mucker 74
Muncy, Raymond 237

N

NAACP 132, 204
National Association of Colored Women 131, 132
National Pants Company 147
National Prison Association 77
National Prison Project 235, 236

Nelson, Scott Reynolds 75, 243
Newgate Prison 20
Newport News 120, 125, 126, 128, 129, 177
New York 20, 27, 29, 40, 43, 65, 77, 93, 109, 120, 121, 122, 135, 145, 211, 224, 235
Norfolk 19, 27, 113, 127, 128, 170, 175, 177, 207, 232
Norfolk and Western Railroad 84
North Carolina 152
North River Canal project 53
Norvall, Jack 52
Nowlin, Thomas 86, 87, 95
NPP. *See* National Prison Project

O

ODGC. *See* Old Dominion Granite Company
Old Dominion Granite Company 88
Oregon 47, 98, 140, 182, 239
oznabrig 26, 27, 31

P

Page, John 30
painters 48
Panopticon 20, 25
Parsons, Samuel 31, 36
Patrick County 223
Patteson, Dr. William A. 54, 90
Peeples, Dr. Edward H. 232
Pegram, Roger 202, 208
Pendleton, Edmund 16
Pendleton, James 54, 67, 70, 71
penitentiary choir 175, 183
Pennock, Capt. William 19

Pennsylvania 16, 17, 40, 228
Petersburg 33, 105, 109, 179
Peyton, C.C. 198, 200, 203, 207, 209
Philadelphia 16, 17, 19, 24, 25, 32,
    45, 47, 54, 64, 71, 135
Philadelphia Society for Assisting
    Distressed Prisoners 16
Pierpont, Francis H. 66
Pig Laws 70
Pittsylvania County 232
pneumonia 76, 82, 83, 243
polygamy 16
Powell, Freida 226
Powell, J.C. 72, 97
Powhatan Thirteen 159, 160, 161
Priddy, Dr. Albert 115
Prince Edward County 26
Prison Discipline Society 31
prisoners of war 63
Prisoner's Relief Society 115
Probst, Arthur 194
Prokofiev, Sergei 165
public guard 38
Puckett, Lee 223

Q

Quakers 16, 18, 71, 77, 204, 205
quilling 47

R

Racial Integrity Act 116
Rawlings, Vincent 180
Rea, F.T. 182, 183
Reconstruction 69, 70, 75
Reformer, The 98
Richmond and Clifton Forge
    Railroad 82

Robb, Charles 138, 141
Robinson, Joseph "Cocky Joe" 224
Rockefeller, Nelson 211
Royster, R.L. 152, 209
Ruffin v. Commonwealth 66, 214
Rush, Benjamin 16
Rutherfoord, Thomas 18

S

Savage, Mosco 110
scars 57, 69, 71, 207
Schofield, General John 70
Schoonmaker, Captain J.M. 65
Schwartz, Herman 235
Scott, Robert G. 48
Scottsboro boys 165
Scottsboro trial 164
scurvy 45, 54, 75, 77
Searcy, Charles 216, 217
segregation 140, 197, 198, 200,
    201, 203, 205, 208, 236
Senate 40, 70, 74
sewage lagoon 44, 46
Seybold, Thomas 172, 173
Shapiro, Jonathon 141, 142
Shockoe 18, 33
shoe-making 29, 32
Shortis, John 22
Shostakovich, Dmitri 165
silicosis 75, 76, 243
Sing Sing Prison 122
skeletons 242
slavery 43, 49, 54, 66, 70, 72, 77, 84
Smeaton, John 19
Smith, Bruce 205
Smith, Henry 123, 187
Smith, Samuel 54
Smithsonian Institute 242, 243

Smyth, Frank, Jr. 156, 157, 164
solitary confinement 15, 16, 17, 20,
        24, 31, 39, 40, 45, 71, 115,
        126, 197, 198, 200, 202, 208,
        209, 210, 211
Southampton State Farm 149
South Carolina 62, 84, 152
Southern Railway 84
Southside Virginia Medical
        Association 109
Spivacke, Harold 185
Spotts, John 52
Spring Street 149, 179, 204, 205
Spring Street Theatre 191
Squirrel Charlie 217, 218
Stafford County 36, 217
Stanley, Thomas 241
Star Clothing and Manufacturing
        175
Starling, Lawrence 154
State Board of Charities 95, 113, 115
State Board of Welfare and
        Institutions 207
State Farm 59, 95, 98, 99, 100,
        104, 110, 144, 145, 148, 151,
        152, 153, 156, 157, 183, 185,
        189, 192, 196, 197, 208, 209
Staunton 33, 55, 101, 110, 228,
        236, 240
Steele, Hiram 105, 106, 108
sterilization 106, 108, 110, 111,
        112, 115
Stiars, William 173, 174
St. Luke's Hospital 102
stripes, the 49, 57, 59, 114
Strode, Dr. Aubrey 115
Strother, George 77
Strothers, Jimmie 183, 184, 185, 187
Sullivan, Bishop Walter 192

Swanson, Claude 121, 122, 123,
        127, 160, 173
syphilis 100, 144

T

"talking through the commodes"
        204
Taylor, George Keith 17
Taylor, Isham 159, 160, 161
tear gas 213
Teeter, Negley 17
Tennessee 69, 84, 97
Terry, General Alfred 70
Thacker Boot and Shoe Company
        112, 113
Thirteenth Amendment 66
Thornton, William 20
"three strikes you're out" 55
ThroTTle 140, 230
Time to Learn 192, 193
toilet 25, 31, 104, 178, 202, 207, 208
Toole, Ottis 226, 228
Toot, William 134
trackliner 74
Trans-Allegheny Lunatic Asylum 53
Tredegar Iron Works 47
Tri-State Gang 134
Tucker Telephone 61
Tuck, William 155
Turner, Early T. 237
Turner, Richard "Dick" 63
Turner, William Dandridge 63
turnkey 32
Turpin, Walter 171, 172, 173, 174
Tyler, James 170
Tyler, J. Hoge 223
typhoid fever 83, 102

U

University of Virginia 102, 109, 221

V

Valentine, Mann 33
vasectomy 106
Victorious, the 35
Virginia Colonization Society 41, 50
Virginia Colony for the Epileptic and Feeble-Minded 115
Virginia Commission of the Arts and Humanities 191
Virginia Commonwealth University 230
Virginia Council on Human Relations 204, 205
Virginia Department of Historic Resources 238
Virginia Historical Society 238
Virginia Medical Society 106, 111

W

Walker, Maggie 132
Walnut Street Jail 17, 32
Walsh, Adam 228
Walsh, John 228
Wansley, Thomas 201, 202, 209, 213
Wardwell, Burnham 70
War of 1812 35
water cure 60
Watson, Dr. J.C. 85
WCTU. *See* Woman's Christian Temperance Union
weavers 47, 52, 78
Weisenfeld and Company 81

Wells, Henry Horatio 70
Western State Hospital 110, 111
Weston State Hospital. *See* Trans-Alleghany Lunatic Asylum
West Virginia 26, 28, 53, 72, 74, 75, 77, 84, 108, 178, 185, 228, 241, 242, 243
WGOE 192
wheelwrights 32, 47, 52
whipped 41, 75, 157
white house 42, 76
Whittle, Judge Kennon C. 163
Wilder, L. Douglas 141
Williams, Jerry 193
Williams, Sam C. 81
Wilson, James 169
Wilson, Melvin 180
Winston, George 22
Withers-Lassiter Good Roads Law 101
Woman's Christian Temperance Union 93
Wood, James 18
Wood, J.B. 112
Wrecking Corp. of America 238, 242
Wythe County 88, 221

Y

Youell, Rice M 146, 148, 150, 152, 156, 157, 184

Z

Zahradnick, Robert 192, 233

ABOUT THE AUTHOR

Dale M. Brumfield is field director for Virginians for Alternatives to the Death Penalty, a nonprofit based in Richmond; a digital archaeologist; and the author of eight books. His work appears regularly in numerous publications, including the *Staunton News Leader*, the *Rappahannock Review*, *USA Today*, *North of the James*, *Richmond* magazine and *Style Weekly*. His two books, *Richmond Independent Press: A History of the Underground Zine Scene* and *Independent Press in Virginia and D.C.: An Underground History*, were both nominated for Library of Virginia Literary Awards in nonfiction.

Dale lives in Doswell, Virginia.